# Designing
# SOCIAL RESEARCH

# Designing
# SOCIAL RESEARCH

## A Guide for the Bewildered

## IAN GREENER

Los Angeles | London | New Delhi
Singapore | Washington DC

SAGE Publications Ltd
1 Oliver's Yard
55 City Road
London EC1Y 1SP

SAGE Publications Inc.
2455 Teller Road
Thousand Oaks, California 91320

SAGE Publications India Pvt Ltd
B 1/I 1 Mohan Cooperative Industrial Area
Mathura Road
New Delhi 110 044

SAGE Publications Asia-Pacific Pte Ltd
33 Pekin Street #02-01
Far East Square
Singapore 048763

**Library of Congress Control Number: 2010936904**

**British Library Cataloguing in Publication data**

A catalogue record for this book is available from the British Library

ISBN 978-1-84920-189-6
ISBN 978-1-84920-190-2

Typeset by C&M Digitals (P) Ltd, Chennai, India
Printed by MPG Books Group, Bodmin, Cornwall
Printed on paper from sustainable resources

For my parents, who taught me how to argue

# Contents

# Tables

# About the author

Ian Greener is a Professor in the School of Applied Social Sciences at Durham University where he leads the provision of research methods teaching on ESRC-accredited courses. Prior to this he worked for a number of UK Higher Education Universities including Manchester and York in Business Schools and Social Science Departments. His main research interest is trying to keep up with the hectic pace of public sector reform both in the UK and internationally, using a range of qualitative, quantitative and mixed methods research strategies to examine continuity and change in public services, and which has led to books on the history of the NHS and public management, and over 50 articles published in a range of international peer-reviewed journals.

Ian lives in York where he spends his time trying to stop his children, Bethany, Emily and Anna, from spending what remains of his money, and walking a spaniel his wife insists he must grow to like. He likes good red wine, Strictly Come Dancing, and computers that work.

# Acknowledgements

Thanks to all the research methods students I've taught at Manchester and Durham, especially those who participated in discussions in classes that led to me changing my opinions. They are the ones who prompted me to write this book. Thank you also to colleagues who got me thinking about the way I do research, including Dave Byrne, Martin Powell, Steve Harrison and Kieran Walshe. I am grateful to Patrick Brindle at Sage for his enthusiasm for the book, and to the anonymous reviewers he found to make suggestions for its improvement. Thank you to Linda Jayne for more than I can say. And, I suppose, to Anna, Bethany and Emily for stopping from arguing for long enough to allow me to write.

# Preface

There were two main reasons for adding to the already groaning shelves made up of social research texts. First, I wanted to write a book that students might actually read, and second, I wanted to give students a multi-disciplinary text that gave practical advice about the process of designing and doing social research, but at the same time grounded students in the vocabulary and philosophy they need to understand what it is they are doing.

My experience of teaching research methods at the Universities of Manchester and Durham suggests that students have a tendency to buy texts and then, intimidated by their sheer size, sell them to the nearest second-hand bookshop almost unread. This is a terrible shame, so my first criterion was to try and keep things, within reason, as brief as I possibly could. Because the subject of research methods is so diverse and complex, what is here is not complete. What I've tried to do is to give a good grounding in debates around research from which students can go to other more advanced texts.

Equally, while teaching research methods I've found myself frustrated by the division between books that are very practical in offering students advice on how to go about social research and those that explore the philosophy of research. Books also often refer to social research concepts in early chapters and then only infrequently afterwards as they get on with the very difficult task of describing all the different methods that are out there. I wanted this book to follow through on the concepts throughout in an attempt to give students a grounding not only in methods, but also in the ideas that underpin them. I want students to be able to engage in a discussion not only about the differences between methods, but in the reason for those differences.

I've tried to present research methods in a multi-disciplinary and multi-perspectival way. This doesn't mean that I subscribe to postmodernism, although I do have a great deal of sympathy with some of its exponents. What it does mean is that I believe strongly that there isn't usually a single best way of doing social research. What students seem to enjoy in classes is exploring problems and ideas from different perspectives, even if they come to the conclusion that, in their particular circumstance, there is one answer that is better than the others. As such, each chapter here explores the dynamics and tensions of doing social research from different angles to try and illustrate how different research traditions and practices go about doing social research in different ways. Of course, this comes with the caveat that the limited range of perspectives I'm able to offer in each chapter is not comprehensive, but does, I hope, give the reader some idea about the diversity and range of approaches to social research.

I've tried to make each chapter as self-contained as I can, recognising that not everyone will want to read every chapter in the book. As a result, some topics (sampling, for example) crop up several times. I hope that the treatment in each case is sufficiently different to still make the discussion interesting, but necessarily some repetition does appear.

# The structure of the book

In the introductory chapter I give an overview of the language of social science research, as well as giving some indications of what makes a good research question. This chapter is important because it covers the foundations upon which the rest of the book is based. Chapter 2 looks at ways of reviewing existing research on the grounds that the beginnings of many projects are found in exploring existing research. Chapter 3 is about surveys and questionnaires on the grounds that they are widespread, but which also raise a number of challenges that are interesting in terms of both quantitative and qualitative research.

Chapter 4 moves on to explore quantitative research design. It considers the importance of numbers, outlines some basic principles in thinking about quantitative research, and considers the use and misuse of quantitative methods. Chapter 5 examines ethnography, in many respects the polar opposite of quantitative methods, considering what ethnography means, the methods used in ethnographic studies and the different ways such studies can be designed.

Chapter 6 considers the problem that just about all social researchers face having collected any kind of qualitative data – what to do with all the words. It outlines grounded theory and discourse analysis as means of dealing with qualitative data, comparing it to historiographic and quantitative techniques for document analysis before asking what a good ethnographic analysis might look like.

Chapters 7 and 8 cover advanced topics – causality, and the role of time and control in social research. The material in these chapters is alluded to in earlier parts of the book, but is expanded here to give researchers a clear idea of the implications of their choices in respect of these issues in design, and the ways that different approaches to social research deal with them.

Chapter 9 deals with ethics in social research, showing how different research bodies conceptualise ethics, and asking what the purpose of ethical statements is, before Chapter 10 considers strategies for writing up social research with a strong emphasis on the techniques of argument formation – an area students often struggle with. Chapter 11 follows on from this to give practical guides to writing reviews and proposals that I hope researchers will find helpful.

The concluding chapter summarises the overall argument of the book.

At the end of each chapter you'll find a section entitled 'Five things to remember' – my attempt to give you the highlights of what each chapter is about, and, in most cases, a discussion of a piece of research or a debate about research that captures in some way the contents of the chapter.

Finally, a word about citing and referencing. My instinct, because of my own disciplinary background, is to pack the text with citations and provide a really long bibliography at the end of the book to show that I have done my own research in writing this book. I haven't done this here because I wanted to try and keep the text free from excessive citation to keep things clearer, but also because I wanted to try and use a more limited range of sources that students might want to go to themselves as illustrative of the range of methods and different perspectives I've used here. I hope this makes the text easier to navigate than it would have otherwise been.

# ONE

## Introduction to social research design – or what are you talking about?

## Introduction

This chapter introduces the key concepts that students need to know in order to be able to begin to think about and discuss social research. First, we will work through some basic terms such as the difference between primary and secondary data, before considering some more philosophical terms. Next, some practical examples of how these concepts can be applied will be given to show that research methods vary considerably in terms of the way they use data, and on their philosophical bases. Finally, the chapter will argue that what is important is that students and researchers understand what I'll call a 'logic of appropriateness' in their work – that no methods are intrinsically better than others, but that the choice of methods is important because some methods suit particular kinds of problems better than others. Being aware of the relationship between method and the problem at hand is therefore extremely important in conducting social research – the central theme of this book.

## Defining terms

Nobody likes jargon. It's depressing to sit in lectures or meetings and to simply not understand what anyone is talking about because they seem intent in stringing together sentences that are based on obscure terms and acronyms that seem designed to obscure rather than improve understanding. Any author therefore has a duty to try and minimise their use of terms to those that are necessary in order for readers to be able to deal with the literature in a subject area, or those which help readers to get some additional analytical purchase on the subject.

There are a bewildering range of terms in social research texts, but for the moment we have to deal with eight in order to get started. As I hope to make clear, I'm not sure that some of these terms always help in understanding social research, but they are necessary if readers are going to begin to engage with the ideas underpinning social research as well as the process and practice of social research itself.

## Primary and secondary research and data

A first question you are likely to be asked when putting together a research proposal or dissertation is, 'What kind of project do you want to do?' One of the key dimensions of this is whether you aim to collect your own data, or you want to use existing data or library resources, often supplemented by theoretical work, to construct your project instead.

These different kinds of social research projects are named after the data they collect: primary and secondary data. Primary research is usually associated with researchers who collect data in some way for themselves. So, if a researcher goes and interviews research participants, or collects data for themselves using a survey, then they will be conducting primary research. Equally, the data that they will collect during this process will be primary data.

If, however, researchers are conducting a review of others' work, or are looking at sources that were collected by someone else, then they are usually regarded as conducting secondary research. The data that they are using (the research papers they are reviewing, or the data that others collected) is secondary data.

These distinctions between primary and secondary research and data are a reasonable starting point, and they are widely used in the literature on research methods (as well as in university departments, which have few problems in making the division between primary and secondary research projects), but the boundary between them isn't as clear and distinct as this simple presentation suggests. Historians, for example, would regard the sources they find in archives as primary data, but those sources were initially collected by others for entirely different reasons than the historian will be putting them to, so it is certainly possible to argue they are really closer to secondary sources.

The distinction between primary and secondary research and data is therefore good as a starting point, and as a way of labelling research in an outline way, but isn't something that needs to detain us for too long. There are other terms which are more important, both in respect of their analytical value and their significance within the research methods literature, so we should move on to them.

## Quantitative, qualitative and mixed-methods research and data

Another common split is between quantitative and qualitative research and data. Quantitative research is primarily concerned with techniques that analyse numbers.

If we are calculating descriptive statistics (calculating averages, probabilities or exploring numerical relationships), then we are doing quantitative research. Quantitative data is the numbers we use as data, or the results of the numeric processes that the research has been though.

Qualitative data is non-numeric data. It is made up of words or images or anything that isn't presently in numeric form. Of course, it's possible to convert just about any non-numeric phenomenon to a number – we can code letters as numbers, count the occurrence of words, express feelings on a scale from 1 (very bad) to 5 (very good). However, qualitative data is often collected because it can capture more naturalistically what research participants wish to express because they are able to use their own words rather than the categories or tick-boxes that researchers have designed.

Quantitative methods carry with them a range of often well-established techniques that can be checked for their statistical robustness, and where the consumers of research want a specific answer, they can be extremely powerful. However, qualitative researchers often argue that social research often can't provide such specific answers, and that instead social knowledge is often contingent and contextual.

Mixed-methods research, as the name implies, suggests a strategy whereby you use both quantitative and qualitative research. It can be a way of overcoming the problems associated with each of the approaches, and is very fashionable at present for exactly this reason. However, it can also create a terrible mess. This is because different methods often lead to the production of different kinds of knowledge, and having more data of different types doesn't always result in better research. It is therefore important that we begin to think about some of the philosophical issues underlying research methods.

## Induction and deduction

Induction and deduction are used in at least two ways in social research methods texts. Inductive research is that which tries to work from data (usually primary data) to build theory – it is a 'bottom up' approach to generating theoretical insight. Deductive research is that which, on the other hand, tests theory through the use of (usually) quantitative data. Inductive research tries to start without clearly defined hypotheses or propositions that the researcher is trying to examine, whereas, for deductive research, because it is based on testing existing theories, will tend to include these elements.

Inductive research tends to be closely associated with a qualitative research strategy. This is because qualitative researchers tend to place a premium on being close to their data and participants by collecting it themselves, and by trying to approach their participants in such as way that any theory they generate is built up from data observation rather than being imposed upon their data from pre-existing theory.

In contrast, deductive research tends to be quantitative, as it involves testing theories and hypotheses using procedures that are sufficiently robust in their own terms to allow this to happen. Quantitative methods tend to have tightly defined procedures that allow testing to occur in ways that would be difficult with qualitative research.

To make things more difficult, it is possible to do deductive qualitative research, and inductive quantitative research, but the majority of work falls within the rule of thumb above – quantitative research tends to be deductive, and qualitative research tends to be inductive. Economists, for example, often analyse government-collected statistics (secondary data) using deductive, quantitative methods. Sociologists, on the other hand, often conduct inductive research, collecting primary data through the use of qualitative methods such as observation or interviews.

To understand the underlying differences between these approaches, we need a few more terms.

## Epistemology, methodology and ontology

The next three terms are perhaps more intrinsically scary. These are complicated-sounding terms that are often more associated with philosophical discussion than with research, and many researchers have successfully gone about their work without having to confront them. Why do we need to know about them?

My argument why these terms are important is this; it is possible to do good research without understanding its philosophical bases, or exactly how research works, but that you significantly increase your chances of doing good research if you understand something about the philosophical assumptions implicit in the process of choosing methods to deal with the particular research problem you are trying to address. Knowing something about the philosophy of social research means that you are more likely to make informed choices about method, and that can only be a good thing. Being aware of some of the key debates around the philosophy of social research will not mean that you always do good research, but will increase your chances of making good methods choices.

Having outlined my position, let's get on with understanding these terms. I'm going to deal with them one at a time before putting them all together to discuss how they fit together in particular ways of conducting social research.

## Epistemology

Epistemology is the theory of knowledge. It is concerned with what knowledge is, and what counts as good knowledge.

So what is good knowledge? At the risk of sounding like I'm equivocating from the beginning, well … it depends. Epistemology examines what counts as truth (if, indeed, anything at all falls into that category), what we can say we know and how we know what we know.

Different methods, and different research strategies, favour different kinds of knowledge. A great deal of scientific discourse has a tendency to present experimental methods as being the most important and significant, and these methods favour knowledge of a particular kind. Considering just about everyone who is reading this book will have conducted an experiment at some point, think for a moment what kind of knowledge experiments generate. We'll deal more with experiments later in the chapter, but for the moment note that experiments are primarily a tool for testing hypothesis and for generating knowledge this is either highly quantitative (where, for example, you are conducting laboratory experiments in psychology) or propositional (where you are trying to find out what happens as a result of introducing a particular intervention or taking a particular action).

Now contrast that with the kind of knowledge that would come from you conducting a series of interviews instead. It is possible to analyse interviews using quantitative techniques, but they are more likely to produce knowledge that is qualitative instead. The knowledge produced from conducting a series of interviews is likely to be far more contingent, and while it may produce propositions, it is more likely to demonstrate the differences in perspective and understanding of the participants than what happened as a result of a particular intervention or change.

As experiments produce knowledge that is more definite, and which is based more on the methods of what we call the natural sciences, does that mean that they are better than interviews? Well, some researchers would certainly argue that. However, my argument is that experiments might well work in some circumstances, but not in others, and that we need to be aware of their limits and problems before we go ahead with them. It may well be that interviews are a better option in dealing with some research questions and in some circumstances. The trick is knowing when. I'll return again to experiments in a moment, but before then we need to deal with two more terms.

## Methodology (and method)

Research methods texts often begin by discussing the difference between methodology and method. Because both words tend to get used a lot in research, it's important to say what each means, as well as their significance more generally. Methods are the tools and techniques that are used in social research practice. Interviews are a social research method, as is the calculation of descriptive statistics.

Methodology, on the other hand, studies methods to work out what we can usefully say about them, and explores their philosophy, application and usage. So when we are examining methods, comparing them or thinking about the kinds of knowledge that they produce, then we are doing methodology. So technically this book is about methodology, but I'm going to be writing about methods most of the time, so will tend to stick to that term rather than its (arguably more pompous) close relative.

To go back to the argument above, and relate it to the section on epistemology, there seems to me to be a strong case for thinking about how particular methods privilege particular kinds of knowledge. The choice of method has to be related to the particular problem before a researcher and the research question that they need to answer, and the choice of research method carries with it implications for the kind of knowledge that the research is able to produce later on. If you want to use statistical methods, then you are less likely to be conducting interviews and more likely to be doing surveys. At this level this sounds like a statement of the obvious, but as the book progresses I hope to demonstrate that method choices are often more subtle than this, but still carry considerable implications for the knowledge that they subsequently produce.

## Ontology

Ontology is the theory of being. That's not a particularly helpful definition, but it again is a starting point. When you are considering questions of ontology you are thinking about issues such as whether the world exists independently of your perceptions of it. As it turns out, this kind of question, I would argue, is extremely important for social research.

Let's revisit for a moment the example of the experimental method we've already discussed above, and which will be discussed at greater length below. Experiments implicitly presume that there is a world independent of our understanding of, and that the goal of social research is to find out about it. This is a common-sense approach to doing research, which is what we can call a 'realist' assumption in that it assumes that the world has a 'real' existence independent of human perceptions of it.

Interviews, however, do not always have to presume a world independent of our perceptions of them. Interviews can be utilised within a range of social research traditions, being used in lots of different ways. In social policy, interviews are often used to find out more about participants in a particular situation, interviewing nurses to find out about healthcare, or unemployed men in social housing to find out about a particular aspect of social exclusion. They will often tend to assume, however, that by talking to people in these situations that research can find out what is 'really' going on (the link to the 'realist' position may therefore even be present in the language of the research programme).

However, other disciplines, for example within Human Geography, might use interviews to find out instead the inter-subjective experience of research participants. The important thing in such a research programme would be to find out about how participants construct their reality – an almost mirror-image situation to the social policy programme, as the emphasis might be on the narratives or stories participants tell one another regardless without any regard as to whether they give a consistent account of the worlds in which they live. In that approach, the existence of an external world is either the product of the participants of the research, or irrelevant to it. In the first instance, the argument would be that the world does not exist in any meaningful way outside of our subject experiences of it – we cannot experience the world except through our own senses. Therefore the world is constructed, rather than coming to us as a given. This means that it is possible to move to the second position, that whether the external world exists or not is actually irrelevant – it is our conceptions of it that matter.

As such, particular methods, and the way that they are used in particular research programmes, carry with them a view of the world that has consequences for what we can claim from the research. Both of the perspectives discussed in this section will be expanded on and discussed in far greater depth in this book. The important thing is that, when you are conducting an interview, you need to be able to link it to your research question, and to conduct it in an appropriate way. If you are trying to find out about what is going on in a particular situation, you may find you have presuppositions in your questions or your analysis about the presence or otherwise of an external world that affect what you are subsequently able to say in your results or conclusions.

## Some general points about research questions

An obvious starting point for any programme in research is the question it is trying to answer. However, in practice, this is something that students and researchers often struggle with. In the worst case, this can end up with researchers trying to find a question that fits with the research that they believe they've done, attempting to retro-fit it as if it was what they had in mind all along.

Clearly having a good research question doesn't mean you automatically do good research, but it does increase the chance that you'll at least know where to start. In addition, it's a good exercise for checking your understanding of the research principles outlined in Chapter 2, as research questions contain a number of implicit assumptions about social research that can either reassure reviewers that you know what you are talking about, or undermine your proposal or idea before it has even begun to get off the ground.

### Questions or hypotheses in quantitative methods

In quantitative designs, researchers use questions and hypotheses to provide sharp focus to the purpose of the study. Remember, quantitative studies are likely to be deductive, and so testing a theory or hypothesis, so the research question they are attempting to answer should follow directly from that aim.

Quantitative research questions tend to be concerned with the variables that the research wants to know about. It will particularly be concerned with the relationships between the variable seen as causing a relationship on another variable where the effect is measured, as well as probably also including a third variable which is being controlled for. So we might ask what the effect of gender on pay is in local government, controlling for education achievement level.

Quantitative hypotheses are predictions the research makes about the expected relationships among the variables that are included in the study. Hypotheses are then tested using statistical procedures which allow researchers to infer whether or not they have been proved.

Research hypotheses are typically either 'null' or 'alternative'. The null hypothesis makes a prediction that no relationship exists in the general population between groups on the variable under question. So, to continue the example above, it would suggest that there is no significant difference between men's and women's pay in local government, controlling for education level.

The alternative hypothesis (sometimes called the directional hypothesis), however, suggests that there is a relationship between the variables under question, and makes a prediction about its direction based on a previous theory or existing literature (which is why quantitative research tends to be deductive). So an alternative hypothesis might be that women are paid less than men in local government, controlling for education attainment level.

Finally, if we suspect there is a relationship between variables, but really don't know from existing literature which direction it is going in, we might make an alternative hypothesis that is non-directional – such as gender is related to pay in local government, controlling for educational level.

So, to summarise, research questions in quantitative methods will ask questions about clearly defined variables, which hypotheses can then test by gathering appropriate data and by using statistical methods.

## Qualitative research questions

Asking research questions in qualitative research is usually a very different process from that in quantitative inquiry.

Qualitative inquiry is likely to be the result in an inductive approach to research. This presents us with an immediate quandary – if we don't know what we expect to find, how can we sensibly ask questions about it?

There is clearly some sense to this, but it is probably overstating the case somewhat. Equally, even if we don't know much about the social context that we want to research, that isn't the same thing as saying that we have no idea what we are trying to find out about it.

It is fair to say that, within qualitative work, research questions are likely to be expressed in a more open and less precise way than in quantitative research, which is usually aiming to test specific theories. In fact, a good starting point for putting together questions in qualitative research is to ask the biggest question you can …

## A central question

The process of qualitative research can often start by asking a big question that you'd like your research to answer. Quantitative researchers often struggle with this, as they are used to specifying precise relationships between clearly defined variables. Qualitative research, in contrast, is more accepting of ambiguities and differences – that's supposed to be its strength.

Asking a general, central question can be a good starting point. To go back to the example above, we might ask, 'What is the effect of gender on pay?' That's certainly a big question.

Now we have specified the general area that we are interested in, we have some key concepts to think about – here we have 'gender', 'pay' and 'public sector'. What we can do now is drill down into each of these concepts to try and generate sub-questions that get us further down the road to a study that is actually possible to research (without unlimited time and unlimited resources).

## Sub-questions

Starting with 'gender', 'pay' and 'public sector' we can now start being a bit more precise about each one. Starting with 'gender' we can think about the dimensions of gender and work out which ones we are most interested in researching here. Are we interested in relatively simple differences between men and women, or in more complex ideas where masculinity and femininity might come into play – in short, are we really saying 'gender' when we mean 'sex', or are we more interested in the more performative category of gender?

Thinking a bit more about pay, we might want to differentiate between full- and part-time work, between permanent and temporary work, between salaried and waged work, or any number of other categories associated with the idea. We will pick up on sub-questions depending on, once we've considered the dimensions of the idea, exactly what it is we want to research.

Finally (in terms of this example, anyway), there is the 'public sector', which could mean all services run by the state, or could be more precise, being local government or health services in a particular area, including those provided by both public and private sectors.

Having thought through our concepts, we can then begin to ask sub-questions that aim at directing the study in a more specific way. We might want to ask, 'How does the performance of masculinity affect salary in local government in York?' That puts together our concepts into a far more specific form than the central question, focusing our attention on the problem in hand.

We can then proceed to generate additional sub-questions such as, 'How does the performance of masculinity in salaried jobs differ from its performance in non-salaried jobs in local government in York?' Now I've got a comparison – two questions that explore the differences in the performance of masculinity in two different settings, those of salaried and non-salaried workers. I can continue to generate sub-questions until I've got all the dimensions that I think are important to cover, but – a word of warning – generating very large numbers of sub-questions is likely to lead to you being rather overwhelmed when it comes to your actual study.

# Some other general guidelines

The language of research questions can reveal a great deal. If you begin questions with 'What' then you seem to be putting together a descriptive question – you are trying to find out 'what' something is like. This is an open question that can be answered using qualitative work, but can also fit with quantitative designs such as surveys that are trying to find out the characteristics of those included. So you might ask:

> What is the average height of eight-year-olds in Newcastle? (which is the basis of a quantitative study)

Questions beginning with 'How' equally tend to be open, but are generally more amenable to qualitative than quantitative research. This is because they are likely to be provoke complex answers, and it may be difficult to come up with a quantitative design to take sufficient account of this. 'How' questions are often linked to attempts to bring above change, and so can acquire a normative aspect quickly. An exception is where 'How' is simply followed by 'many', in which case you effectively neutralise the complexity quickly. So we might ask:

> How does gender affect pay in local government in York? (which suggests to me a pretty open inquiry not based on existing theory)

Or:

> How many women working in local government in York receive below median-level pay? (which suggests to me a quantitative project).

'Why' questions are a source of some debate. Some writers suggest that they are amenable to quantitative research, and this is the case provided that the causes and effects can be modelled in such a way as to prove or disprove an existing theory, and that the causes and effects tend to occur together so that their relationship can be shown statistically.

The question: 'Why do more women receive below median-level pay in local government in York?' could be answered using a quantitative survey tool that could provide several possible answers from existing theory or literature that participants in the research could answer (although finding the best group to answer might be a challenge here). Equally, however, it could be answered using qualitative research strategies such as a semi-structured interview, where the question could be asked directly, and participants answer in their own words (a strategy that, of course, is also possible using open-response questions in a survey).

For this reason, I tend to associate 'why' questions with either quantitative tools such as surveys, where we already know a great deal about the case in general (low pay and gender), and where we are looking to confirm a specific theory that we might be testing (due to career breaks to have children), but they are also useful in qualitative work as they allow participants to respond directly and give their own ideas and interpretations of the question.

# Some practical examples of how questions, methods and philosophy combine

Examples of the importance of the concepts described so far in this chapter have already been given, but it's worth spending some more time on this to make the links as clear as possible. Three will be given here. It is worth stressing that, in order to work through these examples I can't possibly do justice to all the nuances and different versions of the examples that I work through. However, I do hope that the examples chosen are not unrealistically over-simplified.

## Experiments

Experiments are a good place to start in thinking about social research, not only because they have already been used in examples above, but also because most people reading this book will have carried out an experiment at some point in their lives. To think about experiments, we have to first disentangle what they are and how they work.

Experiments are usually associated with natural sciences – a first association readers might have is that of finding out the boiling point of water at school, or attempting to distil pure ethanol in chemistry class (or was that just me?). Experiments are a method that involves putting forward a hypothesis and null hypothesis of what the experiment is designed to test. So, to follow the natural science example we might propose that water boils at 100 degrees centigrade. What then happens is that a test of that hypothesis is designed to control for the variables within it. So we would be careful to be able to measure the temperature of water as accurately as we sensibly could, find a reliable heat source and be able to put the water in a container that will conduct heat without disrupting the experiment by polluting the water. We will also need a clear definition of what 'boils' means. We will then have a process by which we apply heat to the water, and be able to measure the temperature at which 'boiling' occurs. Once we have repeated this test sufficient times, we will be able to say that we have tested our hypothesis, and be able to draw a conclusion from the experiment that either confirms the hypothesis or the null hypothesis.

## Stages of experimentation

Experiments therefore have three phases. First, there is the stage of working out what it is you are going to test, and forming a hypothesis and null hypothesis.

This is a creative process which is inductive in nature in that it is attempting to think of a specific phenomenon that is worth investigating that might be representative of a general phenomenon. In social research, for example, we might be interested in post-industrialisation as a general phenomenon and want to investigate it, but have to come up with a specific hypothesis that allows us to address this general phenomenon, such as 'former coal-mining communities tend to suffer considerable decline unless they receive significant state investment'.

Once we have come up with stage one, we can move on to stage two – designing the specific test of the hypotheses we have come up with in stage two. This is a deductive stage in that it attempts to show, given our general proposition, how our specific example fits within them. So to continue the post-industrialisation example, we might examine the incomes or wealth of a range of communities that have lost their coal-mining industries, where some have had significant state investment and some not.

This takes us onto the third stage, carrying out the research itself, the carrying out of the experiment.

The final stage is that of interpreting our results. This is again an inductive process – trying to work out from the numbers we have collected what they mean by finding appropriate analytical tools. We can then compare our results to our hypotheses and find out what the case appears to be.

## The philosophical basis of experimentation

There are several key elements to experiments that have to be taken into account in the light of this chapter's discussion to consider their suitability for social research as well as for natural science research. First, there are a range of philosophical assumptions. Experiments are based on the idea that there is an independent reality which we can access and investigate – or 'realism' – and is an ontological assumption (it assumes something about the world, rather than our knowledge of the world). From this assumption comes the claim that knowledge is good if it represents that reality – an idea known as the correspondence theory of truth. We know something is true if, by investigating it empirically, it seems to be the case. There is therefore a privileging of empirical investigation as a means of advancing knowledge. If we can't measure a particular social phenomenon accurately, or there are other barriers to doing empirical research, then experiments might not be appropriate. The combination of all of these ideas together is often referred to as positivism.

## Features of experimentation

Experiments also have two specific features that are important. First, there is the idea that the external reality that we are testing can be controlled so as to allow individual elements within it to be investigated. A difficult question is whether social phenomena more generally can be controlled in this way. Experiments assume that a 'closed' system can be created, or that a particular social phenomenon can be sufficiently controlled so that it can be tested one variable at a time. It makes sense to wonder whether this is often the case – at any moment in time countless things are often going on in social situations, so it can be very difficult to isolate the effect of just one variable. Recent research in experimental economics (Ariely, 2008) has shown remarkable creativity in achieving controls and closing social systems down so that the effect of one variable can be shown, but whether this is generalisable to other situations is a difficult question. If we can't control variables, then can we conduct a social experiment? Is it possible, given the multiple influences and factors often engaging with us in social situations, to measure their effects one at a time?

A second key question related to experiments is their treatment of causation. Causation is, in simple terms, a model of how we construct a model of how one thing can be said (or not said) to cause another thing. The model of causation experiments (along with lots of other kinds of social research) depend upon is called 'constant conjunction'. Constant conjunction is the idea that we can say that one thing leads to another if the two things tend to occur in sequence, together, in lots of different contexts. If I find that applying heat to water leads to it getting warmer in lots of different situations, then I might conclude that the heat is making the water warmer. If I find that introducing performance targets into public organisations makes them focus more on meeting targets than providing good service, and this seems to happen in a range of different settings, then I might be able to conclude that the targets are leading to the change in service (albeit within the 'closed system' constraint described above).

## Assumptions in experimentation

Experiments therefore contain a complex bundle of assumptions about the world. They are an example of quantitative research strategy, and are deductive as they involve testing a theory or hypothesis. Experiments are realist in that they presume that the world exists independently of our conceptions of it, and that we can access that world more or less accurately through our experience of it, so that good knowledge is that which describes the world (empiricism).

Experiments might appear to be an obvious way of conducting research, but questions about their appropriateness can be raised immediately upon considering the philosophical assumptions underlying them. Experiments presume an external world, and regard knowledge as being good if it can be shown to correspond to it (the correspondence theory of truth). They therefore privilege empirical knowledge, and so require us to be able to empirically measure the phenomena we are looking to investigate, as well as assuming that causes and effects tend to occur together – if there is a gap between them then this poses difficult problems. This usually means that, in order to conduct an experiment we must be able to control the presumed external reality so that we can measure the effect of single variables upon it.

But what if any of these conditions doesn't work? Does that mean that we can't conduct an experiment? The theoretical answer to this is probably 'no'. If you compromise the design, then you risk claiming findings that are unjustifiable according to the method. The practical answer, however, is 'maybe', because you can try and argue that the condition you are breaching isn't so serious as to compromise the entire design. You must, however, be able to show how you are going to justify your experimental design choice given the breaches of condition that your question might lead to.

## Class analysis

### Basic ideas

Class analysis is not really a method in social science research, but more a tradition within sociology and political science that makes use of, and which favours, particular methods. Class analysis is associated with the Marxist tradition which states that underlying many of the recurring problems in society is the exploitation of one class (the proletariat) by another (the bourgeoisie). What this boils down to is that one class in society, a minority in terms of numbers but certainly not in terms of income or wealth, is able to dominate another, the majority of those who have to work for a living. The interesting question that comes from this is how this persists even though the majority of people seem to get rather a bad deal from it.

### How class analysis is different to experimental methods

Like experimental design, the methods of class analysis assume a reality independent of human perceptions of it, but unlike experiments it suggests that accessing that reality might be problematic. A moment's thought shows why this is the case – if it were straightforward to discover the truth of the situation according to class analysis, that one class in society was exploiting another, then the exploited would have done something about it by now. So whereas class analysis would propose that although there is an external reality, it needs to find different methods to experimental analysis that allow us to access it because participants' beliefs, ideas and concepts might prevent them from seeing it. In sum, class analysis, at least in its contemporary realist guises (Sayer, 2005), would suggest that although social classes exist independently of our conceptions of them, our interpretation of them might differ from individual to individual or group to group.

### Methods in class analysis

The methods involved in class analysis also have a different model of causation to experimental work. Causation will be explored more in a later chapter, but for the moment we can bring out something of the contrast between constant conjunction models and the generative model (Pawson, 2006b) often used in class analysis. Rather than causes always appearing alongside their results, as in constant conjunction models, they might have rather more complex relationships. A generative model suggests that mechanisms are at work which might shape our behaviour and interactions with others which might not be immediately obvious, or even occurring at the same place and time, but which are significant nonetheless. Our social class, for example, as well as having direct implications in terms of the financial resources that we have access to, might shape our attitude towards others, our beliefs about our role in society, our expectations of how far we should take our schooling, our ideas about what careers might be possible and a variety of other factors that can channel us through our life. Class analysis suggests that the social position we are born into matters profoundly – we have choices about where we go from there, but we have to recognise that they are not completely free choices. To paraphrase Marx, we make choices, but not necessarily in conditions of our own choosing.

Class analysis therefore has to proceed along rather different lines to an experiment. It has to use methods that seek regularities which shape our behaviour, but may have far more complex relationships than we can find using experiments. It might utilise quantitative methods, for example, to show how particular groups are being systematically discriminated against through benefits systems or employment opportunities. Qualitative research could attempt to explore how belief systems differ from one social group to another, and to show what difference this might make in society. Theoretical work in political science may make little specific use of empirical work at all, instead exploring how the particular combinations of structures present in society have causal effects on those living within them (as in Jessop, 2002).

Class analysts would tend to suggest that experimental designs are usually inappropriate in social research. They would argue that it is not possible to access reality in a straightforward way through empirical research, and that the constant conjunction model doesn't work because class often manifests itself in ways that can be difficult to measure straightforwardly and require a more creative approach to interpreting causality that involves looking for regularities rather than strict sequences of one thing following another.

## The philosophical basis of class analysis

Class analysis, then, works in a rather different way to experimental methods. Class analysis applies a particular theory about the world, that social relations are driven by class, and attempts to present a compelling account along these lines. This is, strictly speaking, neither deductive nor inductive in terms of its reasoning, although it is closer to deductive than to inductive in that it is using a pre-existing theory.

Class analysis is, strictly speaking, an abductive research strategy, requiring a creative interpretation of the world from a particular perspective. Abduction is different from induction or deduction because it is not constructing a theory from the data (as with induction) or testing an existing theory using hypotheses (as with deduction) – instead it is an interpretive process for understanding how the world works that stands or falls on how well it is able to explain what is going on (Danermark et al., 2001: 85–88).

Class analysis is, like experimental methods, realist, in that it presumes an external world. However, unlike experiments, it suggests that accessing that external world is not always easy because we have to do so through our interpretive world – and that means that it is possible to conceal the class factors that analysts in this tradition believe drive the world. So at the same time as being realist, class analysis is interpretive in that it requires us to interpret the external world rather than being able to access it straightforwardly, as with the empiricism of experimental methods. Class analysis also tends to be normative in that it seeks to emancipate people through a better understanding of their class position – by understanding that there is a relatively small number of people who have the majority of the world's resources, we might want to act upon this knowledge and do something about it. This is a position known as 'critical realism' – where we not only accept there is a world external to our understanding of it, but also that we should be doing something about the inequalities and unfairness that results from a better understanding of it.

Finally, because causes and effects do not tend to occur together in class analysis, and the class system acts upon our lives in complex and diverse ways, the constant conjunction model of causation used in experimental methods cannot work. Instead it was a generative model of causation instead that seeks to find the mechanisms that affect our lives, and which might be the result of long chains of events rather than simple linkages. The link between the number of hours our parents spent reading to us as a child, along with the number of books in the house and the availability of reading materials, and subsequent educational achievement might be complex and take years to become clear – a simple constant conjunction model is unlikely to work. But by viewing those factors as generative mechanisms that eventually lead to different educational outcomes, a less firm link is made that makes us concentrate on the many ways that reading and access to books might be important in a child's development.

## Actor-network theory

### Basic ideas

Actor-network theory takes a very different approach to understanding the social world than either experiments or class analysis. Actor-network theory's roots lie far more in anthropology than in scientific experimentation or Marxism, and as such it is concerned with providing detailed descriptions of social contexts that explicitly attempt to avoid theory as much as possible.

## Philosophy and actor-network theory

Actor-network theory can be characterised as being incredulous towards realist claims that we are able to access the world in any kind of unmediated form (Law, 2004). Instead, it argues that as the social world is necessarily viewed by us from our own perspectives, and instead of trying to generate theories that simply underplay the complexity of the social world, we should instead focus on attempting to describe what is going on in all its mess and cacophony.

Actor-network theorists defy characterisation, but this perspective can be seen to have a great deal in common with idealism – the view that ideas are the only reality we are able to experience. As such, the social world, rather than being a source of and location for objective research (as with experiments) or a location for class oppression (as with class analysis), is the result of our inter-subjective experience – more in common with the human geographic approach described earlier in the chapter. If reality is determined inter-subjectively, then it is appropriate for research to be about understanding each other's ideas, and understanding that they won't link together neatly but overlap and contradict one another, not because one is more truthful than the other, but because the world is open to multiple interpretations.

Idealism means being concerned not with attempting to find truth in an objective external world, but instead focusing on the perceptions and ideas people hold. It would argue that there are limits to the extent to which we can understand each other's experience because we have each had different lives that have led to different subjectivities. In particular, actor-network research is concerned with respecting the voice of overlooked and repressed actors, and with inductively generating careful description from observation and careful note-keeping, with the maximum respect paid to those who work with researchers to generate the data.

## Methods in actor-network theory

Because of its roots in anthropology, actor-network writers tend to suggest detailed ethnographies are the most appropriate way of researching the social world (see, for example, Latour, 2005). Methods books that advocate the approach take researchers through detailed processes for note-taking and record-keeping along these lines, and then provide guidance as to how their accounts can be structured to reflect the complexities of the world that they find (see Mol, 2002, for a combination of both actor-network account and methodological discussion).

There is also implicitly a different model of causality present in actor-network analysis that we might refer to as discursive causation. Because of the belief that reality is inter-discursively constructed, then causation also follows the same pattern, meaning that causes are often the result of oppressive practices and concepts that must be located, exposed and changed. If we can change our concepts and practices, then we can reach a fairer and more equal society. Causes lie within these concepts and practices, and it is these that must be addressed.

**Table 1.1** Different approaches to social research

|  | Experiments | Class analysis | Actor-network analysis |
|---|---|---|---|
| Assumption about external world | External world exists, and is accessible to empirical research | External world exists, but is not always easily accessible to empirical research | External world is the result of our concepts and its existence or otherwise is largely irrelevant |
| Favoured method type | Quantitative, empirical | Quantitative and qualitative, interpretive | Favours qualitative, descriptive over quantitative |
| Favoured type of knowledge | Numeric, hypothesis-derived. | Numeric and discursive, class-derived | Discursive, emancipatory accounts |
| View of social system | Product of the effect of variables that can be controlled | Product of class-based mechanisms that empirical research cannot reveal | Product of inter-subjective mechanisms through concepts and practices |
| Model of causation | Constant conjunction | Generative causation | Discursive causation |
| Research strategy | Deductive | Abductive | Inductive |

A comparison between experiments, class analysis and actor-network theory is shown in Table 1.1.

What this amounts to is that different methods not only have different research agendas and procedures, but also that they look at the world in different ways. Thinking about these differences considering the philosophical ideas above provides us with a way of informing our choices, but also explaining why it is that different approaches to social research often seem to talk past one another – it is because they are thinking about the social world in very different ways.

# What's the problem, and how are you going to research it? A logic of appropriateness

## Experiments and the scientific method

A good starting point for thinking about how you are going to go about social research, then, is to think about the assumptions that you hold about research. Do you believe that social research is about approximating the scientific method as closely as possible, discovering real phenomena in the social world as writing it up as an objective, independent researcher? If so, then experiments are likely, of the three versions of social research considered here, to be the most appealing to you. In disciplines that have taken their inspiration from scientific methodology, such as psychology and economics, these methods tend to be most widely used. This type of research has produced remarkable insights into how humans behave, and has prestigious awards such as the Nobel Prize for Economics available to it.

However, this view of research is not exempt from criticisms, and its advocates have to understand different perspectives than their own. All researchers should be able to take part in informed discussions considering whether there are any limits to the fields in which their methods can be used, and what the limitations of using those methods might be. Future chapters continue this discussion.

## Class analysis and realism

The class analysis position described above is most associated with contemporary realism (including critical realism). Realism explicitly suggests that there is a need to separate out ontology from epistemology and methodology (for a full exploration see Archer, 1995). Realists acknowledge that there is a world external to our perceptions of it (and ontological claim), but also that we can have different perceptions of that world (an epistemological claim).

What is needed, according to realists, is research strategies that acknowledge that reality is both complex and open to differing interpretations. This points firmly in favour of mixed-methods research, often with quantitative approaches that look for societal patterns that may not be immediately obvious, and qualitative methods that attempt to find out how those patterns impact on people's lives. To revisit the class analysis example, there is still a great deal of work to be done tracking the very many ways that education affects our life chances, with quantitative research being able to look for patterns between educational results, life expectancy, lifetime income, susceptibility to illness and a range of other factors, complemented by qualitative research that can attempt to examine these interplays 'close up' – by looking at whether hospitals treat patients of different social class in different ways, for example.

However, just because realism forms a 'middle way' here between the scientific, hypothetico-deductive model and the idealism of actor-network theory, it doesn't mean it is without problems. Contemporary texts on the philosophy of social research often suggest realism is that most persuasive of the approaches available in social science (Benton and Craib, 2001) but it is also possibly the most complex. Realists, because of the generative model of causation, can occasionally appear as if they are able to find their own pet theory in any dataset – a complex model of causation allows there to be considerable distance in space and time between causes and effects, running the risk of researchers imposing their own ideas on every social issue they investigate. Class researchers might have a tendency to see class at the root of every issue, gender researchers see gender and ethnicity researchers ethnicity.

Equally, combining methods is a fraught business raising lots of questions about purpose and fit that must be handled thoughtfully and carefully (see Chapter 12). Just because mixed-methods research is currently fashionable, and supported by a realist approach, it doesn't mean it is always appropriate or the right thing to do.

## Actor-network theory and idealism

I've identified actor-network theory as being idealist in nature, and for the purposes of our example, the tradition in research that I identified represents a third perspective on social research – one that emphasises the importance of subjective knowledge, and which celebrates difference. Actor-network research seeks to examine our inter-subjectivity and raise awareness of how the categories which we use to divide up our experience can create unfair power relationships.

Again, as with experimental and realist perspectives, there is a great deal to be said in favour of actor-network analysis. Our concepts do undoubtedly influence the way we experience our lives, and detailed accounts that show difference in the social world can go a long way to show how this affects our understanding of it. However, its idealist starting point leaves it open to criticisms from realists that it has little to say about the actuality of social inequalities, concentrating too much on the experience of them so that problems of poverty and health are reduced to interpretations rather than having a physical basis. Equally, a complaint against its subjectivist epistemology would be that, in respective others' standpoints, it leaves no room for criticisms of practices that researchers from other social research traditions believe should be roundly condemned. If you accept that others have a standpoint or perspective different from yours, and that you cannot fully understand their world because you lack their subjectivity, then what right do you have to criticise them, even if they behave in a way that people from your own cultural background might find barbaric and cruel? There are answers to these questions, but they require actor-network researchers to be aware of alternative approaches to social research and to be able to understand their research in relation to them.

## Conclusion

In all, what I'm trying to ask for is for researchers from different perspectives to gain an understanding of how their approaches differ, and for this to promote dialogue rather than conflict. Social researchers will disagree about the best way to do social research, but understanding our differences gives us a better chance of learning from them and of doing better research in the future as a result.

## Five things to remember about this chapter

1  Social research embraces a wide variety of positions and has a number of terms you will have to get to grips with in order to be able to understand what you are being asked to do.
2  Research projects tend to initially be split into those that are primary and those that are secondary. Primary research projects get researchers to collect their own data, whereas secondary research projects are those that re-use existing data or get researchers to come up with a new perspective on existing data.

DESIGNING SOCIAL RESEARCH

3  Research projects that try and build theory from data are inductive, and tend to be qualitative (although this is not always the case), as they are based on trying to capture the fine-grained nature of the world through methods such as observation and interviewing.

4  Research projects that try and test existing theory are deductive, and tend to be quantitative (although, again, this isn't always the case), as they are based on using robust procedures to prove statistically whether a particular hypothesis can be supported or not. The experimental method is the archetype here.

5  These different methods have very different underlying philosophies, and it is important to have an understanding of these differences, not because it will allow you to show how clever you are, but because it can help you to design social research so that it is more coherent and so has a better chance of success. Knowing all the philosophy in the world can't guarantee that you do a good project, but it can prevent you from making mistakes, such as claiming that you are going to prove or disprove a theory by using a method which simply doesn't offer this as a possibility. As it would be odd to try and generate an in-depth understanding of a social setting using an experimental design (odd, but not impossible), it would be odd to try and test a theory using qualitative data because words, videos or other recordings, the primary forms of qualitative data, can't really be used to prove or disprove anything.

# TWO

## Reviewing what other people have said – or how can I tell if others' research is any good?

### Introduction

As soon as you begin to engage with a new area of research, you are in the position of having to review what others have said. Even if you are planning research yourself, the first thing you will have to do is to find out what other researchers have already said about the topic (not least to find out if what you plan to do might already have been comprehensively researched already).

If you're writing a grant proposal you'll need to be able to show that what you are asking for money for adds to existing knowledge in some way, and if you are putting together a proposal for a studentship of some kind, you are much more likely to get the money if you can locate your proposed study in relation to the existing literature. There is a separate chapter later in the book that deals with the process of writing up research proposals, but because reviewing what existing research says is broader than that, and will be a part of just about any research project that you are ever involved with, it deserves a chapter to itself.

The chapter proceeds as follows. First, it deals with the nuts and bolts of reviewing – how to tell if a source has credibility, and some strategies for taking notes on your sources. It then considers how you can go about looking for inspiration for your own research projects from published research, before moving on to consider a generic list of criteria for what you are looking for when assessing others' research. After this, it discusses the process by which research gets assessed in the academic world and asks questions of what kind of work gets published the easiest. Finally, it covers the topic of how you might go about writing the review section of your proposal/thesis/dissertation and gives some ideas for making this successful, before concluding.

# Nuts and bolts

Okay, so you want to find out about a new area of research. What do you do? Most of my students seem to now start off by typing some key words into Google, and seeing what happens as a result. Failing that, their first port of call might be Wikipedia. Is this a good strategy? Yes and no (but probably mostly 'no').

First of all, if you are going to use Google, then you need to be careful. Google gives you the whole internet, so anybody who has ever published a website on your topic will appear on your list of hits eventually. This includes world authorities on your subject, but also groups whose job it is to lobby government (who are therefore hugely biased) and people who have talked about the topic on their own website or blog (this doesn't mean their ideas aren't good, but it does mean their thoughts have never been subjected to any kind of scrutiny). Google can give you a quick introduction to a subject, but you have to be extremely careful in examining the providence of the sites you are looking at – you're going to have to check that the material you are reading is actually any good. How do you do this? You need to find out who it is that wrote the stuff you are reading, what their credentials are, and whether the website has been set up to represent a group of people who are more interested in expressing a particular opinion than trying to present a balanced argument. You have to treat every single web page with considerable caution. Fortunately, there's a better option.

Instead of using Google, use Google Scholar instead. Look at the main Google website, and click on the 'other' tab next to the search box, then on 'Scholar'. Now type in your search. Instead of searching the whole internet, you just searched Google's academic database, so what you are seeing is typically the most-cited work in the world that includes your search terms. What this means is that the research Google Scholar is showing you has been recognised as worthy of discussion or remark in other academic papers. This doesn't mean it is good – other academics could be citing it as an example of a piece of poor research, but this is less likely than it being recognised as being an important piece of work in its field. So what you've found is a piece of work that is probably written by an expert in the field, has probably been through a substantial process of academic review and has been published in a source that gives it credibility. All good news. Now for the bad news. You might not be able to read it straight away.

Google Scholar gives you references to work that is published in sources such as academic journals, book chapters and research reports of other kinds. Just because work is listed there, it doesn't mean you can necessarily read it. A link may take you to the journal's home page, for example, but you will still need a subscription to that journal to be able to read the piece it is referring you to. If you are a student registered at a university, your university might be able to give you access to the journal through its library website. If your library doesn't stock it, you might be able to request the piece (or a copy of it) using a document supply service through the library. In the case of a book, you might be able to see parts of it through

Google Books, to borrow the whole thing from your university or local library, or if you are a registered student, request the book using an inter-library loan. In the case of something like a government report or a research document, you might be lucky in that if you go to that government's website you might be able to download a copy for free, or if not, then you'll have to get a hold of a copy in the same way as you would a book. If all else fails, try looking up the authors of the piece for their homepage, where you might find copies of the pieces (or of pieces which are very similar) available for download.

As well as Google Scholar there are also a range of bibliographic databases that, if you are a registered student, your library might have varying levels of access to, including ingentaconnect, ebscohost, bids, web of science and ovid. Again, these databases won't necessarily be able to give you access to articles as well as to references (although they will sometimes), but will require you to work through the references you find in a similar way as I've outlined above.

All of this is rather more of a hassle than just reading what comes up in vanilla Google, but it does give you access to much better work for the vast majority of cases, and it will mean that you get access to academic work that people reading your work are likely to treat more seriously.

I also said above that I have a problem with Wikipedia (as do most, but by no means all, academics). Actually, there are two problems. The first is that you don't know who wrote the entry for the subject you are examining – it could have been anyone, from a world-leading expert to someone who got bored in their lunchbreak and decided to have a bit of fun writing about something about which they know nothing. You might get lucky, you might not. My second problem is that you are approaching academic work by looking up something in an encyclopaedia. There is likely to be a considerable amount of research on your research topic that has been carefully written up, reviewed and published, but instead of looking at that, by going to Wikipedia you are effectively saying, 'I'm too lazy to read anything that has depth or complexity, instead I'm going to look at a general encylopaedia'. Wikipedia might provide you with a starting point for a research area, but that's all, and you have to treat what it says with considerable caution because you don't know who wrote any particular entry.


## The hierarchy of evidence

Okay, so you've got some research in your area. How do you know if it's any good? The simple answer is always to read it carefully and to think about it while you're reading it, and I'll come to some strategies for that in a moment. However, there are some generic things you can do to assess the quality of sources that you encounter using Google Scholar, other bibliographic databases and, for that matter, Google.

The hierarchy of evidence is a way of thinking about the quality of sources. It's pretty crude, but it is a starting point that students often find helpful.

At the top of the hierarchy are peer-reviewed journal articles and monographs published by good quality publishing houses. A peer-reviewed journal is one that sends out articles submitted to it for examination by academics in the field, getting their opinion of whether the piece is any good or not, and if it is not publishable, whether it ought to be rejected by the editors of the journal, or whether it can be rewritten sufficiently to be publishable. The important thing is that these journals are checking the pieces submitted to them to see by getting the views of experts in the field. This means that anything they publish is much more likely to be good than web pages selected by Google. A monograph from a respected publisher is likely to have been through a similar review process when the book was proposed to the publisher, but also after the author had written it. Publishers named after prominent universities are likely to have prestige (Oxford, Cambridge, Harvard, etc.) and specialist academic publishers who have careful processes are also likely to be high quality (Sage, Palgrave, Policy Press and so on). If a work has been cited a large number of times, be it a journal article or a book, then it is likely to be a piece that you are expected to know and to have an opinion about in your subject area, so you really ought to read it.

Of course, not all journals are equally prestigious and not all publishers as important. You can get an understanding of where journals stand in relation to one another by looking up their citation ranking in Web of Knowledge (if your library has access to it), and this information is often available on the journal's website. Getting to know which journals are well regarded in a particular subject is part of the process of researching it. The most-cited journals in many fields tend to be American, and it is important that you get access to them to see what the current debates in your field are. However, there are lots of other journals out there, many of which might be extremely specialist or have a lower impact than the leading journals in the field. As long as these journals are peer-reviewed are published by credible publishers, then they too are worth looking at.

Next down on the hierarchy are non-peer-reviewed journals and edited collections. Non-peer reviewed journals might be practitioner journals which often contain shorter pieces which are trying to present a particular point of view rather than a full piece of research. Edited collections are made up of a collection of papers which may or may not be linked together by theme or a common subject. Good edited collections will have peer-review processes, but this is not always the case, and collections can be marred by including work that perhaps should not have been published without further revision. Because of this unevenness, in general they aren't as credible as monographs, but there are exceptions, and some very highly cited and important book chapters are out there.

On the same level as these publications is a lot of what is called the 'grey' literature – often government-funded research in particular areas that have published reports to investigate particular problems. This kind of work has probably been extensively reviewed and competitively bid for in order to attract funding, but processes of peer review are not usually as rigorous for the final report. It is likely, however, that this type of work has been written by experts in the field, and so is often of very high quality. Reports from research organisations also fall into this category, but have to be treated a little more carefully because research organisations often have a particular political slant or focus, and this can lead to work being published that may have prejudged its answers and has not been peer reviewed.

Next down the hierarchy might be quality newspapers and popular books. Quality newspapers often have contributors that are experts, but the pieces published there tend to be fairly short and with little space given to discuss research in full. A lot of research pieces in newspapers are based on longer academic publications, and so it is worth reading them, but getting hold of the original, full-length publication to find out more. Encyclopaedias, where they have respected editors and contributors, also tend to fall into this category, providing a short definition or piece that provides a bare minimum in its own right, and so may give a starting point with further references to find out more about a subject.

Finally, there are lower-quality newspapers, magazines and general online sources. These are likely to be written by people who are not experts in the field, may be put together to present a particular view of the world not particularly informed by research, and include errors or misleading information. You need to treat them extremely carefully.

## Reading efficiently and critically, and taking notes

Having assembled a range of sources and got a preliminary understanding of whether they are likely to be good or not, you are now in a position to begin to read through them. You need to be able to do this efficiently and critically.

You are likely to get far more out of published research if you read it several times selectively rather than reading it through from beginning to end once. Work published in academic journals will contain an abstract, or summary of what the research is about usually including its main findings, and which is a good place to start reading. Then you might want to read the introduction to see what the authors are saying the paper is about, and jump to the conclusion or discussion section and find out more about the paper's main findings. If, after this, you think it isn't really relevant to your topic or your ideas, you can put it to one side and move on to something else. If it is, however, you can begin to ask the paper a series of questions as you read through it. How was the research done? What kind of methods did it use? Does the argument seem well worked out to you? Do the conclusions follow from the data or arguments? Does the paper actually do what the author or authors said it was doing?

The important thing is for you to engage with the research rather then reading it through in a passive way. This should hopefully move you to making notes on it. If you are reading your own copy of a journal piece, writing your comments on it as you work through is a good idea – it forces you to be concise because you won't have much space, but at the same time gives you reminders about your interaction with the paper. It is also possible to do this on a PC – lots of pdf-reading software allows you to add notes (you'll have to pay for this if you use a Windows-based machine, but it comes free with a Mac), but this doesn't work particularly well for me – I'd rather write on a paper copy.

If you own the book you are reading, I'd also recommend you write all over it. I know that this reduces the resale value of the text, and you may feel it somehow disrespectful to write on a book, but it really is the best way of engaging with an author, and you can always use a pencil if you want to have the option of selling in the future. If you don't own the copy of the journal or book, then you'll have to be a bit more organised and either take paper notes or type notes into a computer, but you should take page references so you can link the notes to the original later on. Some bibliography software (such as Endnote) has a 'note' field and this can be a very good way of keeping your notes in a database for future reference, so is certainly worth considering.

# So is the study any good?

Academic journal pieces tend to be around 8,000 words, which may sound like a lot, but can seem like very few words when you are trying to communicate a complicated idea or a lengthy piece of fieldwork. As such, no matter how well written, they are likely to contain compromises. Data can't be fully reported, methods are likely to be presented quickly, and conclusions are likely to be briefer than the author(s) would have ideally liked. However, the generic questions mentioned above are still salient, and are worth spending some time with.

## What is the research question or problem?

The author(s) should tell you fairly early on in the piece exactly what it is the research is trying to achieve. This gives a focus to the piece, but also allows you, as a reader, to get some idea of what is going on. When the author tells you what the piece is about, you should be reasonably expected to be able to hold them to it – to be able, once you've read it, to link the claims made in the conclusion with what was said in the introduction (and abstract). Authors will also typically try and give a reason why the topic is important. You need to think whether this seems like a sensible claim or not to you.

Once you've established what kind of question the research is asking you are then able to work out whether the methods it uses seem to be appropriate in answering it.

## Are the methods appropriate?

Chapter 1 of this book suggested that research is much more likely to be successful if it is based on an informed understanding of method. Good methods do not necessarily produce good research, but bad methods or inappropriate methods stand a much weaker chance of producing anything worthwhile. To see whether the methods were appropriate you need to revisit the research question or problem, and see whether or not the method links with it. If the research is about finding out about how people see the world in a particular social situation, but is based on quantitative data that makes no reference or effort to talk to people, then it seems you have grounds for being suspicious. Much of this book is about thinking through the appropriateness of method, so I won't give further examples of problems here – they will become more apparent as we work through the rest of the book. However, you should always be able to ask the question of whether the research question is going to be answered using the methods used.

## Is data reported accurately?

It can be difficult to see whether data is accurately reported in a paper as the authors have so much control over the presentation of data, but what you can do is see if some thought has gone into the way data is included. If a diverse group of people have been interviewed, for example, is the data included diverse? If not, why not? If a large quantitative data set has been collected, how has that data been summarised and presented, and is this appropriate? Various averages, for example, are wonderful ways of summarising data, but may not be at all representative of the data – think of the mean of 0, 0, 0, 0, 0, 10, 10, 10, 10, 10, which bears little resemblance to any particular data point in the series. So when you look at the reporting of data you need to be thinking whether it seems to you to be appropriate and accurate.

## Do the conclusions follow from the data?

Once you've looked at the presentation of the data and the conclusions, you will be in a position to assess whether the conclusions are adequately supported by the data the author(s) present. Do the conclusions seem to logically follow, with a clear and fair discussion appearing about how the author(s) moved from one to the other, or does it seem to you that they represent something of a leap of faith, and have little relationship to one another? Does it seem to you that the author(s) were genuinely trying to come to a conclusion on the basis of the evidence in the paper, or had they made their minds up regardless of what the data said?

## Was the problem or question in the introduction addressed?

When you get to the end of the paper you are in a position to say whether or not the paper achieved its goals. Did it address the problem it claimed to set out to consider, or did it go off on a tangent and do lots of other things instead? If there was a specific question raised in the introduction, did the paper answer it, or go some way to answering it?

### Does any study meet all of these criteria?

A simple answer to this question is, no, probably not. The important thing is to be able to discuss a paper's strengths and weaknesses, and to be able to come to your own informed conclusions as to how good a piece of research you believe it to be. All research has limitations, be they associated with word length, or having to deal with the process of peer review, which can sometimes lead, through the suggestions of other researchers, to the paper becoming less focused than it originally was in order to deal with the suggestions of reviewers. Equally, genuinely innovative work may actually be difficult to publish because it does not fit with the established tradition or accepted practice within the field, and this can lead to researchers being deliberately conservative in order to be able to get their work into journals and books. However, the criteria above are a good start in assessing whether published research is of good quality or not. Of course, you should also apply these questions to your own work and see how well your research comes out ...

# Writing a review

Once you've read a number of sources and taken notes of various kinds, you should be in a position to write a review of what others have said in the field. If you are writing an essay this will show that you have done some work (which is something any marker will be looking for), and if you are writing a dissertation or thesis, you are probably going to have to include a specific section you have labelled 'literature review' or something similar in your plan or outline.

So how should a review be written? To a very significant extent, this depends on what the purpose of the view is. It is therefore worth revisiting the three perspectives outlined in Chapter 1 in order to get some sense of similarities and differences.

### A scientific view of a review

#### Systematic reviews

Within some research areas the process of review has an additional importance. Researchers in the field of social policy or business and management, for example, might be asked to put together a review that is designed to inform future decisions from either policy-makers or specific organisations. In social research, the process of review has become something of a contentious one because of the difficulty of transferring techniques used, particularly in scientific or medical studies into areas where they may not work.

Systematic reviews attempt to assess and summarise existing research into a form to establish what the best evidence says about a particular intervention. In medicine they are used to combine studies about clinical interventions to try and find out how efficacious they are (or are not). They work by carefully assessing the research methods used in each study from its published data, with a built-in preference for quantitative studies with rigorous sampling and collection methods because of their potential to be combined and synthesised. Studies that do not report their methods clearly enough, or which are not regarded as being sufficiently rigorous, are disregarded and, in effect, a larger study synthesised from existing studies that is larger than any of the individual projects upon which it is based, and the results re-analysed. Clinical practice can then be changed, if necessary, in the light of the new review. Reviews of this kind have made a considerable impact on some areas of medical practice, and are hugely valuable as a result.

However, whether such techniques can be used in social research reviews is far more open to question. There are several problems. First, it is not that common for published social research to give a detailed account of its research methods, and so assessing pieces on their description of them is often inappropriate. Because of word-length restrictions in journals, research methods often receive relatively little coverage. Indeed, I know of some authors who claim to write the same research methods sections for every paper they publish as they have found a form of words that peer-reviewers appear to accept without argument. I am not for a minute suggesting that this is good practice, but do think that this means that social research methods sections are not always a good guide to how the research was actually done.

Second, social research papers often contain either bespoke surveys or qualitative data that is very rooted in the particular context in which it was collected, and so it is not clear how this data could be summarised or analysed or combined with other studies. Indeed, if the argument for carrying out qualitative studies is often given that it allows richer and more contextually sensitive data to be collected, then this would appear to go directly against the principles of systematic review. If the aim of qualitative research is to create detailed, contextual descriptions, then it isn't at all clear that combining such studies, and so losing much of that contextual description, is such a good idea.

Third, it may well be that social research is producing a different kind of knowledge than medical research. Whereas systematic reviews are often concerned with experimental results where interactions between clinical interventions and individuals take place in as closed a system as possible, with clear boundaries set up to try and make each case as comparable to the next as possible, social research takes place in open and complex systems, where isolating the effect of individual interventions is extremely difficult. Instead of producing results that demonstrate law-like behaviour and have a model of constant conjunction causation, instead behaviour might be contingent upon circumstance, and even then, always open to negotiation, and an alternative model of causation more appropriate in which factors combine in a non-linear and less obvious ways to influence events. Even clinical trials often struggle to achieve a research environment sufficiently closed from environmental influences so that factors such as participants falling ill from diseases or viruses that had nothing to do with the trial, or being under stress through work, cannot be excluded. Given that most social research takes place in much more open systems than clinical trials, there is the potential for the behaviour of research participants to be influenced by a massive range of factors outside those under the control (or awareness) of researchers. Synthesising findings from work which emphasises the contingency and fragility of the social world (which is often the case), in order to try and produce law-like propositions, seems like an odd thing to do.

As such, although the scientific view of conducting a review is still probably, at least implicitly, what many social researchers think of when summarising others' work, there are very considerable problems with it that researchers need to have answers to if they are going to review from that perspective. What can different perspectives bring to the review process?

## A realist view of reviewing

The work of Ray Pawson (Pawson, 2006a, 2006b; Pawson and Tilley, 1997) presents the best worked-out alternative statements of reviewing to the systematic approach. Pawson suggests that complex interventions need to be broken down into their contexts, the mechanisms that are being reviewed and the outcomes that have resulted. What this allows is for mechanisms in apparently different areas of social research to be compared between different contexts to see how outcomes vary as a result.

An example perhaps best illustrates Pawson's approach. If we were reviewing the governmental approach that has become known as 'naming and shaming', we would be, as social researchers, examining how governments attempt to prevent certain social ills by publicising the names of those individuals or organisations regarded as being problematic to incentivise them to avoid being exposed as such. However, this mechanism works differently in different contexts; where those potentially 'named' wish to retain their anonymity or respectability the approach might work – as with the case of married men who visit prostitutes for example.

However, in other contexts the approach might fail completely – as with youth offenders in the UK who received Anti-Social Behaviour Orders (ASBOs) as a result of their activities, but came to regard this label as a badge of honour rather than of shame – as an achievement and recognition of their status as a danger to the local community. Being 'named and shamed' had very different outcomes in very different contexts, and it is the job in a review to try and work out how social phenomena play themselves out depending on where and when they occur.

Pawson's approach to reviewing would suggest that, instead of trying to judge studies in terms of their scientific validity, we should be looking to see how they vary by context, and to try and see how what we are investigating plays itself out differently depending on that context. If we were investigating social class, for example, we might want to see how it manifests itself in a diverse range of set-tings in order to try and see how differing contexts of research affect it, with what outcome and so generate a complex understanding of it. Instead of looking for similar research and assess scientific quality, as in the systematic review model, we look for differing research about the same idea or theory, and assess it on the basis of what it can contribute to our emerging theory about the phenomenon. A review conducted in this way produces a very, very different approach and result to research reviewed using systematic approaches.

## An idealist view of a review

A third view of what a review is about might be based on an idealist perspective. In this situation, reviews hold empirically a much reduced role, but theoretically are extremely important. From an idealist perspective, reviews of others' work can probably contribute very little empirically to our understanding of our own research as they will be concerned with other people's interpretation of their own places and times. We would expect those interpretations to be very different from our own. Saying that because something tends to empirically be the case in another research setting does not hold at all for our own – in fact we should be wary of such claims because of the danger that they might influence our own thinking.

What other research can contribute to our understanding is an awareness of the concepts, ideas and methods that are associated with a particular field, so that we can reflexively examine both our own, and our research subject's, understandings of them. It is important to find out how women, for example, experience organisations, what narratives they tell about their lives within them, and how those narratives combined concepts and discourses that help to describe and shape their worlds. It may actually be irrelevant whether particular organisations are held to be exemplars of good employment practices. What matters in this research is the experiences of women within them.

As such, idealist reviews will be about finding out which concepts, narratives and stories subjects use to describe their lives, about how they construct their subjectivity. Once a researcher knows about these, it allows them to explore both their own reactions and attitudes to them, as well to explore these topics with new research subjects. Research is not geared to establishing objective truths through reviews, as is the aim to varying extents in both the systematic and realist approaches. It is about exploring interpretations and understandings instead.

What these three approaches show (Table 2.1) is that there is no single answer as to what constitutes a good review, or what work the review should do. If you are expected to write at all conventionally, however, there are some principles that are worth thinking about in relation to your work.

## Organisation

Before you start writing, you need to spend some time thinking about how your review is going to be organised. You are going to need a structure, otherwise it will read as if you are presenting a mass of material that you've read that has no direction

**Table 2.1**  Different methods of review

|  | Systematic review | Realist review | Idealist review |
| --- | --- | --- | --- |
| Concerned with | Highest quality empirical evidence | Potential contribution of research to emerging programme theory | Concepts, ideas, narratives, stories, in research |
| Criteria for inclusion in review | Closeness to randomised-controlled trial | Potential contribution when compared to other research | Distinctiveness and innovativeness of research in showing differing subjectivities |
| Scope of study | All the research that meets the required scientific standard | Research that provides a diverse range of understandings of mechanism under investigation | Research that contributed theoretically or conceptually to the subjectivities of those in related areas |
| Standard approach to review | Synthesis | Comparison | Literary, aesthetic |

and no main themes, and so will severely try the patience of anyone who has to spend time going through it.

A good general first principle is that literature reviews are 'funnel'-shaped. What this means is that they start out by considering a general problem or area, and then get more specific as they go on. So you might begin a review on looking at classroom literacy, for example, by first discussing education policy more broadly to give a context for literacy, before focusing down onto the topic in hand. This has the advantage of demonstrating that you are able to locate the specific project within its field, as well as establishing your credibility as a researcher in the broader context.

You also need to consider the role that your literature review has in the broader article, thesis or dissertation you are writing. If it is a part of a longer piece its role will be to show that you are an expert on the existing literature, but also to link in to your own work. One way to achieve this is to ensure that the literature review ends by highlighting a problem or gap that needs investigating, and that you are able, through your own work, to address this. This approach also gives your review a flow that takes the reader on to the next section of your work.

## Using themes in your work

As well as thinking about the organisation of your work, you need to show that you are adding value to the original studies in some way through their presentation in your work. One way in which you can claim to achieve this is through summary – you are presumably not going to reproduce each entire study in your review or it will fill your allowable word length very quickly. It is a useful exercise to be able to summarise the main points, findings or arguments of existing work, but simply listing a number of studies one after the other in your review isn't good enough. Another approach is to think about what the studies you have summarised have in common and difference, and then to organise your review according to these themes. This allows you to compare studies, showing what the existing literature says thematically, and provides a structure to your review which you can then potentially further summarise in a conclusion, bringing out problems and gaps which your own work can address. If the review is meant to be free-standing, it needs to be clear about what its key findings are, demonstrating the links between those findings and the research upon which they are based.

## Displaying good scholarship

It is also important to show the reader that you understand the field you are reviewing, not only in terms of what others have written within it, but also in terms of how you are going about reviewing it. Think about the differences in reviewing approaches discussed above, and which your own review might be closest to.

Equally, consider what research in your area is the most important for your review. This might be because it is the most significant empirical or theoretical contribution, but it might also be because it is the most-cited work, or the most recent research. Think about what each of those different contributions adds to your review, and what different assumptions about reviewing each of them holds.

Of course, we might want to argue for several or even none of the above criteria for our review. But our thinking about what is good scholarship does affect the way we go about reviewing, what we include, and what we exclude. Table 2.2 summarises these points.

# Conclusion

Even the apparently straightforward process of reviewing others' work, something that is necessary in nearly every essay, dissertation, paper, book or thesis that we write, conceals a great deal. What is important, again, is that researchers have a sense of why it is they are conducting their review, what kind of review they want (or are expected) to produce, what they intend to do with that review and what their understanding of the contribution of others' work is meant to be.

**Table 2.2**   Assumptions about what is important in a review

| Research contribution | Assumption |
| --- | --- |
| Most important empirical contribution | That research is about finding out about what is going on in a particular area – often descriptive, may also be realist (assuming a world about which we can objectively conduct empirical research) |
| Most important theoretical contribution | That we must explain rather than describe, and that producing theory is the aim of social research |
| Most highly-cited work | That work that is widely cited is the best work in the field |
| Most recent research | That work that is up-to-date is the most relevant |

Mixing up the approaches presented in this chapter is relatively common, but can lead to reviews that appear to be inconsistent or even incoherent. Having a clear idea of what it is you are trying to achieve from a review before you begin, and of the issues you are likely to encounter along the way, is likely to give you a much better chance of being successful.

## Five things to remember about this chapter

1   Not all sources are regarded as being of the same standing to academic audiences. If research comes from a good source it is more likely to be good, but it is not a guarantee.
2   You really aren't likely to impress anyone by citing Wikipedia. You probably have access to far more specialist and rigorous sources, so why aren't you using them?
3   If you are going to use Google to search for research, use Google Scholar rather than regular Google, but do remember that you probably have access to a library with specialist academic databases in your research area.
4   Judging whether a piece of research is any good needs you to understand it on its own terms – so you need to be able to recognise what it is trying to achieve, and to work out whether it has achieved it or not.
5   There are different ways of reviewing bodies of research – you need to understand the differences between a systematic review and a realistic review, for example, and to be able to say which is more appropriate to the task that you have in hand.

## Example – 'Qualitative research and the evidence base of policy'

In 'Qualitative research and the evidence base of policy', Graham and McDermott (2005) explore difficulties of using qualitative research for evidence, particularly in how it might be utilised in policy interventions. As such, their paper is concerned not only with how qualitative research might be reviewed, but also whether the results of that review can be used to design or implement government policy.

The explicit approach taken within the paper is to map and synthesise qualitative research through a systematic review process – that is one based on the principles found in quantitative studies, especially those in medicine. The authors describe the four stages needed to achieve this; 'i. searching the literature, using a set of search terms developed through an initial scoping review … ii. applying inclusion/exclusion criteria to the studies located through the search … iii. quality appraising the studies which meet the inclusion criteria and … iv. synthesising the findings which meet the quality criteria' (p. 27). For the first two stages, the researchers adopted the methods used in quantitative studies more or less directly. They found search terms relevant to the review, searched electronic databases along with grey literature and made use of experts in the field known to the researchers. They then created inclusion criteria that whittled down the 4,000 studies identified as possibly relevant in stage one, narrowing the date range, and using those relevant to the scope of the study specifically, reducing it to 98 relevant studies.

For the next two stages of the review, they utilised 'techniques which have been developed expressly for qualitative syntheses' (p. 27). The authors put together a process of quality appraisal of the studies that included 'a clear description of the study context, sample selection and characteristics, and methods of data collection and analysis; evidence of attempts to assess the validity and reliability of the analysis; and the inclusion of sufficient original data ... to make clear how the researchers built interpretations from them' (p. 27). This reduced the review from 98 to 10 studies.

For the last review stage, they attempted a 'synthesis' which 'summarised the findings of each study in a matrix, which enabled us to cross-check whether related issues were indentified in other studies. From this summative synthesis, we were able to identify a set of experiences which ran across the studies. We grouped these recurrent experiences under broad (and overlapping) headings ...' (p. 28).

In all then, the qualitative review process used exactly the same techniques as a quantitative systematic review for the first two stages and adapted versions of the techniques for the last two. The interesting question this raises is how appropriate is adapting quantitative techniques for the review of qualitative data?

The first two stages of the review appear relatively uncontentious. In order to conduct a review, it is necessary to come up with some search terms and to conduct a search for relevant materials. Coming up with the terms, as we have seen, can be a difficult process, and knowing which databases are most relevant also sometimes involves some trial and error. Equally, identifying which papers fit the scope of the review can also be a source of some disagreement, but abstracts should give some guidance of whether the particular study is relevant to the subject and purpose of the review, so some basic inclusion/exclusion criteria can usually be agreed and applied. On the whole, the search and inclusion/exclusion stages of a review tend to be the easiest to reach agreement on between researchers.

The second two stages, however, are harder to reach a consensus on. The third stage – where quality criteria were applied, represents a particular challenge in qualitative research. As we noted in this chapter, in clinical research – in many respects the originating discipline of the systematic review process – research methods sections of papers are crucial because they make clear what kind of study was carried out (whether it was a trial and then whether the trial was randomised, or double-blind, etc.), and the systematic review process makes it clear, based on the logic of clinical work, which kinds of research it will favour. This logic is known throughout the whole of clinical research, and although some disagreements exist (for example, Greenhalgh and Peacock, 2005), is generally accepted amongst clinical researchers. No such consensus exists amongst social scientists. As such, criteria might vary by discipline, by journal or by research area.

Just because criteria can't be easily agreed, however, it doesn't mean that we shouldn't try and come up with some. However, it does mean that any attempting to apply criteria in a discipline like sociology, where plurality and diversity are likely to be favoured above meticulous reporting of methods (even if the methods in the study were rigorous) is likely to result in dispute and debate more than in clinical studies, where the template might be far more accepted and regarded by researchers as important.

However, the problem does remain that, given there is no consensus on what kinds of studies are favoured, then is it sensible to apply criteria to them for inclusion and exclusion that the authors themselves might have been unaware of, or actively disagreed with? In Graham and McDermott's review, 88 studies were rejected on the grounds of being insufficient quality, with quality being defined in terms of 'a clear description of the study context, sample selection and characteristics, and methods of data collection and analysis; evidence of attempts to assess the validity and reliability of the analysis; and the inclusion of sufficient original data ... to make clear how the researchers built interpretations from them' (p. 27).

Now there is much to commend this list, but equally, as we have seen above, there is also much to commend alternative lists of what constitutes good research. Equally, the list is rather vague, and could be applied by different researchers in very different ways. It is worth asking the extent to which, had researchers from a different team applied these criteria, they would have come up with the same 10 studies for the final review that Graham and McDermott did.

The last stage of the review process described by Graham and McDermott makes a great deal of sense – to compare the studies across headings generated from those studies, and include those elements that appeared most. However, this approach can be usefully contrasted with Pawson's approach to view which might be more interested in papers that present differing understandings of the research area because of the additional theoretical interest they might offer us.

Qualitative reviewing does present us reviewers with a series of challenges. The review processes suggested in the chapter can lead to very different methods of conducting reviews. However, this doesn't mean that we should advocate an 'anything goes' approach. Thinking through the purpose of the review, the theoretical assumptions held by the reviewer and the disciplines that the review will encompass and the methods used in those disciplines, may lead to very different reviews embracing very different methods. As with most areas of social research, there really are no magic solutions.

# THREE

## Surveys and questionnaires – or how can I conduct research with people at a distance?

### Introduction

Surveys and questionnaires are, in many disciplines and in many subject areas, almost the common-sense approach to doing social research. Businesses ask us to fill in surveys as to how effective their service was, and public organisations send out questionnaires asking us how well they are doing, what they could be doing better and what we would like them to do in the future. Given their extraordinarily widespread usage, it is remarkable how badly surveys and questionnaires are often done. We have all been sent forms that seem to go on forever, having little regard for the time subjects have to take in filling them in, surveys where questions don't seem to make much sense, or questionnaires which don't provide us with any chance to explain that answers we give, leading to us becoming frustrated and either throwing the form away rather than returning it, or leaving an online form half-filled in.

This chapter considers when and where it is appropriate to use questionnaires, gives some pointers on how they can be designed to get them returned and filled in, and considers how to ask questions that subjects won't find confusing. It then moves on to explore some contentious issues in relation to this type of research, including sampling, response rates and the role of anonymity, before coming to a conclusion about when surveys and questionnaires are appropriate, how they can be used and what assumptions about social research they contain.

### The use of questionnaires – the best (and worst) of quantitative (and qualitative) social research

#### Surveys and questionnaires

An initial distinction that we have to begin with is the difference between a survey and a questionnaire. This isn't a difference that we need to get too preoccupied with, as in many disciplines the terms are used more or less synonymously, but technically a survey is a research design that takes a cross-sectional approach. This means it is based on a sample, with the aim being to have as large a sample as is necessary to capture all of the variation in the population; that it occurs at a single point in time (or as near as possible to a single point in time); it is predominantly quantitative; and the aim is to seek patterns within that quantitative data. A questionnaire is a type of survey – but there are many other examples of survey design, including quantitative explorations of text (as with content analysis) and highly structured observation, as might be used in organisational analysis in time and motion studies.

A questionnaire is a type of survey involving, unsurprisingly, asking subjects to respond to a range of questions, often in a self-completion form. Questionnaires represent the best and worst of social research. They are widely used because they are relatively simple to put together and they are cheap because they often don't involve researchers having to find time to gather data personally, as they would have to do for interviews or participant observation. They are versatile because they can be used in a variety of ways right across the social science disciplines, and because they can produce data that can be used to test hypotheses as well as gather qualitative responses. Questionnaires are widely used, and there are good guides offering advice on how to construct them. However, they are also just about impossible to get perfect – different subjects respond to different words and concepts in different ways, and you get only one chance at asking your questions. Unlike an interview, you don't get to clarify when subjects don't appear to understand what it is you are asking, so any mistakes acquire a rather embarrassing permanence and any omissions will be absent for everyone you send the questions to. It is easy to put together questionnaires, but also easy to get them very wrong.

## Perspectives on questionnaires

Choosing to use a questionnaire in a research design is a choice that carries with it a series of assumptions. Different kinds of questionnaires have different presumptions about the kind of knowledge they are trying to produce, and it is important that the implications of these choices are thought through.

Chapter 1 argues that different approaches to social research produce different kinds of knowledge. We can illustrate this by making use of three different perspectives and comparing what difference they might make in a questionnaire design.

### Three perspectives on social research

A hypothetico-deductive perspective, as the name suggests, is based on an experimental method, with a view that social research is about testing hypotheses using deductive methods. This is most likely to favour a quantitative approach.

A hypothetico-deductive perspective on a questionnaire will privilege the testing of hypotheses, which themselves will be derived from existing theory. Quantitative data will be preferred because of the relative lack of ambiguity in terms of testing hypotheses, and so the design of the questionnaire will tend towards closed-response questions (see below). The aim of the study will be theory generation through hypotheses testing.

A realist approach, in contrast, would accept along with the hypothetico-deductive view that the point of social research is to find out about the external world, but suggest that our ability to gain access to the world is limited by our perceptions of it. As such, social research in this perspective requires us to find underlying, generative causes of behaviour that cannot be simply modelled using experiments.

A realist perspective on questionnaire design will also privilege theory testing, but is much more likely to utilise mixed methods than one based solely around a hypothetico-deductive design. The quantitative element of a questionnaire will serve purposes such as looking for potential generative mechanisms by seeking promising patterns between measurable variables, whilst at the same time acknowledging the difficulties in finding measurable indicators of complex social phenomena. A quantitative survey might be useful in a mixed-methods design, preceding qualitative research in order to find promising patterns of variables that can be subject to more detailed analysis through it. However, realists also acknowledge that interpretations of the external world vary between research subjects and societal groups, and so it will also be necessary to conduct qualitative work, which questionnaires can be a part of through open-response questions, in order to capture differences in interpretation and understanding which are likely to exist.

Finally, an idealist perspective would go further again, suggesting that speculation about some kind of real world is largely pointless because we can never gain access to it except through our own senses and ideas. As such, the point of social research is to understand our subjectivities and interpretations of the world.

An idealist perspective on questionnaires is likely to be more problematic about their use. Idealists may believe that a pre-designed questionnaire is unlikely to be able to adequately capture the inter-subjectivity of the social world – with participant observation and unstructured interviews being preferred. Where questionnaires are used, they will prefer open-response questions in order to allow research subjects to speak using their own words, and to impose the very minimum of the researcher's concepts and ideas upon the research.

The three perspectives on surveys are compared in Table 3.1.

As such, questionnaires vary considerably depending on the perspective the researcher takes on their research. But the use of questionnaires also varies considerably on their purpose in social research. It is to this topic that the chapter therefore turns.

**Table 3.1** Different perspectives on questionnaire design

| | Hypothetico-deductive | Realist | Idealist |
|---|---|---|---|
| Aim of study | Testing of theory (deduction) | Finding the appropriate theory (abduction) | Finding out participants' interpretations of the world (induction) |
| Favoured methods | Quantitative | Mixed methods | Qualitative |
| Types of question | Closed-response questions | Open- and closed-response questions | Open-response questions |
| Example | Measuring income, height, weight – anything that can be placed into a category and correlations with other categories sought | Looking for relationships in complex social phenomena – social deprivation, education, inequality | Exploring participants' understandings of gender, ethnicity |
| Typical problem | Categories not being appropriate for what is attempting to be measured | Difficulties in combining methods and complexity of design | Lots of open-response questions may result in non-completions |

# Designing questionnaires

The purpose of a questionnaire in your research design will considerably affect its design and use. There are a number of possible purposes. Are you trying to scope (or initially explore the boundaries of) an area that you don't know much about? Are you testing hypotheses that you have generated from existing research or from your own ideas? Do you want to test a series of propositions that you have about a particular social area? Are you testing a new instrument or concept you want to use to measure a particular social phenomenon? Are you trying to estimate the attributes of a population from the sample you are investigating? Flexibility is a significant strength of questionnaire research, but it can also be a weakness where researchers try and achieve too many goals with the same instrument.

A scoping questionnaire might be as qualitative as quantitative in order to allow participants to make as many open-ended responses as possible and to avoid researchers imposing their ideas unnecessarily upon the instrument, and so the possible responses that can be made. We have all seen questionnaires that don't provide us with the option that we really want to choose – I prefer to think of myself as being European rather than British, but often I'm not given this option in questionnaires.

To test a series of propositions, questionnaires can be set up in a more quantitative way to collect responses on the extent to which subjects agree with those propositions (and variations on them). This is one of the most straightforward and widely used forms of questionnaire. So we might be asked how much (or little) we agree with the sentence that Margaret Thatcher was the best post-war British Prime Minister (not at all, a little, quite a lot, a great deal). To validate an instrument, a questionnaire can be distributed to a group that is regarded, because of previous research, to have the characteristics that the instrument is designed to measure, in order to see whether the instrument appears to capture that characteristic or not. So, an instrument designed to measure the degree of formality in an organisation might be issued to an organisation previous research has shown to be hierarchical and rule-following, as well as to one which we believe to have the opposite characteristics, to see if those differences are captured.

To estimate the attributes of a population from a sample, which is another popular use of questionnaires, we need to pay even more attention to sampling than usual in order to make sure inferences from sample to population are statistically valid. We might be interested, for example, in trying to assess a political party's chances in the next election, and so attempt to construct a sample that is representative of the population of the voting country in order to achieve that goal. We might utilise a questionnaire designed to measure stress in a particular workplace, such as a university, and so send that instrument to a sample of staff in such a place. We can then compare results with other universities, as well as between departments within that university.

So the aim of a questionnaire is likely to shape a range of design issues within it, including the extent to which it utilises open and closed responses, the extent to which sampling is a significant issue and the type of questions we ask within it. These issues can now be explored in more depth.

## Open and closed responses

Open-ended questions are those where subjects are asked to give a response in their own terms. There are two main reasons for doing this. The first is that you wish to gather information about a topic where it is impractical to give all of the possible options in the questionnaire. If we want to know someone's name, it doesn't make a lot of sense to try and list all the possibilities, but simply to allow them to give it. A second reason for using open responses is to avoid imposing the researcher's ideas and concepts upon the respondent. This means that researchers get data back that is in the respondents' own words, and which therefore might contain vital clues to the concepts and words they believe are appropriate rather than imposing what the researcher thinks is relevant.

So instead of asking, 'Is recycling an excellent idea, a good idea, something you don't feel strongly about, or a bad idea?', and getting respondents to tick appropriate boxes through a closed-response system, we might ask, 'What do you think about recycling?' to try and get a more nuanced view that allows respondents to use their own evaluative words and ideas.

Closed-ended questions ask respondents, in contrast, to give their answers according to possibilities that the researcher has predefined, as in the first recycling question above. This requires the researcher to have a good idea of the likely responses to the questions, and to make sure that they are covered in the options that are available to respondents. If the advantage of open-ended questions is that they allow respondents to use their own words and concepts, the advantages of closed-ended questions is that they reduce ambiguity by allowing greater precision in question-asking, they allow respondents to be asked similar questions several times to cross-check for validity and consistency, and they are far easier to interpret. Closed-ended questions can be answered quickly, meaning that respondents are more likely to answer several of them than open-ended questions, and as long as you have come up with appropriate answering options, you can collect a great deal of easy-to-analyse data extremely efficiently.

Both open- and closed-ended questions have their disadvantages. Open-ended questions take longer to answer, so questionnaires that extensively utilise them risk not being completed. Equally, they require far more care and time to analyse adequately, and may require researchers with different skills to work together in order to achieve rigour in both quantitative and qualitative aspects of the questionnaire. Closed-ended questions fall down when the response options offered to respondents are inadequate, and they always carry the risk of respondents not being able to give unexpected answers, so limiting the range of responses that can appear. Closed-ended questions also have to be extremely clear in terms of both the questions that they ask and the responses that are allowed, with designs being carefully tested to check for ambiguities and confusions. Open-ended questions also need to be checked carefully, but offer some chance of collecting useful data even where there are problems in question phrasing as respondents still have the opportunities to express thoughts in their own words, whereas misunderstandings in closed-ended questions may be difficult or even impossible to pick up. Complex social science concepts can be interpreted in a wide variety of ways, and can be the source of considerable confusion if not used carefully, and using local language, or indeed failing to use local language where appropriate, can result in respondent confusion and gathering poor quality data.

An example of a questionnaire going wrong which relates to my own work is through the student surveys of my courses. Every year, without fail, a student will fill in the university-designed survey incorrectly so that I get some (unintentional) bad grades because the student, in a rush, simply ticked the 1s on the list, thinking they were the highest rating, when the 5s were instead. They will then leave a comment at the end saying that the course was good, not realising that their response to the closed-ended questions was entirely the wrong way around.

The language and concepts used in questionnaires, both in their instructions and their questions, is therefore extremely important. It is vital that researchers make use of existing studies and pilots in order to find out not only what likely respondents regard as the important questions that they believe should be asked about the research area, but also the way that they need to be phrased, and the responses that they need to be offered. Preliminary interviews or focus groups can be extremely useful in this respect where they allow potential respondents to use their own words and ideas, as is carrying out a pilot study of the questionnaire to try and look out for problems in design before the main study begins.

# Getting questions really clear

It isn't possible to take readers through a complete guide on how to write questions. What I can do, however, is point out several mistakes that are often made, and then ask readers to look at their own questions to assess the extent to which they suffer from them. As I suggested above, no questionnaire is ever going to be perfect. What we can do, however, is to try and make it as error-free as possible.

## Ambiguity and vagueness

Any aspect of ambiguity will mean that your respondents won't know what was asked of them, and so any answers they do provide will detract, rather than add, to your research. In closed-response questions this is especially important because respondents may not have the opportunity to tell the researcher of the problems they are having filling in that question.

Let's say you have created a question that asks respondents to judge how often they feel stress during a working day. You might then attach frequencies to that question of 'frequently, often, infrequently and never'. However, there are problems in terms of the question and response here. Unless we are being clear about 'stress' elsewhere in the questionnaire, we are leaving it open to widely different interpretations. That might be part of our research design, if we are interested in stress as a subjective experience rather than as an objective condition, but we must be explicit about what it is we are trying to find out. Equally, having responses such as 'frequently' poses a number of problems for our research. How often is frequently exactly? Once an hour? Once a minute? That leads to an additional ambiguity and so difference between respondents. Again, if we are interested in the subjective experience of stress, that might not be a problem – we are getting an assessment both of the subjective condition and its subject frequency. However, it does present problems in comparing respondents' answers, which may be one of the main aims of constructing the questionnaire in the first place.

A second source of ambiguity comes when asking questions about concepts which might be interpreted differently between respondents, or even misunderstood by them. If we are to ask about the 'organisational culture' of the place where people work, this might be interpreted in lots of different ways, or even regarded as a term that has no meaning for particular respondents. This might be made even worse by asking respondents if they believe that the 'organisational culture' is 'weak' or 'strong'. We might then run the risk of having ambiguities, again, for both our possible responses and the terms we are asking about.

## Hypothetical questions and abstractness

There are lots of circumstances where we might ask a respondent to imagine themselves in a particular situation and to give their reaction or response to it. However, the more abstract the hypothetical situation, the more difficult it might be getting a consistent or sensible response. Many people, quite reasonably, will not answer questions when asked to imagine scenarios they believe to be unlikely or ridiculous, and we have to be careful to make sure that we don't alienate people when they are doing us the favour of filling in our questionnaire.

Questionnaires examining, for example, theories of justice can fall into this trap. The work of John Rawls (1995) sets up an 'original position' in which he asks us to imagine that we have to come up with a fair way of distributing society's resources with the life experiences that we have now, but not knowing what position or role in society that we would have. This is designed to try and get us to think about what would be fair in a society, based not on the position we presently occupy, but on the assumption that we could end up being born into any position with it. Now we might want to find out how people respond to Rawls's 'original position', and research has already attempted to do this (Freeman, 2005). But asking people to make such a complex suspension of belief is extremely difficult, and may end up with them asking why on earth they are doing it, and not wanting to participate.

## Leading questions

There are two categories of leading questions – questions that attempt to impose a view upon the respondent and get them to agree or disagree, and questions that less obviously lead respondents down a particular path of reasoning and so influence the answers that they give.

The first category of leading questions comes when a question asks something like, 'Given the present government has failed to tackle crime, are you more likely to vote Republican at the next election?' What is going on here is that the question is trying to smuggle in a presupposition as a fact and to get the respondent to react to that. The previous question could also be worded, 'Assuming that the present government has failed to tackle crime ...' or, 'If the present government failed to tackle crime ...'. Equally, leading questions can be more subtle, asking questions along the line of, 'Do you agree that the present government has failed to tackle crime?', which again contain a presupposition around which the respondent has to try and orient themselves before they answer.

A second problem with leading questions comes through the sequence with which questions appear in the questionnaire. This can be explicit, or rather subtle. An example of an explicit sequence of leading questions would be to compare the questions in Table 3.2 (reading each sequence in turn from top to bottom). This example makes widespread use of leading questions in an obvious way, but also, through the sequence of questions, could lead to a very different response to the third question, even from the same respondent. It is important to ask if your questionnaire is leading people to answer in a particular way because of the questions you have asked them *before*.

A more subtle form of leading questions comes because of 'anchoring', or the way that humans appear to base their current answers on the answers they gave a few moments ago. This is clearly related to the kind of leading sequences shown

**Table 3.2**   Two question sequences

| Sequence one | Sequence two |
| --- | --- |
| Is it fair for one person to take another's life? | Is it right that jailing convicted murderers have to be paid for by taxpayers who have done nothing wrong? |
| Does killing another person, in your opinion, contravene religious or moral laws? | Do you agree that the murderers of children and policemen should get away with only life imprisonment, with the potential to receive a reduced sentence if they behave well in prison? |
| Should the death penalty be introduced for murder in the UK? | Should the death penalty be introduced for murder in the UK? |

above, but can also occur through less obvious means. If you start filling a questionnaire with closed responses in a particular range, unless you are paying close attention, you might continue down the page or form in roughly the same range – anchoring your answer to the first response you gave. Another example of this is given by Dan Ariely (2008). If you ask someone to think of the last three digits of their social security or national insurance code, and then ask them to estimate something that they are unlikely to know, such as the birth year of Ivan the Terrible, those with smaller numbers in the last three digits of their code are likely to guess lower than those that have higher numbers in the last three digits. We can be quite subtly influenced by number sequences.

What this means is that if we ask respondents to think about numbers or frequencies in question after question, they are likely to 'anchor' and so answer in clusters of about the same values rather than thinking about each one individually. We need to safeguard against this by having section breaks in the questionnaire where we introduce new topics, by having checks to validate answers in different sections, or by mixing up open- and closed-response questions.

## Value judgements

A similar problem to that of leading questions is where questions express particular value judgements, again to safeguard against imposing the researcher's view of the world on participants.

## Asking two (or more) questions in one

It can be extremely tempting, in order to keep questionnaires short, for researchers to try and jam as much material as possible into a question. However, where this leads into asking two or more questions at once, it can again lead to poor data being collected. So were we to ask, 'Do you agree that the government is doing enough to raise awareness of environmental problems, and should refuse collection be better geared to aid recycling?', it might appear on some readings that the (rather long) question is about the same subject, when the two parts of the question could lead to different answers from the same respondents. People might, for example, disagree with the idea that the government is doing enough to raise awareness of environment problems, but agree with refuse collection being reorganised to make recycling more straightforward. How are they meant to answer the (double) question then?

## Hidden assumptions

Again, similar to leading questions, poor questions can contain assumptions about participants that can lead to them becoming annoyed at the questions, and not filling in the questionnaire. 'What is your job?' is fine for people in work, but those out of work might find it to be thoughtless.

## Sensitive issues

If you are going to ask people about issues that they find sensitive, then you are going to decrease your chances of them filling in your questions. Sensitive issues vary culturally, so there is a real need to be thoughtful about what they might be for the group you are investigating. Questions about sex and sexuality, death, religion and those which imply some kind of neglect or other failing on the part of respondents are obvious candidates in most places, however, to raise sensitive issues. If you are investigating such areas, a great deal of thought and care need to be taken to avoid giving offence or causing embarrassment.

# Common response forms

Having thought about your questions, you need to then have several options about how you can get participants to fill in their responses. Where you are asking for open responses, then you need to get the question right, but also to allow sufficient space for participants to fill in their reply. Giving too little space is going to result in frustration and a sense from your respondents that you don't really want to know what they have to say.

Closed-response forms come in a number of formats. In categorical formats, respondents can tick or circle items that you list for them, choosing more than one if the question allows. You can ask people to circle one category for age groups or to answer whether they consider themselves male or female, but may want them to tick or circle more than one answer to a question that tries to find out which from a list of items they have purchased in the last week.

## Rating scales

Rating scales are commonly used in questionnaires to get respondents to answer whether they agree with statements with ratings such as 'strongly agree, agree, uncertain, disagree, strongly disagree'. Whether to offer an 'uncertain' or 'don't know' option on such scales is a source of considerable debate. Intuitively it seems to make sense to give respondents this option as, about some things, we are genuinely indifferent. What does seem important, however, is that you consider whether including such an option for the question you are asking is going to help with your research. In some circumstances, indifference might be an important response. In others, you might believe that it is important to get respondents to express an opinion that tends to one end of your rating scale or another.

A ranking format asks respondents to examine a list of items and specify either which are the most important from the list, or to rank all of the items in order of importance. So we might ask the public to rank which social issues they believe are most worthy of government support, or which characteristics of a new product would be of most benefit to them. In general, though, the more items that appear on a ranking list, and the more items you ask them to rank within it, the more likely people are going to get fed up in trying to come up with an answer. Keeping the list short, but including options that are relevant, is the challenge here.

Think of, for example, a survey that attempts to find out which improvements the local council should fund. A list of five items (new bus stop, new street lights, speed cameras, more frequent rubbish collections, more speed bumps) would be more easily ranked than a list of ten items, but might omit the improvement that people would like the most (such as more frequent police patrols) – so the list would be easier to rank, but lose its legitimacy in achieving the aim of the research in the first place.

## Questionnaire design

Questionnaire design varies considerably depending on a variety of factors explored above, but again a few general things can be suggested.

I have already mentioned the importance of thinking about question order above – there is now a great deal of evidence suggesting that the order you ask your questions in will affect the results you get. You need to consider this carefully to try and avoid leading respondents down particular paths. However, there are also some other general considerations.

First, if you are relying upon particular aspects of the questionnaire to be returned to you in order to be able to carry out even basic analysis, then it makes sense to ask these questions as early as possible. Even if it isn't completely filled in, the form may still be able to contribute valuable data to the project. Second, it may help to put relatively straightforward questions at the end of your questionnaire, as people will be able to fill them in without having to give the matter much thought – putting complex and difficult questions at the end is likely to result in them not being filled in. Equally, putting sensitive questions right at the beginning of a questionnaire is likely to lead to a low response rate because of the risk of them appearing abrupt and cold.

How long a questionnaire should be depends considerably on the subject area and how important people regard it as being. Having a very short form has the advantage of people not perceiving it to be much work, and so increasing the likelihood of them filling it in. However, short forms can also appear frivolous, especially where they are about topics that respondents regard as being important to them. As a general rule, though, think about who is going to be responding to your questionnaire, and how long they are prepared to give to your research. Questionnaires that are too long run the considerable risk of ending up in the nearest bin.

## Filter questions

The use of filter questions is a feature of questionnaire design that can help keep questions focused on the characteristics so far given by respondents, but can run the risk of making your form more complicated. Filter questions (where you say, if you answered 'yes' to question 1, go to question 5, for example) can help your questionnaire retain relevance for respondents – no-one wants to fill in a form that asks them lots of irrelevant questions and seems to have been poorly thought out. However, filter questions make the process of filling the form in more complex, so need to be used with care, or respondents may get confused and start filling in the form incorrectly, again leading to data coming back incomplete or incorrect.

## Question density

Question density is another feature of design that needs some attention. If you are trying to cram as many questions as possible onto your form, there is a tendency to use smaller fonts and to allow little space for open-response form answers, but that, as noted above, is an error. If you find that your questions do not fit onto the space you have allowed for them, then you need to think again about your design.

Having explored many of the issues that arise in relation to the design of questionnaires it is worth thinking through some of problems that can arise in terms of analysing and presenting your results.

# Analysing and reporting questionnaire responses

One of the most common problems researchers find when analysing their first questionnaire is how to both examine each question's responses individually and to tell a coherent story about what the results as a whole seem to add up to. This often results in researchers presenting a blow-by-blow analysis of the answers to each question individually, giving both statistical and graphical treatment of each result, before moving on to the next.

Conventions on how questionnaire results should be presented do vary from discipline to discipline. However, it is important for researchers to bear in mind the research questions which prompted the questionnaire design in the first place, and to make sure that the analysis and presentation of results are geared to answering those questions rather than getting subsumed in exploring every dimension of every question that ended up on the final form. What your readers will want to know about is what you have found about your research area, not your thoughts on your detailed analysis of every single question in your questionnaire. Of course, once you have presented your interpretation of the results, you need to be able to justify it by showing your analysis of questions, but even then it is often better to show data the links responses on several questions rather than expecting your reader to work through your results by showing every kind of analysis you performed on every question on your questionnaire. Think carefully about what results seem to you to be especially important or interesting, make clear to your reader what those are and make sure that you present the analysis or tests that back up those findings.

Think carefully also about your presentation of results. There is a strong tendency for you to want to present your reader with every test you have performed on your data in the name of completeness, and to show all the hard work you have done. But would you want to read such an account? It is a good discipline for you to try and work out what the headlines are from the research you've conducted, and to explain as concisely as you reasonably can your answers to your research questions. Once you know this, you can work out what evidence you need to show to support those claims and what the best way of presenting that evidence will be. Think about who your audience is – a peer-reviewed journal will require different types of evidence and different presentations of that evidence than a public lecture or practitioner journal.

## Reflexivity and questionnaires

Questionnaires, as we began by saying, represent the very best of social research, but also potentially the worst. One problem that I think is particularly worth thinking about is how particular instruments can become ingrained as an adequate or good tool in a research area, and so become used without thought within it.

It is surely important, even if there is a generally accepted tool within a particular research area, for it to be used in a careful way. Using an established tool has a number of advantages – it produces straightforward comparisons with previous work, it avoids the need for a new form to be designed, and so can mean that new research is both quicker and cheaper than it would otherwise have been. However, it can also lead to particular tools being used without any particular justification other than the fact that they have already been used. The argument of this book is that research methods need to have a logic of appropriateness, and the thoughtless use of any kind of research tool or method isn't a good move. Being reflexive about methods means thinking about their usage in each new research project and each new design. If social research is going to be taken seriously, then social researchers need to use methods and tools not because they have been used before, but because they are fit for the task at hand.

# Contentious issues

There are still a few more difficult issues that social researchers doing questionnaires need to consider. These issues will not always arise, but having a view on them will lead to more informed decisions being taken when they do.

## Sampling and sample sizes

Issues of sampling and sample sizes vary considerably between academic disciplines. Chapter 4 deals in more depth with sampling, but again, what I want to stress at this point is that the sampling method chosen for a project is appropriate to the goals of the research. Assuming that a random sample is the only way of conducting research is going to mean a great deal of research that could be done in environments where this simply isn't possible, won't be done. Equally, assuming that, to be valid, sample sizes have to be big isn't a good starting point. What researchers need to do is to work out what kind of claims they want to make about their questionnaire results, what kind of data they are trying to collect using them, and make sure that the claims they can make from it are defendable and appropriate. Quantitative and qualitative research designs might require very different sampling strategies. There are no automatically right answers.

## Response rates

A related question to the one above concerns what response rate is required for a result to be valid. Again, the matter requires thought and care. Ideally, researchers need to be able to show that the group that has responded to a questionnaire has the characteristics required by the study. A quantitative measure of this might be whether the response group is representative of the sample chosen (in the sense of being a stratified sample of it) with, of course, the sample itself being representative of the population. If particular characteristics are missing from the respondent group compared to those of the sample, then there is a problem, and further, targeted questionnaire distribution might be necessary to try and address this.

If researchers can show that their response group is representative of their sample, and that their sampling method was reliable, then they have a good footing for arguing that their results too are reliable. The important thing is for researchers to think about what kind of a case they need to make in order to make that claim – what are the norms within their discipline, and what are the norms within their research area?

## Anonymity

Last, there is perhaps the most thorny issue of all – anonymity. It is common sense in many disciplines for questionnaires to be conducted anonymously. The arguments in favour of this can be put under the headings of anonymity being both practical and ethical. The practical argument is that offering anonymity will lead to respondents being more honest, and feeling that they can say what they believe without being concerned whether their answers will in some way be used against them. The ethical argument is that respondents should have assurances that participating in research will have no adverse consequences for them, that their responses can result in no subsequent harm and that they have a right to anonymity generally.

What possible arguments are there against these points? In many respects, they do appear to be common sense. However, objections can be made against them.

In terms of the practical arguments, it is also the case that anonymity can lead to less honesty in research participants rather than more. Again, the work of Ariely (2008) has shown that people taking part in research can behave in remarkably dishonest ways when the assurance of anonymity is in place. Research participants have been shown to be more likely to steal and to lie about test results they have taken, for example, when they believe they are anonymous. The idea that anonymity leads to greater honesty is a proposition that needs a great deal more testing before it can be regarded as common sense.

The ethical argument for anonymity is a strong one, not least because it is backed by many research codes of conduct (see Chapter 9) and so requires a strong counter-argument for it not to be a standard part of research design. Again, though, there are possible objections. One situation where anonymity becomes problematic is where respondents use their anonymity to make racist, sexist or even illegal statements. We can take the view that this is a part of everyday life, and so we should turn a blind eye, or ask the question at what point the ethical idea of confidentiality might be trumped by these other considerations. If, in a student questionnaire, some respondents make comments about lecturing staff that can be fairly regarded as indecent, are these grounds for breaching confidentiality and asking those students to account for their behaviour? If in a questionnaire it becomes apparent that particular respondents have knowledge about unsolved crime, or have the intention to commit crime, is that consideration more important than anonymity? If a group of politicians fill in questionnaires and some of them divulge information that makes them, by the law of that country, unfit to hold office, would that mean that their anonymity should still be retained?

Again, these questions do not have easy answers. Researchers need to be thinking about the issues that they raise, however, and to be able to provide an explanation of the choices that they make when difficult issues arise in their own work. Codes of conduct provide answers to problems such as anonymity that can help us with ethical dilemmas, but not necessarily give defendable answers.

## Conclusion – working with the good and bad of questionnaires

Questionnaires are deservedly a popular and effective way of conducting research. However, they must be chosen for the right reasons, based on them being the most appropriate tool for the research problem to be addressed, and temptations to use 'off the peg' instruments should be resisted unless those designs can be shown to be the best for the research job in hand.

Different perspectives can be taken on research design that lead to them having very different roles within a research design, or perhaps even ruling them out completely. It is important researchers understand why they are using a questionnaire, how it fits with other method choices they are making, and what they are seeking to claim by collecting questionnaire data.

Questionnaires are deceptive in that they can be designed quickly, but are just about impossible to get perfect. An almost overwhelming range of difficulties present themselves very quickly, most of which boil down to the problem that in many other forms of research, interactions with participants allow confusions and mistakes to be clarified, whereas with questionnaires you may get just one attempt to get that person to respond to your questions. Any ambiguities, leading questions or errors in sequencing or presenting questions will be there for all those who participate, and it may not be possible (or desirable), where a mistake happens, to get your respondents to fill in a corrected questionnaire.

Questionnaires also raise difficult issues around sampling, response rates and anonymity, the first two of which will be a part of any study, the last arises only occasionally. However, these issues highlight the concern that, because questionnaires can be done so quickly, a magic formula can be found to address all the research issues likely to arise. Where research is done without thought, it is less likely to be good research.

## Five things to remember about this chapter

1 Questionnaires are popular because they are a relatively cheap and efficient way of gathering a lot of data quickly.
2 Questionnaire design carries with it a series of assumptions; questionnaires that have lots of closed-response questions based on scales are very different philosophically from those that ask open questions asking respondents to answer in their own words.
3 Getting questions right is extremely important – unlike interviews you won't get a chance to elaborate or clarify if your question is ambiguous or misleading.
4 You need to pay attention not only to the wording of individual questions but also to the sequence in which they appear if you are to avoid leading your respondents to particular answers.
5 What is an acceptable response rate and sampling system varies according to the type of research you are carrying out. You need to find out norms for each in the respective field if you want to publish your work there, or to make a successful grant proposal.

# Example – *The Paradox of Choice*

Barry Schwartz's book *The Paradox of Choice* (2004) illustrates both the pitfalls and importance of questionnaires. Schwartz explores research, examining the extent to which the public want to be able to exercise choice in healthcare systems when they fall ill. This is an important area because a great deal of health policy in both the US and UK seems to explicitly presume that people want to choose where and how they are treated when sick.

What Schwartz's work suggests is, when asked prospectively (or before they are actually sick), the overwhelming majority of people say that they would want to be able to make choices should they fall ill. This is exactly what governments want us to do – to drive improvements in healthcare systems by choosing the providers of care who are the most responsive, or who have the best records in treating patients, so that standards are driven up for everyone as a result. This part of the work Schwartz describes fits exactly with the way we have been reforming our healthcare systems.

However, there is an additional part to the research. When asked whether they would like choice when they actually fall ill, especially with a serious condition such as cancer, the overwhelming majority of people say they *do not* want a choice.

So, it turns out, the important thing about survey work in this area is to make sure that you ask not only the right questions, in the right sequence, but also *at the right time*. There is little point in giving people choices they may express they want when they are healthy, if, at the time they actually have to make those choices, they no longer wish to. Only by having a research process that captures these differences can we get a sensible picture of how patient choice can (or cannot) work in health reform.

Does this mean that choice-based reforms of healthcare are taking us in the wrong direction? Not entirely. Schwartz's research makes us ask important questions about whether we want more choice in all aspects of our lives. But at the same time, coming to the conclusion that choice in healthcare is a bad idea are premature (and not the central thrust of Schwartz's book). There are situations where we can be genuinely empowered by having choices about our care – patients with chronic diseases, such as multiple sclerosis or cystic fibrosis, often develop high levels of expertise about them, but also about their own bodies' responses to the treatments available. In these circumstances they can become genuine experts in their own right, and so are probably better able to make choices about their treatment than many of the clinicians they come into contact with.

In other words, it isn't that we don't want, or can't make, choices about healthcare – it is that different conditions and different people need healthcare systems to support them in different ways, and presuming either that we all want choice, or that none of us want it, are equally unlikely. You probably know people who arm themselves with printouts of diagnosis and treatment information from the internet before going to see a doctor, and they clearly will demand a wider range of choices than those of us who take the view that we ought to ask our doctors what they think is wrong with us first. We should probably be suspicious of any research finding that suggests it is possible to generalise sufficiently to take into account such a wide range of views.

# FOUR

## Elements of quantitative design: sampling and statistics – or what can I do with numbers?

### Introduction

Quantitative methods, more than any other approach to social research covered in this book, are based on tools and techniques that establish their credibility and rigour on the clear procedures and principles by which they should be carried out. What I can't do in this chapter is go through the standard toolbox of quantitative data techniques – there is a range of books that do this in far greater depth than I can achieve here, and which do an excellent job to that end (my personal favourite is Blaikie, 2003). What I can do is to show how quantitative methods techniques face many of the same problems as the rest of the methods discussed in the book, and to try and work through some of them in a way that will better inform students about their choice in the future.

The chapter proceeds as follows: first, we'll consider why numbers carry so much status, and why they are so well regarded in social research. We'll examine how they change the nature of a research programme, examining both the benefits and drawbacks that result. Next we'll consider sampling, thinking about how it varies between quantitative and qualitative research and thinking about the implications of those differences. Then we'll look at some basic descriptive statistics before reaching the chapter's conclusions. Let's start by asking why are numbers so important and what are they good for?

### Numbers and their importance

#### The importance of quantitative research

Quantitative social research gains its status and importance from being able to prove or disprove theory, and to produce specific answers to questions. If you want to conduct an experiment, or measure the country's gross domestic product to see if any economic growth has taken place, you ask a quantitative researcher. Quantitative research is rightly regarded as being extremely important by research funders. The UK Economic and Social Research Council have put it forward as a priority area for the training of doctoral students, and it is probably fair to say that including a robust quantitative component in a grant proposal significantly increases the chances of its success. Quantitative research is not only important, but is widely regarded as being important by social research funders (and potential academic and non-academic employers).

## Controversies

Numbers, however, have a tendency to provoke extreme reactions. On the one hand, a sizeable group of social researchers regard anything with a number on as reductionist, simplificatory and entirely inappropriate when considering social phenomena. They suggest that the world is too complex and diverse to be captured using numbers, and that any application of them creates distance between social researchers and the phenomenon that they are looking to examine because of the simplifications and conceptualisations that are required. They look askance at quantitative researchers, wondering what on earth it is they think they are doing. Another group of social researchers, however, celebrate that numbers make it possible to find trends in large populations that might be impossible to pick out using other research strategies, and enjoy the rigour and re-usability of numeric techniques that can seek out patterns in data and which can produce data sets that can be combined and re-analysed to create findings of even greater importance. Quantitative-minded researchers look amazed at qualitative researchers, wondering why they don't take large-scale medical trials and statistical studies of income inequality with the seriousness they believe they deserve.

## The ubiquity of numbers

We all depend on a basic level of numeracy in our everyday lives. We would not be too impressed if we requested a bank balance from a cash machine and it said we were a 'little bit' overdrawn rather than giving us an exact figure. Equally, we wouldn't like a payslip saying we had got a 'reasonable' amount of money that month, but not telling us how much. Numbers are good because they are precise, and because we can do amazing things like add them up, multiply them and independently of one another (hopefully) come to the same end result in a way that would be possible were we to be manipulating textual data. Numbers are extremely powerful representations, and as a result have a certain status in our society. We are more persuaded by people who are able to give precise results instead of saying 'more than' or 'very much', and we are impressed by people who can perform complex statistical techniques well – adding to the status of this type of research.

# What are numbers good for?

Quantitative research methods provide a range of established tools for measuring social phenomena which can be counted in some way or another. Even if you are the most rigorous defender of qualitative research methods, it often makes sense to count things. Instead of writing 'many participants' or 'few research subjects', both of which can lead reviewers to ask exactly what you are talking about because of their vagueness, it can help to say how many. We do this by simply counting.

However, as we've already noted in previous chapters, quantitative research methods allow you to do far more than this. They are extremely good at answering 'what'-type questions – that is questions that try and work out 'what' is going on in a social context. As long as you can count something, you can do quantitative research.

## Variables

The things that we count in quantitative research are called variables. The use of variables comes with a number of assumptions attached to it. First, we are assuming that the variable actually captures the world in some kind of way. This may or may not be the case – it will depend on how complex the social phenomenon we are trying to capture is. I'm pretty sure there is exactly one dog in the room with me as I write this, but I might be prepared to concede that, under certain circumstances, such as the Kennel Club redefining dogginess, that it might be possible he could be reclassified as something else. Equally, there are six chairs, one table, one sofa, and so on (if this sounds like a big office, I'm working from home). These categorisations, unless we really want to be difficult, aren't too problematic.

So if I want to know how many students I have on a course, and what the drop-out rate is at the end of term, I can count the students at the beginning of the term, and at the end, and work out what proportion of the students have left. This isn't entirely without problems, as with any social research. I have to make sure that the number I counted at the beginning of term included students who were registered but might have been ill when I did the count, and I might have some issues about late-arriving students to deal with. Equally, I might have to make a decision whether or not to count part-time students as being weighted at the same level as full-time students. Then, at the end of term, I'll have to go through the same considerations as well as verifying that students who aren't present really have left. But in principle, I can work out a drop-out rate.

Once I have an agreed process for working out the drop-out rate for my class, I can compare it to drop-out rates for other classes. I can find out average drop-out rates. I can compare drop-out rates across terms and across time. This is the strength of quantitative research – as soon as I have standardised a procedure, I can collect data and perform comparisons quickly and reasonably unproblematically.

More than this, I can, by collecting a little more data about my students, go much further. I can look to see if drop-outs occur amongst particular groups more than others. I can see if drop-out rates are related to exam marks or to age, or any other item of data I have available. I can easily track changes to the data across time and see if these relationships change or are the same.

Quantitative research allows me to do some remarkable things, especially now we have software packages like Excel and SPSS, with remarkable ease. However, to understand how to use quantitative research, we do need to understand its philosophical underpinnings.

## The philosophy of quantitative research

Numbers are used in a number of ways in social research that are worth thinking about carefully. The most common strategy for doing quantitative social research is to create a variable, a category which we are going to use to count the instances of a particular item or phenomenon and assign a numeric value to. This is a fancy way of saying that we give names to things that we count. However, there are also some interesting things going on philosophically here.

First, there is the question of whether numbers have a different kind of existence to words and other non-numeric data. I'm not going to dwell too long on this question which has been the focus of debate amongst philosophers for hundreds or even thousands of years; however, there are two, broadly defined positions.

The first is that numbers are ontologically special, that because we can link numbers to real objects, add one more object and independently get the same result as each other, that numbers represent a special kind of logic that has its own existence. Numbers in this view represent a very pure kind of way of knowing the world. Intuitively this certainly carries some weight – numbers do seem to follow rules incredibly well, and to have a special kind of power. This view was held by Frege and Russell who spent much of their lives attempting to demonstrate the underlying logical principles of number.

However, there is also the view that numbers are just symbols like words, and that the relationships between them is nothing more than custom – that there is no master logic to them that goes beyond this. This view was held by Wittgenstein in his later works, which is interesting because of his thorough mastery of both mechanics and philosophy, and who advanced some remarkable arguments about mathematical theorems to support his position. The importance of this debate does not necessarily lie in finding out who was right, and whether or not numbers do represent something ontologically different to words, but that it seems that we should not take even the apparently obvious characteristics often associated with numbers and quantitative techniques for granted.

Numbers have a special role in our society. We believe them and even suspend our critical faculties when confronted by them, no matter how sensible or silly they might be. It is best to try and retain an open mind, and to work from there.

## Variables as proxies

When we create a variable we seem to be accepting the existence of a reality external to ourselves – a world in which the things we are counting exist. Any kind of quantitative design seems therefore to operate according to some kind of realism – the presumption that the world exists independently of our ideas about it. Variables, in turn, are regarded as being more or less accurate representations of that reality depending on how closely they represent it. This is objectivity decided by the correspondence theory of truth – a variable is a good one if it captures reality as well as possible (or at least better than the alternatives). Variables are therefore a realist idea based on the correspondence theory of truth, but there is a double assumption going on – first, that there is a real thing out there that the variable can measure, and second that the variable is a good proxy for it. Variables derive their importance from their ability to be a good proxy – it is crucial we remember this or we risk mixing up the representation (the variable) with the phenomenon (the thing it is meant to be representing).

Mixing up variables with the phenomenon is surprisingly widespread. We might regard the result of an IQ test as the same thing as intelligence, or the value-at-risk calculation financial institutions reported to their boards each day as really representing the extent of the risk of the financial positions organisations such as Bear Stearns and Lehman Brothers held. However, neither of these variables is the same thing as the phenomenon – IQ is not intelligence, and value-at-risk, as it turned out, failed completely to represent the risk attached to the financial positions held by Bear or Lehman – both of whom ended up effectively bankrupt.

## How we treat variables

A hugely important first point, then, comes in how variables are treated in a particular quantitative research programme. We can assume variables to be synonymous with reality to the point where they become inseparable – an empiricist position where the differences between our concepts and the world are not deemed relevant or important. In the light of what this book has had to say so far this is at least problematic. On one level some categories of variables seem to be relatively straightforward – it is surely possible to count how many students there are in a room provided we can agree both what a student is and what space it is exactly that constitutes the room in question. Most of the time this isn't too hard; however, at other moments it can be surprisingly contested. If there are part-time students, for example, should they count the same as full-time ones, or less (or even more?). If a classroom has a partition that is open at present, does the space count as one or two classrooms? If you are returning student statistics to a funder of courses, the first question (how many students?) takes on considerable significance. If you are trying to assess space utilisation or charge departments for their use of rooms, then the second question is extremely important (how much space?).

A lot of our categories don't cause us too many problems most of the time, but that doesn't mean that in some circumstances they can prove to be rather elusive. We must be extremely careful that the very sensible reasons that we used in deciding how to define our variables are actually still relevant during the research.

## Internal and external validity

The problem of whether the definition of our variable fits the phenomenon we are seeking to investigate is not unique to quantitative research. It does highlight a specific problem that tends to arise more frequently in quantitative research, however – that of focusing too much on internal validity at the expense of external validity. Internal validity considers how well the model being tested corresponds to established practice for the research techniques it offers. For example, whole books exist explicating the techniques involved in the statistic processes looking for relationships between variables, correlation and regression, and the tests that can be applied to both the data and its results to try and make sure that the results are as rigorous as possible (Gujarati, 2009). Where a research programme makes use of an established method, examining the results and applying tests in line with a protocol, then it has a much better chance of assuring internal validity.

External validity examines whether the model researchers have painstakingly examined and constructed has any relevance to the phenomenon it is meant to be investigating. Lawson (1995) argues that economists, for example, have become so obsessed with creating elegant theoretical mathematical models of the economy, which have considerable claims to rigour from their internal validity in terms of the mathematical techniques they utilise and their correspondence to economic theory more generally, that they have forgotten to check whether their models are actually of any use in explaining or predicting the behaviour of the actual economy. It does seem rather remarkable that economists assessed each other's work as being of such high quality in the UK 2008 research assessment exercise at exactly the time that a global economic meltdown occurred that none of their models appeared to predict.

An alternative position to the empiricist view of variables, where they represent reality more or less unproblematically, is advanced by Byrne (2003), who suggests that the name 'variable' should be abolished and that we should instead be exploring 'variate traces'. The difference between the two is not just one of terminology, but is more deeply grounded than that.

A variable, for Byrne, is a reified relationship between a concept and a number that takes on a life of its own and creates a tendency for researchers to make claims that are grounded more in statistical theory than in any relationship between their concepts and the world. Byrne suggests that we need to take a realist view towards considering social research, but that we need to regard the relationship between our concepts and the world far more carefully. A 'variate trace' is a concept that captures a particular aspect of the world at a particular time. It is literally a trace of reality, acknowledging that it is not the reality itself, but a conceptualisation of it, leaving open the debate as to whether and how well it represents that reality. A good trace captures something about the external world, while a bad one does not. This is not entirely based on the correspondence theory of truth, as the concept does not simply capture reality by representing it in a simple relationship.

A variate trace we call social class, as with any variable that we create with the same name, is not to be confused with the reality of social class in the world – it is a representation of it that more or less captures it. Byrne suggests that representations are not reality because reality is organised around open systems that overlap and interfere with one another creating an environment that is complex (in the sense of being non-linear). It is technically possible to create a non-linear model that represents that reality, but reality is so radically over-determined, having so many variables that interrelate with one another, that it is almost impossible to come up with any model that captures it.

## Numbers are indicators of regularities

Quantitative analysis is often associated with the hypothetico-deductive paradigm that suggests that the purpose of research is to test hypotheses and so to advance knowledge by showing what knowledge does, or does not, reflect reality. Knowledge is cumulative and tested by empirical testing. Numbers are an integral part of this – they give us results that are measurable and allow tests that try and replicate them. A considerable amount of quantitative research is deductive in that it is testing hypotheses that are themselves drawn from enacting specific cases of general theories (Bryman, 2001) There is apparently a seamless link from general theory to specific experiment, which creates results that prove to disprove the point under question, and which further theoretical elaboration as necessary.

## Inductive quantitative research?

However, it is increasingly the case that quantitative data is not being examined by researchers in this deductive way. As our movements in society are more and more measured and recorded, and governments and private industry gain access to increasing amounts of numeric data, it is not testing theories that becomes important but instead looking for regularities within it. Data mining was first used by large retailers to look for patterns in the shopping habits of their customers to try and find which products they tended to buy together to allow stores to be designed to try and put them together for convenience, or possibly even further apart to try and get customers to buy additional products on the path between the two products. This is an inductive approach to quantitative analysis that may test theories about social behaviour once they have been derived, but places a strong premium on deriving those theories from the data itself. This is looking for patterns in pre-collected data to better understand it (see Ayres, 2008, and the example at the end of this chapter).

That so much good quantitative research is increasingly being conducted in what appears to be an inductive way suggests that the principle that quantitative analysis has to be deductive is probably as suspect as is the principle that qualitative research has to be inductive. In the same way as it is impossible to do qualitative research in a purely inductive way, which would involve the investigator emptying their head of all concepts before they start to allow ideas to emerge solely from the data, it is not possible (or even desirable) to approach quantitative research in a purely deductive way. Once we have got over the need for quantitative research to correspond solely to a hypothetico-deductive model, and approach data in a more open-minded, curious way, then the possibilities of searching for patterns for data open up and new insights can be generated. What this suggests is not an inductive or a deductive model of research, but instead a retroductive model (Danermark et al., 2001) in which alternative theories are tested against the data to find the one with the closest or most explanatory fit. This involves a mixture of creative imagination (in coming up with new theories to test) and rigorous analysis (as theories are tested against the data), and is probably closer to what makes good quantitative research in practice – a mixture of methodological rigour through analysis and imagination in coming up with new ideas to test.

This points to a situation where quantitative research, in much the same way as qualitative research, becomes a process of looking for regularities in data. Just because we have found a regularity, however, it doesn't mean that we have found something that is meaningful in any other context. What it does indicate is that we have found a relationship in the data that is probably worthy of further investigation that may, or may not, produce something that leads to either theoretical insight, or to a better description of the phenomenon under investigation, depending on what the aim, and underlying philosophy of the research was.

# Sampling

One of the key ways in which the design of a quantitative research project is assessed is in terms of the way that it samples data. Because quantitative research is trying to represent reality, you need to make sure that the data you collect is collected to try and achieve this. There are a number of ways of trying to achieve this, and it is crucial that you have an argument about which strategy you are following and what it means in terms of your design.

## Random and stratified sampling

### Random sampling

There is a view often held by students that all sampling is based upon trying to find a group that is representative of a population as a whole, and that the only way to achieve this is through a process of random sampling that includes enough data collection for any bias to be ruled out. This is certainly one approach, but the issue more generally needs to be thought through rather more carefully than this. Once again, the appropriate sampling strategy depends upon the aim of the research, the expected audience of the research and the underlying assumptions of the research programme.

Random sampling, as the name implies, is based on the idea that the best way to remove bias from those that you include in your research is to include all members of the population, and to select those who you wish to include through a random process. Because everyone has, in principle at least, the same chance of being selected, then bias where it occurs should be balanced out amongst those chosen provided the sample is big enough. Random sampling can be done in a number of ways – a computer can be used to pick out individuals to be included according to a random algorithm, or names drawn out of a hat (provided you can find one big enough and you've made sure you mixed them all up sufficiently).

## Stratified sampling

Related to random sampling is stratified sampling, where the population is divided up into characteristics that are regarded as being key to the study (be they age, gender, ethnicity, or whatever else), and then each category is randomly sampled within that in order to get participants. This strategy can cause significant difficulties in research where the categories chosen are, in themselves, fairly small within the population as a whole. In a comparative study between two localities, one with a large non-white population and one with a small one, the second site will have much smaller group of non-white respondents to be able to sample from. This increases the chance of the population itself having within it biases (which might be based on geographic space, age, income or a range of other factors), and if the population itself contains biases, then the sample almost certainly will. Equally, even if it is the case that the population as a whole is without biases, then its small size might mean that it is difficult to get an adequate number of responses from it in order to produce a reliable sample.

In general, though, stratified sampling is a more reliable and informed way of going about sampling than simple random sampling – the research group is being selected in a way that links to the research question and so is being thought about in a more careful and systematic way than relying upon randomness to rule out bias during the study.

## Other means of sampling

In addition to random and stratified sampling, there are approaches that are often more associated with qualitative work, but which often occur in practice in quantitative studies as well, especially in questionnaire-based research.

Convenience sampling occurs where, instead of trying to select participants according to either randomness or stratification, you pick participants based, as the name suggests, on the basis of convenience. This is a very pragmatic approach to research which, to a very considerable extent, throws out the idea that a sample must be representative of a population as a whole. It acknowledges that in some situations it is impossible to be sampling in reference to a population at large, or even questions whether the population at large is a relevant concept when sampling. These are important points and need to be dealt with each in turn.

It may not be possible to sample in reference to a population where a researcher is not able to access population-level data. This might happen when work is taking place within an organisation, for example where access has been granted for research, but that organisation isn't willing to divulge private information about employees with respect to variables such as income, age or a variety of other factors that might be relevant where the researcher would prefer to carry out stratified sampling. Equally, a more pragmatic approach might need to be carried out because those within the organisation might be unwilling to participate in the research unless someone else who has already participated is willing to recommend it, and this will necessarily mean that the research has to proceed slowly, through a gradually expanding network of respondents rather than trying to sample across the entire organisation. Of course, it might well be that sampling within those who have participated might be carried out later on, with only those who meet a sampling frame being included in the analysis, but this is a rather wasteful approach to research, and might involve missing out collected data where inductive analysis of it might come up with patterns within the data that could be informative and insightful. Convenience sampling is, to summarise, often used to generate research in situations where information about populations is not available, or where access to a research setting might be limited or difficult.

Equally, whether the concept of a population from which to sample from is relevant has also to be questioned in some views of research. If you were engaged to look at employee opinions in a large multinational firm, for example, then it might be possible to come up with a sampling frame to cover every function, every managerial level, every type of organisation within the firm and every national setting, but after coming up with such a grid you might wonder whether it made sense to consider the large multinational firm as being, in itself, a meaningful population to sample within. This is because the population at large is so diverse that any sampling method is not going to produce anything that is in any meaningful sense representative of it.

If you accept this logic, that a diverse population makes sampling meaningless, then it is not too big a leap to suggest that convenience sampling is at least as appropriate as random sampling in these circumstances. To think through these claims we need to think about sampling errors in more detail.

## Sampling errors and bias

Sampling errors occur where differences occur between the sample selected for research, and the population as a whole. These can occur within random samples through bad luck where the sample selected is found to have a systematic factor running through it that makes it unrepresentative. So randomly sampling men in a population might lead to those chosen to participate all being smokers, or all being under the average size. These factors may or may not affect the research as they might not be relevant or causal within it, but they will mean that, in terms of this factor at least, the sample is not representative of this population. A random sample does not get rid of chance, but simply tries to deal with it by hoping that, if the sample is large enough, errors will be self-cancelling – that for every very tall individual included there will be a very small individual as well.

Sampling bias is the tendency for the sampling process to favour the selection of participants that have particular characteristics. This isn't the same as sampling error, which is more or less due to bad luck. In sampling bias there is a systematic problem within the sampling method that leads to the sample chosen being unrepresentative of the population. One reason for this might be due to inaccurate data being held in the population records that lead to problems in sampling. So if, in a given urban area, research was being conducted that involved sending out questionnaires to everyone in a locality, but the lists of house occupiers and addresses were found to be systematically inaccurate because they excluded particular streets or because particular groups had moved out between the lists being assembled and the research being carried out, that would lead to sampling bias.

A second kind of sampling bias can emerge between sampling and response. A sample can be drawn up that is representative of the population, but where only certain types of respondents within the sample respond. This might be due to some groups being apathetic to the aims of the research and others, who have a particular grievance about the issue being researched responding in large numbers. It may be down to some respondents systematically having more time than others, so particular groups within an organisation might respond more than others. This can lead to the potential problem that those with more time to respond can end up disproportionately dominating results.

## Sampling in diverse populations

To return to the issue of whether it is possible within a diverse population to draw up a reliable sample, then issues of both sampling error and sampling bias can be explored to consider that problem. If a population is hugely diverse then sampling error, where a systematic bias of one group over another occurs, is certainly relevant. Just because a population as a whole is diverse, it doesn't let researchers off the hook and allow them just to examine participants of one kind only. What it may do instead is suggest that they might have to be systematic in trying to speak to as diverse a range of participants as possible on the argument that a diverse population requires a diverse sampling strategy, whilst acknowledging that it might be impossible for the sample ever to be strictly representative of the population as a whole. This may call for researchers to be pragmatic in trying to look at their data and work out which factors seem to cause differences in responses between participants, and to set about an iterative sampling strategy of trying to work out what appears to make differences between participant groups, what doesn't, and moving toward a strategy that, following grounded theory, might be termed theoretical sampling where the researcher looks for participants who are able to advance the emerging ideas within the study, or to test theories, rather than aiming for strict representativeness.

Issues of sampling bias can also inform research where a diverse population exists. Once again, the most sensible answer in this case appears for researchers to be proactively examining their data and trying to account for similarities and differences between responses in an iterative way. This allows researchers to examine whether a particular factor, such as respondents all coming from the same street or streets (to revisit the urban example above) seems to reflect upon the results by making a conscious effort to compare those findings with others from a different locality. Theories and ideas would look for patterns and emergent ideas, as well as testing pre-formulated theories and hypotheses. This also means that errors where some particular groups seem to respond to surveys more than others should be taken into account, as this would be considered theoretically, and so further research required to take into account the responses of groups with low response rates.

## Convenience sampling

The strategy suggested above does not reject convenience sampling – where access is limited, or where little is known about the area being researched (and so the population is not known in advance), it is certainly appropriate. However, it does seem sensible that convenience sampling be carried out reflexively so that researchers are as aware of the characteristics of those that are participating in research as much as possible so that appropriate comparisons, theory building or thick description is carried out.

Having carried out some research, the next problem is working out how to analyse the data. What I can't do here, as I've said earlier, is to take readers through a large range of quantitative methods techniques – there are plenty of books out there that will do this. What I can do is to begin a process of thinking about the assumptions underlying some of these methods that hopefully will illuminate their usefulness (or not) in dealing with the particular research problem in hand.

# Some issues in quantitative analysis – basic descriptive statistics

Basic descriptive statistics are easy to calculate, even for large data sets, now that we have spreadsheets and specialist software packages such as SPSS. A few clicks and whole lists of summary statistics appear. This is great, but also something of a problem, because it moves the emphasis in quantitative research somewhat away from the mechanics of calculating the numbers (which were a major part of the way I learned statistics as both an accountant and as an undergraduate and postgraduate), and to understanding the results of the analysis (which were always important, but once the processes involved in calculating numbers largely disappear they are literally all we are left with).

A good analogy here is provided by the sociologist Richard Sennett (2009). Sennett suggests that the increase in the use of Computer Aided Design (CAD) packages in building design has led to architects and engineers tending to lose the craft of what is involved in good design – what was once emphasised by drawing and redrawing, by calculating and recalculating loads and tolerances and thinking about how the elements within the building fitted together through the repeated process of having to change things by hand, is in danger of getting lost. Now that designers are able to change textures with a click and move beams around without having to apply much thought, Sennett suggests, there is danger that they lose the craft of good design. He provides examples of buildings that undoubtedly look good on a computer screen, but are actually fairly dysfunctional in practice, and whose faults might have been picked up had the process been carried out more by hand by skilled designers, and less by moving around building elements on a screen.

My argument is that this can also happen in statistical analysis. In no way am I suggesting that researchers should go back to pens and paper and perform all calculations by hand. What I am saying is that, as calculation processes get lost through computerisation, then so does an intuitive process of working out whether the results coming from data seem to be expected or unexpected, or even relevant to the research problem. Results need to be handled with caution.

## Representing data

A much overlooked but great way of beginning to think about a data set is to find an appropriate way of graphically representing it. In an era when most analysis is done on computer packages, this can be surprisingly straightforward. If you have grouped data, put it in a bar chart and see what it looks like. If you are looking at how a variable changes over time, graph it and look to see if there appears to be a pattern. If you are looking for relationships between variables, graph the data and see if they seem to change together, either at the same time or with a lag. Graphing data is a great way of beginning to understand it – and it is extremely quick if the data is in a spreadsheet or statistics package.

Beyond this, a good second step is to calculate some basic descriptive statistics.

## Means, modes and medians

### The mean

The most calculated statistic is probably the mean. The mean is, as every student knows, the sum of the data items divided by the number of data items present (a calculation varied slightly where frequency interval data is used). The calculation of the mean is a very appealing process – we go from lots of numbers down to one through a straightforward process, and that number intuitively feels like it is related in an obvious way to the individual data items. The calculation of a mean, however, can end up obscuring as much as it reveals.

The key question, as with sampling, is one of representativeness. If the mean doesn't look like any of the individual data items then we need to think carefully as to whether it is actually any use in representing it. Where data tends to occupy extreme results on a scale, the mean may not represent it at all – think of the mean of 0, 0, 0, 0, 0, 10, 10, 10, 10, 10. In this case the mean is 5, but that tells us next to nothing about the data series as a whole. That's clearly a problem.

A second problem of representation comes from the careless use of the mean in calculating a number that is of a different data type to the original data. Data that is made up of discrete numbers (whole numbers or integers), such as number of children, will often result in a mean calculation that results in a non-whole number that may be treated as continuous data if used in further calculations. According to the US Bureau of Statistics, the 2000 census indicates that the mean number of children per family is 1.86 (although with considerable variation between States). The problem is that this number doesn't represent any American family, none of which actually have this number of children. The number therefore has to be treated with a little caution in terms of its ability to represent its data, especially where that data is to be used in further calculations. In calculating world averages of number of family per children, for example, this would result in continuous data from other countries and the US being further subject to the mean calculation with the end result being a number that might represent exactly no-one.

### The mode and the median

One way out of this is to bear in mind that the mean isn't the only way of calculating the average of a data set – something that a program such as Excel doesn't help with as it insists on calling the function that calculates the mean 'average'. As well as the mean, there is also the mode and the median, which tend to get overlooked a great deal but may be as (or even more) valuable than the mean. The calculation of the median for an ungrouped data set involves putting it in rank order and then finding the middle value (in terms of sequence). Where there is an even number of data points or data is already grouped, there are additional complications that I won't deal with here. What the median calculation does is come up with a representational figure in a different way to the mean calculation, and which may or may not tell us more. In the data series 0, 0, 0, 0, 0, 10, 10, 10, 10, 10 the mean is 5, and so is the median value is the number of data items (10), plus one (taking us to 11), divided by 2 (5.5 value). The 5.5th value is half way between the fifth and sixth value of the set when ranked, which here is 5, a number which is about as representative as the mean (i.e. not very). Things improve with less extreme data series. So the mean of 3, 3, 3, 3, 4, 5, 5, 5, 6 is 4.11, which, if we're talking about number of children may not be that helpful. The median value, however, is the fifth value when the data is put in rank order, 4, which at least is a discrete (whole) number, and so is of the same type as the data. However, a quick look at the data suggests that this may not be the most representative of the set as other numbers (3 and 5) occur more frequently.

The mode is the most frequently occurring value in a data set. In the data set above, the modal value is 3. If this were numbers of children, it would give us the most frequently occurring number of children, which would tell us something different about the data than either the mean or the median. It would tell us, if you like, the most popular number of children, where the median tells us the middle value of the data when listed in order, and the mean tries to give us a representative number based on what seems to most of us to be an intuitively appropriate calculation. The three averages give us different numbers for this data set. Instead of being a source of consternation, however, this is better thought of as an interesting starting point for thinking about the analysis of the data – it leads us on to think about how the data is 'skewed' one way or another, and to a more informed discussion about how best to represent these numbers.

## The standard deviation

Once we have calculated the three averages described above, a next logical step is to calculate the standard deviation of the data. The standard deviation is the average distance of our data from the mean, and is the result of a fairly convoluted series of calculations when done manually, or rather more straightforwardly the STDEV function in Excel.

The important thing is that the standard deviation tells us how far, on average, our data is away from the mean. So with data series where you have the data series described above: 0, 0, 0, 0, 0, 10, 10, 10, 10, 10, we get a mean of 5, but also a standard deviation of 5.3. A low standard deviation in relation to the mean indicates that the data is, on average, close to the mean, and a high standard deviation in relation to the mean that the data is further away. Here, the standard deviation is bigger than the mean itself, suggesting that the data is some distance away from the mean on average – which a quick look at our data confirms.

In contrast, the data series 3, 3, 3, 3, 4, 5, 5, 5, 6 has a mean of 4.11 as we noted above, but a standard deviation of 1.17. This tells us that the data is, on average, 1.17 away from a mean of 4.11, suggesting that the mean is more representative of the data as a whole – which again a quick look at the data confirms.

The standard deviation is also the basis of the measurement of confidence in statistical calculations, and so is hugely important. We don't have space to go into discussions around the complexities of confidence intervals here, and especially of their use and misuse. I would strongly recommend Nassim Nicholas Taleb's (2008) *The Black Swan* as further reading on this topic though.

What you do next with your data depends on what you want to test it for. You might be looking for correlations between data series, or to conduct any number of statistical tests. I can't help you with those in a book of this length – but can encourage you to take a thoughtful approach to doing your quantitative research, remembering that the variables you calculate are not real in themselves, and that relationships you may find are not proof of anything in themselves. I'm afraid there are no magic bullets to representing data series – what is important is to go through a careful process of analysis and thought, and not to make claims that don't seem to match the data you are presenting.

# Conclusion

Quantitative methods are a hugely important part of social science. However, they present at least as many difficulties and confusions as qualitative methods, and researchers need to treat the techniques it offers with considerable care. Numbers appear to carry an authority that words can often lack, and so claims that are made using them need to be treated to a serious level of scrutiny.

Basic quantitative techniques that involve counting, basic descriptive statistics and graphing numbers to try and look for patterns within data series are important tools for understanding what the numbers we have collected are telling us. A positivistic perspective on quantitative methods suggests that we aren't doing social research unless we are measuring things using numbers, and that numbers can be good measures of reality. Despite the fact this view has become increasingly disputed amongst social scientists over the last forty years, quantitative methods are often used unreflexively and inappropriately. There are many good arguments for saying that the root of the financial crisis of 2007 onwards lie in inappropriate quantitative models being allowed to get completely out of hand (Triana, 2009). In particular, Gaussian modelling based on assumptions that data nearly fits normal distributions when the empirical evidence suggests that it does not, appears to have become a particularly widespread source of error (Mandelbrot, 2008).

But despite their widespread misuse, quantitative methods still offer us a means of seeking regularities in data sets that other methods can overlook, and a means of testing and developing theory that qualitative researchers have been reluctant to engage with. This can be viewed as a positive or a negative – interpretivist researchers would argue that we already have too much theory, and that quantitative attempts to produce more are entirely unhelpful. However, the potential of areas such as complexity theory to help us understand the dynamics of social systems is considerable and omitting this from our set of tools to understand the world would be a missed opportunity.

## Five things to remember about this chapter

1 Quantitative research is extremely well regarded by funders and within academia because of its ability to test hypotheses and follow rigorous, established research techniques.
2 Quantitative methods use variables to specify models of how the world is taken to be, and then to work out how those variables statistically relate to one another.
3 Sampling is extremely important in quantitative methods, and it is crucial you understand the different sampling techniques and the appropriate sample size you need to conduct the kind of quantitative research you wish to utilise.
4 Basic descriptive statistics can add a great deal to research of all kinds because they help researchers avoid writing things like 'many respondents' and 'respondents often say', which aren't terribly persuasive.
5 Researchers using quantitative techniques need to become experts in the techniques and tests involved in those specific techniques. Quantitative techniques are designed to have strong internal validity, so it is crucial that researchers understand how this works for their specific technique, as well as making sure that external validity is not lost in the quest for methodological perfection.

## Example – *Super Crunchers*

If you are interested in how, in an age of large data sets and powerful computers, quantitative techniques are being applied across a range of business and governmental areas, then Ian Ayres's 2008 book *Super Crunchers* is a fun introduction.

One of Ayres's many examples is that of dating websites (Chapter 1). He describes how eHarmony aims to 'find out what kind of person you are and then matches you with others who the data say are the most compatible'. As such eHarmony is aiming not, as traditional dating websites do, to match you against conscious and articulated preferences in what you are seeking from a partner, but instead on the basis of what eHarmony, in its advertising literature, calls 'deep compatibility'.

eHarmony's founder studied 5,000 married people in the late 1990s and, from data about them, constructed a predictive model of compatibility based on 29 variables related to issues such as emotional temperament, social style, cognitive mode and relationship skills. The model is based on regression analysis, taking raw historical data and finding causal factors within it, and aims to 'match compatible people by suing personality and character traits that people may not even know they have or be able to articulate' – so the website might well match you with someone who never imagined as a partner.

eHarmony is not the only data-driven relationship website out there. Perfectmatch works on a mixed basis; it bases its recommendations on historical data about matches that have worked, but on a modified basis of the Myers–Briggs personality test. It is therefore both inductive (using historical data to make matches) but also deductive (assigning people to categories using the test). True.com, according to Ayres, works on a basis more similar to eHarmony by collecting data on 99 relationship factors and feeding the results into a regression formula to calculate a compatibility index score.

Despite being aimed at the same goal (finding member couples who might get on in a relationship) the three websites make very different recommendations – eHarmony tends to match like-with-like, but Perfectmatch and true.com look for complementary personalities. However, it is hard to tell who has the most successful record in matching couples because the industry keeps both its analysis and the data on which its analysis is based secret – understandable as the models are, in effect, the driver of their business models.

What all three sites share, however, is that their models are to some extent dependent on data-based decision making in a way that attempts to transcend the conscious preferences of participants to achieve success in matching them with others. To some extent, all of the models they use are inductive in that they start with the data of successful couples and use regression techniques to try and find out what makes them successful, rather than starting out with prior theory. They all, to various extents, use theories about successful relationships to construct their models (with Perfectmatch being the most explicit mix of inductive and deductive modelling, with the latter being based on the Myers–Briggs personality test), but they all give the users a data-driven match based on factors that they would probably never have taken into account themselves. They are all, then, a very modern mix of inductive (seeking regressions in data sets) and deductive (testing models or making use of existing ideas about compatibility) methods for conducting quantitative research.

However, you should as a social researcher have some misgivings about what is going on with these dating websites. One of the mantras taught on good quantitative method causes is that *correlation is not causation*. If the research underpinning the dating models above had found what they think are the ingredients of successful relationships, as measured by the variables they use, then that is, indeed, a remarkable achievement. But just because a sample of successful relationships have particular relationships between a range of measured variables, that does not mean that those relationships will hold with other couples, or that they will hold in the future.

We really have no idea, as Ayres points out, whether these models actually work or not. We simply don't have the data to show whether one model is better than another, and given commercial confidentiality, it's unlikely that the different models are going to divulge their success rates. And how would we measure success? By the number of relationships lasting over, say, six months? By the number of marriages? By the number of marriages that last over ten years? These different measures of success come with a range of different cultural assumptions (about cohabitation versus marriage, and we haven't even brought children into the picture yet!). Ayres has given us a fun example, but one which probably doesn't bear much scrutiny on further analysis. It might be fun to take a test to find out how allegedly compatible you are with a potential partner, but it seems rather unlikely that such models are able to predict anything about our individual relationship futures.

# FIVE

## Ethnography as a research approach – or what do I gain from watching people and talking to them?

### Introduction

The term 'ethnography' covers a variety of practices and methods in qualitative research (Hammersley, 1991). A very weak interpretation uses it as a term that is synonymous for all qualitative research – so doing ethnographic research is simply doing qualitative research. This seems a rather poor use of the term – if you mean you are doing qualitative research in the broader sense, why not simply use the term 'qualitative research'? At the other end of the spectrum from this view are social scientists who believe that 'ethnography' is something that only trained anthropologists can carry out, with it being based on extensive periods of continuous fieldwork in a setting foreign to the researcher in some kind of way. In this view, researchers have to earn their right to call their research ethnography through lengthy periods of fieldwork where they try and immerse themselves in the almost infinite detail of day-to-day life of their research participants with the view that only this kind of immersion and depth can create the right to be able to describe what is going on. There is more to commend this view than the polar opposite, where ethnography is simply a synonym for all qualitative research, but it jumps to the opposite extreme – instead of being over-inclusive it is over-exclusive. It would suggest that only anthropologists with long periods of time available for immersive fieldwork can conduct ethnographies, and this doesn't seem a terribly helpful starting point either. What is more important, surely, is working out what it is about ethnographic research that characterises it, and then working out whether it can be done in a particular situation given the challenges this imposes on us in terms of research ability and time.

Another difficulty with the term ethnography is that it is often used to describe both a research process and research output. So I can say that I'm doing ethnographic research (a process), and the end result of this will be an ethnography (an output). This isn't a problem unique to ethnography – we talk about conducting a case study (a process) and can publish a case study (an output) as well. What this split does mean, in either case, is that we have to be careful in being clear whether we are referring to the process or the output, acknowledging that there are interrelationships between the two – the one can't be done without the other.

# What is ethnography?

One way into considering what an ethnography is, and what it involves, is to contrast it with quantitative methodology. From the previous chapter, we know that quantitative methods need to be based on carefully constructed samples in order to achieve statistical significance, and are about looking for patterns and generalisations within those data series. If quantitative methods are being used as a part of a hypothetico-deductive (or positivistic) model, where we put forward a hypothesis and then seek to test them through data analysis using tools and techniques such as regression or modelling, then we are setting up questions in advance of data analysis that we seek to answer through the use of quantitative methods. Quantitative methods seek to achieve analytical rigour through the statistical significance they can generate, and the ability of the methods to provide numerate answers to the hypothesis being generated.

Ethnography, in very many respects, is the opposite of all of this. First of all it is likely to involve a very small sample – it is not unusual for ethnography to take place on one site only, for it to be an inductive process in which the researcher attempts to conduct his or her work with as few initial concepts as possible, letting people speak using their own words as much as is practicably possible, and with the explicit aim of producing descriptions of what the researcher finds before him or her that are as rich and as detailed as possible. Ethnographers seek to achieve rigour by allowing the sites of their investigations to speak in as authentic form as they can achieve, preferably without the minimal interference of pre-formulated social science concepts.

# When would I want to use an ethnography?

Ethnographies tend to be used when either we know little about a particular social context, or where we need to achieve detailed, fine-grained understanding of it. Knowing very little about a social context means that deductive, quantitative research is difficult to achieve because we don't know much about the situation, and so existing theory may or may not be valid. In this situation, it is possibly best to try to adopt an inductive research strategy, at least until we have a better sense of the research area. Ethnography offers such a strategy.

Equally, if we want to achieve a fine-grained understanding of a social situation, it is more difficult to achieve this using a quantitative rather than qualitative research approach. Quantitative approaches tend to direct us to what we are looking for – they form a strong link between research questions and method – so a test for correlation will look for a relationship between two variables, but little else. Even if we are conducting inductive quantitative research (see previous chapter) then we still have to specify what kind of test we are applying to the data before we begin, and so cannot be completely open minded about what the data might say.

Ethnography seeks not only to find out answers to 'what' questions, but also to 'how' and even 'why' questions – it attempts to gain its legitimacy by giving the researcher an in-depth, immersive understanding of a social context achieved by spending an often considerable time with those that live or work within it. Ethnographers argue that this level of understanding simply cannot be achieved through the use of quantitative techniques.

## What does it mean to conduct an ethnography?

Ethnography embraces a range of methods through from participant observation through to observation, interviews, focus groups and documentary analysis that we will soon work through one at a time. Ethnography's claims to validity depend on the researcher being able to reproduce in as authentic a form as possible, the setting which he or she has researched. This validity claim clearly has implications for the specific methods conducted in the research, as well as the means by which we conduct sampling, a subject to which we will turn next.

### Sampling

Sampling is an area which is potentially challenging to account for in ethnographic terms. Ethnographies, because of their labour-consuming nature, will seldom be designed using a framework that corresponds to a random or stratified system of sampling. To do this would mean that a large number of sites would need investigating, and this would require a very large research team and so be extremely expensive as a result. Equally, within sites ethnography often uses techniques such as 'snowball' sampling, where contacts made the researcher suggest further potential participants, or 'convenience' sampling, where those that the researcher knows are willing to participate are chosen. The basis of these sampling techniques are completely different to the random or stratified approach, they depend on research being approached in a naturalistic manner, but with the acknowledgement that research sites can often be difficult to enter and do research in.

## Ethnography as participation

A researcher being able to conduct herself as a competent participant in the research setting might certainly provide an indication that she has learned the behaviours, attitudes and codes of conduct that are appropriate, and so can claim to hold some authority. However, this does not also mean that she can articulate and explain them to others – being able to fit in does not mean you can always explain what it is you are doing to fit. So being able to do ethnographic research does not automatically mean that you can produce a good ethnography at the end of it – a significant problem for researchers wanting to conduct research in this way. Equally, the amount of data collected intensively visiting a study site can be almost overwhelming, and is clearly going to mean that some of it has to be left out in the subsequent ethnographic account. If the standard for validity for ethnography is based upon its closeness to the research site, then this raises difficult problems about how to explain what can be found there, and what to leave out of the subsequent account.

Equally, doing ethnographic research as a participant raises ethical questions for the research – are you effectively deceiving others in your research site if you don't tell them you are a researcher, and if you do tell them, do you effectively ruin the chances of carrying out an ethnography because your interactions will always be compromised by others knowing you are researching them?

## Ethnography as observation

Doing ethnographic research through observation means that the researcher has to explain to those she is researching what she is doing, and then hope that they are prepared to go about their business in front of her. Researchers writing up ethnographic research often include a sentence in their methods section along the lines of 'Participants were informed of the research being carried out, but after a period of adjustments where the presence of the researcher influenced what was going on, seemed to carry on as normal as if the researcher's presence was no longer significant or interfering with what they were doing.' This is clearly what observational methods are looking to achieve – to capture behaviour in the research site in a naturalistic way so the researcher is able to claim later on that their account is an accurate representation of the site.

## Interviews

Carrying out interviews in an ethnographic research process is potentially even more problematic. Interviews are not naturalistic data-collection methods – they involve the creation of a rather odd situation in which one party asks questions of another, and often recording the result using a device of some kind or another. As such, do they have a place in ethnography? The argument against interviews has effectively already been made – that they are not naturalistic, and that they collect artificial data. There is certainly a great deal of sense in this viewpoint – if you are basing your claims to validity upon being able to produce a naturalistic account of a site, then why would you go about collecting data in a non-naturalistic way?

## Why use interviews?

There are several possible reasons for conducting interviews. First, if you are researching events that occurred in the past, then you are not going to be able to observe them first-hand. Using participant observation does not entirely limit you to the present as interactions with others are likely to involve discussions about things that have happened in the past, and may reveal stories and accounts that can help fill in previous events. If you are using primarily observational methods, however, you may have to depend upon accounts of the past naturally occurring as you watch, and this may lead to substantial gaps in what you are able to say. An interview, on the other hand, allows you to be extremely focused in asking specific questions about previous events, and so provide valuable context on the present situation.

Second, interviews may allow participants who do not have much opportunity to speak in everyday settings in the research site to speak for themselves. Some people may feel that in public their views are not welcome, or even that their views could harm them personally or professionally if voiced to others in the research setting. An interview may provide a way to ameliorate this problem, giving voice to people who might otherwise be overlooked or excluded.

Third, it is hard to get away from the fact that interviews, when organised well, can be an efficient way to conduct research. It seems difficult to argue that a study conducted entirely through interviews could call itself an ethnography, and make claims to produce a reliable account of a site as a result, but it does make sense for interviews to be able to supplement other methods to help fill in gaps and give research participants a chance to speak that they may not have in naturalistic settings.

## Focus groups

A focus group is a kind of group interview where there are several participants, and the interviewer acts instead as a moderator or facilitator to try to get a discussion going around a defined topic. The emphasis is on group interaction and the production of shared meaning. Focus groups present particular challenges in terms of recording (as it can be difficult to separate out voices), and should probably have a maximum of about ten people before they get so unwieldy that it is difficult to explore interactions any more.

## Advantages of focus groups

The advantage of focus groups is that they can achieve a more naturalistic environment than interviews in which the interviewer plays a much reduced role. However, this naturalism can be over-emphasised – participants have still been typically brought to a contrived setting and will know that they are either being recorded or notes are being taken of their contributions. Equally, however, focus groups, because of their stress on inter-subjective exchange, can be a preferred method within areas such as feminist analysis. The construction of meaning in focus groups is achieved, provided the facilitator can play a relatively minor role, by the participants themselves, a move that addresses power imbalances between the researcher and the researched as well as giving the maximum space for shared meanings to emerge.

## Disadvantages of focus groups

These advantages, however, come with problems attached to them as well. Because the interviewer has less control of a focus group than an interview, it is easier to lose control over proceedings. If researchers are trying to take a highly structured approach to conducting their work, this can be a significant problem as getting through a schedule of topics might be difficult where group dynamics do not permit it. Equally, as mentioned above, they are difficult to record and transcribe, as well as being more difficult to organise than a single interview, simply because more people have to be involved. Finally, although focus groups can be useful in showing the construction of shared meaning, they can also present situations where 'group-think' dominates and some participants feel unable to contribute because of particular vocal or dominant individuals. In such situations facilitators may need to take a more direct role, but this presents challenges for the method if it is claiming validity from being based on the emergence of participants' meaning.

## Documentary analysis

Documentary analysis might seem in some respects the antithesis of ethnography. Instead of involving the live situations of observation or participant observation, it often involves lonely work of going through large volumes of paperwork or computer files where it may seem that inspiration and insight appear relatively rarely. However, the documents that an organisation or research site produces can tell us a great deal about it. Sitting down and going through the minutes of meetings, and looking at the way that the research site attempts to describe its roles and activities on paper, allows researchers to get a sense of the history of the site they are in, as well as seeing what it routinely talked about, which images, stories and events are referred to frequently, and which appear infrequently or hardly at all. The language research sites use to describe themselves can tell us a great deal – is very active language used, or more heavy, passive, bureaucratic language. Are there rule books or codes of conduct? Are there organisational charts, and how are they presented? Do people have titles, and how they are used? All of these things can reveal a great deal. Documentary analysis can provide a great deal of valuable material on the context of the research site, but more than this, illuminate the data collected by other methods by helping to provide more detail about what is going on.

What we can see from the above is that the fundamental characteristics of ethnography are its claim to validity being based upon closeness to the research site coming through naturalistic methods, the variety of methods it uses in attempting to achieving this, and the difficulties that come when trying to convert the very large amount of data that ethnographies collect into an ethnography, the result of the research, at the end.

# Philosophical debates around ethnography

Ethnography raises some particularly acute problems philosophically because it can be justified, as a research process, from a range of possible positions. As with our chapter on questionnaires and surveys, we can see how different perspectives consider ethnography. Examining each allows us to understand the very significant differences that exist in terms of the way that the term ethnography is used, and the different ways of producing an ethnography at the end of the process.

## Realist ethnography

A realist approach to ethnography (such as that suggested by the contributors to Carter and New, 2004) starts with the assumption that there is a reality independent of the researcher and the research participants at the particular site under investigation. This reality, independent of our individual conceptions of it, is the topic of investigation for the research. A realist ethnography is therefore about attempting to capture as true a picture as possible of that reality, with the model of truth in question being that of the correspondence theory – that something is true if it accurately represents the reality independent of it. Realist ethnographers are prepared to accept that accounts participants give of past and present events differ, but have no problem with some of those accounts being more true than others. They will tend to prefer stratified modes of sampling with the elements of the stratification being based on theories that they might be attempting to test in the research field. Equally, they recognise that much of reality might be the product of shared interpretive understandings of it, but would still hold that some of those interpretations are more true than others. The product of a realist ethnography is an account of events that aspires to be as true as possible, with the researcher as the ultimate arbiter of what is true or not, bounded by their understanding of the reality being researched.

## Idealist ethnography

Idealist ethnographers regard the shared understandings and interpretations that are constructed by research participants to be the most significant element. This kind of ethnography is about capturing and exploring those shared understandings, with the question of whether they represent some external reality or not being secondary or even unimportant. What is important is allowing research participants to speak through the ethnography (both process and product), and to capture and present their understandings of the world as authentically as possible. What is meant here by 'authentic' can be difficult to say, however – in rejecting realism this cannot simply be about producing the account closest to the truth, but instead is often about attempting to capture the spirit or essence of what participants have discussed, often by feeding back researcher interpretations to them and allowing those interpretations to be modified iteratively until agreement is reached.

Sampling in this form of ethnography is likely to be a secondary consideration, with use of snowball or convenience sampling being common, and a view taken that attempting to achieve any kind of representativeness is likely to be pointless. The product of an idealist ethnography is therefore the shared understandings between participants and researchers that the research has produced, often without claims to truth, but instead validity being assessed through the collaborative processes of research between researchers and participants, and the resulting understandings that can be articulated as a result.

## Postmodern ethnography?

There is also a version of ethnography that has much in common with postmodernism because of its scepticism towards realism and the possibility of creating generalisable knowledge. This version of ethnography starts in many respects at the polar opposite to positivist ethnography, being incredulous about realist claims to knowledge (Law, 2004). Given that we never have unmediated contact with the world, can we possibly claim to be able to judge whether the accounts of those we research are true or not? Similarly to idealist ethnography, what is true or not is not that important; what is important is for the researcher to be able to chronicle in as much detail as possible what is going on at the particular site they are investigating. The researcher's job is not to conceptualise, or judge, or to claim any kind of authority, but to describe what is happening. Reality is not singular, but multi-perspectival. What this means is that the account, for example, of Australian aboriginals of the history of their land is as valuable as geologists' accounts of the formation of rocks in that country. They are two stories about the same thing. It is the ethnographer's job to go in and describe what is happening at the sites being investigated, the stories that people tell and the way that buildings or open spaces are laid out. It is the ethnographer's job to tell what is going on from as wide a range of perspectives as is practical because of the complexity and messiness of reality, which does not come pre-packaged to us in neat boxes, but instead in a flurry of activity. The product of a postmodern ethnography would attempt to capture this messiness of reality, not privileging the researcher's account, and acknowledging that the end result is never going to be even representative of what was being researched.

**Table 5.1**   Perspectives on ethnographic design

|  | Positivist | Realist | Idealist | Postmodern |
|---|---|---|---|---|
| View of truth | Empirical | Correspondence theory | Authenticism | Narrative |
| Sampling method | Random | Stratified | Snowball | Convenience or snowball |
| Key element | Representativeness | Theory building | Perspectival | Descriptive power |

## Positivist ethnography?

A positivist approach to ethnography is something that appears rather incongruous, and in some respects at least is a contradiction in terms. If by 'ethnography' we mean a qualitative research method that gains its legitimacy from close observation in a naturalistic setting that attempts to capture the subjectivities of research subjects, then achieving this goal in a positivistic manner is difficult to achieve. However, there are qualitative researchers who might describe what they do as ethnography, but at the same time embrace many of the principles of positivism. They may attempt to utilise randomised sampling and observation techniques, for example, which standardise the collection of data within and between sites as much as possible.

A positivist ethnography will make extensive use of counting, will conduct interviews in highly structured forms and then code the data as quantitatively as possible, using techniques usually labelled 'content analysis', and will treat the data they are researching in an experimental manner by trying to find controls that allow for systematic comparison between cases or incidents of data. Such an approach presumes an external reality that is independent of researchers' (or subjects') conceptions of it, but that can be captured using scientific methods.

A comparison between the different perspectives on ethnography is shown Table 5.1.

## What do the differences in approach mean for the resulting ethnography?

Two questions of particular salience arise from the differences in the approach to ethnography stemming from the application of alternative philosophical ideas to it: what is ethnography (the research process) seeking to produce exactly as its product (the ethnography) and how, when we have produced something, can we tell if it has any value or not?

### What is ethnography aiming to produce exactly?

The product of an ethnography can vary between a researcher-driven account of what he or she believes to be the facts of what went on at the research site, to a series of agreed accounts of the experiences and interpretations of research participants, to a multi-perspectival mix of stories, pictures, photographs and narrative that attempts to convey a sense of what it is like at the site in all its complexity.

Whereas a realist version of ethnography has something in common with a police investigation, an idealist ethnography is often closer to a novel that attempts to convey the stories that research participants have to tell about their lives, and a postmodern ethnography attempts to convey the experience of being at a research site, with all its contradictions and confusions. The criteria for a positivist ethnography might be about assessing its scientific rigour – if other researchers were to analyse the data collected by the research team, would they come up with the same results? Are all the claims made in the ethnography demonstrably associated with measurable results from the studies? These are very different research products. Each has its own criteria for success.

## How is an ethnography to be assessed?

A positivist ethnography is assessed in terms of its scientific rigour, defined in terms of its measurable ability to reproduce what was found at the research site. Quantitative data will be preferred because it will be regarded as less ambiguous, and qualitative data may be coded quantitatively in order to try and demonstrate greater rigour in analysis. A good positivist ethnography will be assessed according to the methods used within it, the reporting of those methods and their fit with the data reported. Ethnography, in this view, should have strong internal validity (it will be able to show clearly how its data and methods combined to produce findings), and any generalisations from the ethnographic sites will be based on statistical sampling, and so claims to external validity can also be made.

A realist ethnography is assessed in terms of how well it explains events at the research site. Stories and narratives can be incorporated, but the researchers' view of events will act as a means of linking them together to provide an account of what the research site is like. Inaccuracies and failures to collect sufficient facts undermine the product, as can the researcher not producing an account that sufficiently explains those facts. The quality of the account is based on its ability to explain events.

An idealist ethnography is attempting to present the interpretations of the research participants, and so is assessed on its ability to achieve this. The researcher's narrative has to step into the background as much as possible and allow the participants to speak. Comparisons between narratives and interpretations might be made, but the researcher is not assumed to hold authority over the researched. The success of the research comes in its ability to portray the interpretations and experiences of the participants, which have often been generated in agreement with the researcher. The end point, then, is a description that meets this goal and which is an authentic as possible account that the researcher can produce in those circumstances.

A postmodern ethnography will be frustrated in having to present reality in a linear fashion, or to simply use words to describe what it has found. It will want to include sounds, images, photographs and whatever media can convey the experience of the site investigated. As with idealist ethnography, the voice of the research participants is paramount, and they must be retained and represented in as authentic form as possible, but they must also be individually respected and heard. Experimental methods of presenting the data will therefore be favoured, and even though the conventional academic formats of presenting ethnographies through journal articles and books will be used, they will be recognised as inappropriate and so innovative writing methods (Mol, 2002) will be utilised where possible, which include multiple narratives on the top and bottom of the page, or even starting simultaneously at the beginning and end of a book and having two accounts working toward the middle (Burrell, 1997).

So, there are a range of different approaches to doing ethnography (the research process), and potentially a range of different results in terms of the final result. But the resulting ethnography also has to be situated amongst other research outputs to try and specify exactly what it is. This raises another question – what kind of research does an ethnographic research project produce?

## What kind of research does an ethnographic research project produce?

To consider this question, it is helpful again to contrast the result of an ethnography with that of some kinds of quantitative research projects. Quantitative research projects, where they take the hypothetico-deductive model, aim as we said earlier, to test hypotheses and produce results in numerate form. This has a definite result – that the research they produce often appears very definite – there is a hypotheses that has been proven or not, and often a summary number or numbers that represent a very large data series in a simplified manner. At the most basic level, for example, averages attempt to represent large lists of numbers by being representative of them and correlation coefficients attempt to give an idea of whether two variables appear to be statistically related to one another. This degree of precision is extremely attractive as it appears to give a clear basis for thinking about the data, but also of course potentially rather dangerous if the summary statistics are not particularly representative of the data as a whole and misinterpretations occur as a result. In principle, however, quantitative studies summarise their results in numerate form, and so tend to produce results that can be further summarised and can be potentially combined with further studies to create meta-studies, as is done in medicine to assess the reliability of clinical interventions across several trials.

Most ethnographic research, however, is very different to this. The logic of ethnographic research is based, in all the versions discussed above, on claiming validity through collecting data naturalistically. It is a claim to authority based on the researcher having experienced, first hand, often over an extended period, what a research site is like. Unless the researchers are taking a positivistic view of ethnography, the result is unlikely to be presentable as straightforward a result as a summary statistic; whoever wishes to understand the result of an ethnographic study is going to have to spend time working through it and thinking about it.

Equally, because of the tradition of non-positivistic forms of ethnography and their roots in anthropology, many ethnographers will be reluctant to want to draw explicit lessons from their researchers, preferring instead to write it up as fairly and representatively as they can, and allowing the reader to draw his or her own conclusions. The realist view of ethnography discussed above is perhaps the exception to this, as it will tend to want to take a view about power relationships or have a concern with fairness in the research setting, but other traditions will not regard this as a good way to proceed because it privileges the view of the researcher at the risk of reducing the role of research participants in the final result.

An important question which comes, again in comparing the results of ethnographies to quantitative research, is whether they can be compared, combined or generalised from. If you are conducting research in a range of similar settings (say, hospitals in the same country) at the same time, you might want to be able to compare the ethnographies to try and look for similarities and differences. This makes a great deal of sense, but it would probably be unwise to try and generate much in the way of generalisable theory from such studies. Ethnographies are very good at generating detail, but this detail makes it difficult to generalise because every attempt to do so will have to be hedged and qualified. This doesn't mean that comparisons aren't useful – they can often be extremely illuminating in helping to develop thinking about ethnographic sites because they ask the question of why some things are done in the same way between sites, and why some things are done differently. Unless there are a very large number of ethnographies being conducted simultaneously though, it doesn't seem likely that generalisations can really be made from comparisons. A similar problem arises in attempts to combine ethnographies. Ethnographies are grounded in the specific, and so finding two sites that are similar enough to combine findings on is likely to be extremely unlikely. Again, comparison is likely to be more fruitful than combination.

So does that mean that ethnographies can only tell us what is going on in a specific time and place in a specific research setting, and that the research has no use at all outside of that particular context? This is an important question. Whereas quantitative research often specifically aims to generate laws and be generalisable, is it the case the ethnographic research is specific and so entirely ungeneralisable? And if so, why should any public body ever fund such research?

It isn't the case that ethnographic research can never be generalisable. There are at least two important counter-arguments. The first is that the detailed accounts and stories generated by ethnographies can often be extremely powerful and persuasive, speaking to us and demanding our attention. By showing us what another place is like, and what other people are experiencing, ethnographic research asks us to empathise and sympathise. In this respect, it is like a good novel, or in the case of postmodern ethnography can be like modern art, film or theatre. It is designed to engage with its audience analytically, but on many other levels as well. These other responses require more time and care from the receiver of the research, but can result in a richer response than quantitative data alone if often able to provoke, even if it can be much more difficult to summarise.

As well as this, by becoming immersed in a particular research setting, it is possible for the researcher, in the participant observation model at least, to be able to become involved in the setting and even change things. In fact some researchers would argue that this is exactly the potential benefit of doing detailed, ethnographic-type research – that it gives the opportunity for social science to matter through the direct involvement of social scientists in research settings (Flyvbjerg, 2001). This is a challenging position – most quantitative social scientists would consider themselves to be aspiring to be expert analysts and advisors rather than even becoming directly involved in the social settings that they are researching, but this has not always been the case – consider Joseph and Seebohm Rowntree's studies of York and their involvement in the local community through their investment in housing for workers and research foundations. Although contentious, and asking difficult questions about the authority of social scientists to intervene in research settings, this does bring out another contrast between quantitative and ethnographic research, and gives another example of how ethnographic research might come to matter – by it becoming a version of action research, in which the point of the research is to both become an expert in the research site and to potentially change things.

## How can you increase the chance of doing good ethnographic research?

Given the variety of approaches labelled as ethnography it is difficult to come up with universal ideas about good practice within it. However, a few principles can be stated about the three main methods within the ethnographic approach that can increase the chance of doing worthwhile research.

### Observation and note-taking

There is a great deal of philosophical difference between an ethnography conducted positivistically, where a great deal of counting of particular events might take place, and one conducted in an anthropological tradition, where the subjectivities of participants are the primary concern. What both approaches share, however, is the need to rigorously record what is going on at the research site. Positivistic approaches will produce forms that researchers will fill in by counting occurrences of events that researchers are testing, but qualitative research needs to demonstrate equal rigour through meticulous note-taking and extensive recording of field notes. The most comprehensive recent account of the process involved in doing anthropological social research appears in Latour's methods book (Latour, 2005), in which he describes the notebooks he keeps and the relationship between them. Even the most ardent positivist would be hard pushed to describe a project conducted in such a manner as being in any way lacking in rigour.

Researchers need to think about the relationship between the aims of their research, the intended or promise outcomes, and the way they go about observing and note-taking. Different kinds of research questions require different kinds of notes to be taken. There is also considerable potential for researchers to gather different kinds of data and to make different kinds of notes, depending on the characteristics of the particular context they find themselves. Anthropological description can be improved by counting some aspects of the research situation (how many people? how many times did something happen?) without compromising the research philosophically – counting things is an entirely valid part of description, so long as researchers are clear about what they are counting and why. Positivistic accounts of research contexts cannot exist independent of descriptions – there will still be a need to describe in any reporting of research, and so a need to have accurate descriptions of research sites. Equally, positivistic ethnographers will need to explain not only what they chose to count, but why. Again, the central point is that taking one approach or another to observation and note-taking does not mean that a researcher can stop thinking about what they are doing – they need to be able to explain it, and demonstrate the appropriateness of their approach.

## Doing good interviews

Interviews are typically described in most methods books as being unstructured, semi-structured or structured. This is a sensible starting point for thinking about them, but the degree to which interviews are structured is a continuum rather than having three convenient labels. Some interviews will be highly prescribed, and others have very little structure at all.

Positivistic approaches to interviewing are more likely to favour structured interviews on the grounds that they allow for more consistent and rigorous comparison between the responses of participants, introducing an element of control into the research. Ideally, according to this view, researchers also need to demonstrate that interviews are being conducted consistently, so that if different researchers are doing interviews at the same site, the differences between their mannerisms and approach to interviewing are minimised to the point where they don't make a difference to the collection of data.

There is a logic to this. We want to be able to compare the results of interviews to explore differences and similarities. The extent to which you believe you can control interview situations across time, space and between researchers will depend to a large extent on whether you believe that interviews are there to achieve objective answers to specific questions in a controllable situation, or whether you believe interviews are there to explore the subjective understanding of a participant in a highly open situation. The former case turns interviews into a form of interactive questionnaire, where the format of what takes place is as prescribed as possible to try to achieve comparability and rigour in an experiment-like form, but the latter would be far more open, with the key criterion being that participants have the best possible opportunity to express their thoughts. In the former case the interviewer is there to control the process and get specific answers; in the latter it is to encourage the participant to express themselves in their own words. The former emphasises control, the latter the establishment of rapport.

It is possible to achieve a mix of structured questions that are likely to establish clear, objective answers, and open questions designed to promote discussion and subject thought. It can be difficult, however, to steer participants between the two, and the two different approaches presume different views of the world – objectivity presumes realism in some form, and subjectivity an approach that allows for differing interpretations of events in a manner that would be problematic for positivistic understandings of interviewing.

## Generic advice on interviews

In terms of general advice, there are a few generic things that can also be said. First, people are more likely to co-operate in interviews if treated with politeness and if they are adequately briefed in what the research is about. Researchers need to ask for appointments or specific amounts of time from their participants and to be as clear as possible about the commitment they are asking for in taking part. Making expectations clear in advance is not only polite, but will create some shared understanding of what is going to take place, and so a greater chance of the interview being conducted successfully.

At the beginning of an interview, researchers should explain the purpose of the interview, answering any questions the participants may have before going on. Again, the better-briefed participants are before the interview itself proceeded, the less chance there is of any problems emerging here. If the researcher wants to record the interview in some form, participants should be both warned while arranging the interview, as well as their permission being sought again before the interview begins. Any concerns about anonymity and the treatment of data should also be addressed.

During an interview a number of difficulties can arise. Where participants appear not to understand questions, clarifications can be made and misunderstandings over questions can be addressed – one of the strengths of the method. The researchers' attitude to problems such as participants digressing or not answering the question asked will depend to a large extent on the perspective researchers have on the interview process in the research design. Refusing to answer specific questions and digression are more of a problem for positivistic designs than for anthropological ones that are more concerned with the subjectivity of participants than whether they are presenting a kind of objective truth within them. A similar issue arises when participants have a tendency to answer every question with a thirty-minute answer – in these circumstances a structured interview design will require a researcher to try to politely keep things on track, whereas for a less structured approach it may not matter as much.

Telephone interviews have become increasingly popular because of their ability to be a half-way house between questionnaires and interviews – allowing an interactive research design without all of the costs of researchers having to go to research sites. Many of the same principles as those above apply, but of course the key difference is that researchers must be more explicit and clear in their questioning as there will be fewer non-verbal cues to inform the discussion, and so a greater possibility of ambiguity. As such, telephone interviews tend to fit more positivistic research designs more neatly than anthropological ones, but a case can be made for their careful use from either perspective, so long as researchers are careful to take account of the implications of not having non-verbal cues to go on.

## To transcribe or not to transcribe?

It is often treated as common sense that interviews must be transcribed, and for those interview transcripts to form the primary data that is generated from them. There is a great deal of sense in this – having a transcript gives a durable text which can be analysed using either traditional or computer-based software methods, as well as converting voices or videos into the form that the final report is likely to take.

There are indisputably a number of advantages to transcribing interviews. However, there are also good arguments against it. First, even the most meticulous transcript loses a great deal compared to the original interview exchange and to the recording of it. There is a danger in using transcripts that much of what makes an interview distinctive get lost – the precise tone of voice, timings, silences. At the very least transcripts need not to lose sight of the recorded representation we have of the interview. Second, there is a valid question to be asked about whether the researcher requires a transcript on every occasion. The principles of grounded theory, for example (see Chapter 5), would suggest that different forms of analysis are appropriate at different stages of a project. During the early stages of analysis, it might be necessary to transcribe and analyse text in a great deal of depth. Later on, though, if the interview seems to be repeating themes that have already appeared, or adding little new theoretically to what has already been discovered, then partial transcription, or even no transcription at all, may be appropriate.

Third, many software packages now allow for computerised voice files to be coded and analysed directly. Notes are then attached directly to the voice file itself. Researchers may still want a detailed transcription of key interviews – particularly those that are relied upon in final reports or in academic outputs – but again the case for transcribing every interview is open to question here. It would certainly make a fascinating project to compare analysis based on transcripts versus analysis based on coding directly to voice files, in order to find out if different interpretations tend to appear, whether some aspects of interviews tend to be over- or under-emphasised in different approaches. Either way, assuming it is automatically the right answer to transcribe interviews in all circumstances demonstrates a lack of thought to which the approach advocated in this book is opposed.

## Documentary analysis

Chapter 6 is primarily concerned with textual data, so the dos and don'ts of documentary analysis won't be discussed at length here. Suffice it to say that, again, the perspective a researcher has on social research will strongly influence what kind of documentary analysis is preferred by them. Positivistic social researchers will often tend to prefer quantitative techniques of documentary analysis, and with text analysis software developing year on year, they will find techniques such as computer-based auto-summary of documents, the ability for software to extract the most frequently appearing terms and the statistically speaking key terms, a boon to analysis. Even researchers who prefer to develop analysis based on approaches such as discourse analysis can find such approaches helpful in 'getting in' to the text (Fairclough, 2000; Greener, 2009), but will want to supplement (or contrast) them with other techniques as well. Documentary analysis is an important part of ethnography, and a great deal can often be learned about research sites from what they say (and don't say) in their texts.

# Conclusion – getting close or producing useless knowledge?

As with other approaches to social research in this book, it is possible to take a variety of perspectives on ethnography, and the perspective that you take will have strong implications for the version of ethnography that you prefer and the way that you proceed with your research.

Ethnography gains its legitimacy from its closeness to the data – it usually tries to build theory inductively rather than entering the field with preconceptions about what will be found, and it relies upon this closeness to produce detail that quantitative research will often be unable to provide.

Ethnographic work can be conducted from a wide range of perspectives, but perhaps what is less important than the differences those perspectives imply is what they can learn from one another. Even the most ardent anthropologist will find it useful to count phenomena sometimes, and the most confident positivist will need to provide descriptions.

What is important is for the researcher to understand what role their ethnographies are meant to be playing in their projects, what the ethnographies are meant to produce in terms of their output and what claims to knowledge they are meant to be making. Once these aspects have been made explicit, there is a much better chance of research proceeding successfully, and for results to meet the expectations of the research projects of which they form a part.

# Five things to remember about this chapter

1 Ethnographies can be multi-method in their own right, embracing observation, interviews, documentary analysis and even participation. Ethnography is a term used to cover a wide variety of methods and approaches to qualitative social research – make sure you know, when you use the term, which sense of it you are using.

2 Interviews are a widely used research method, but that doesn't mean they are always the most appropriate tool. Make sure you link your method to your research questions and that you prepare adequately when interviewing.

3 Sampling in qualitative research is often very different to sampling in quantitative research. You need to understand the differences and arguments on each side to make sure you use appropriate sampling strategies.

4 Ethnographies can have strong internal validity, depending upon the extent to which researchers take rigorous notes and show clear linkages between those notes and their findings to ensure that there is ample evidence to support their findings.

5 The extent to which you can generalise from an ethnography is a contentious topic. You need to understand the debates around this and be able to discuss under what circumstances (if any) it might be appropriate to generalise from qualitative data.

## Example – *Reading Ethnographic Research*

Martyn Hammersley is one of the most prolific and insightful academics writing about ethnographic research. In his *Reading Ethnographic Research* (1998) he explores a number of important topics, ranging from the nature of ethnography through to how readers understand ethnographic accounts and standards for assessing the validity of ethnographic research. This section explores his treatment of what makes good ethnographic research, paying particular attention to Chapter 3 of that book.

Hammersley's approach to assessing ethnographic research starts with some ontological assumptions that have strong implications for the way he believes ethnographic works can be considered. Hammersley advocates what he terms 'subtle realism' in which 'No knowledge is certain, but knowledge claims can be made in terms of their likely truth' and 'There are phenomena independent of us as researchers or readers of which we can have such knowledge' (p. 66). Following from this position, Hammersley then suggests three steps for considering the first measure by which ethnographic accounts can be judged: their validity. He suggests that assessing validity is made up three steps:

1 How plausible the account is, or 'whether or not it is very likely to be true given what we currently take to be well-established knowledge' (p. 67). It follows from this that the further away from well-established knowledge an ethnographic account takes us, the greater will be the need to provide evidence to support those claims. In other situations, however, 'we can reasonably accept them at face value' (p. 67).

2 How credible the account is, or 'whether it seems likely that the ethnographer's judgement of matters relating to the claim are accurate given the nature of the phenomena concerned, the circumstances of the research, the characteristics of the researcher, and so on' (p. 67).

Hammersley suggests that the main claims of a study need to be treated particularly carefully in terms of establishing their credibility.

3 The less plausible or credible the research, the greater the evidence we will require to be convinced of its validity.

Hammersley notes that this three-step process is very similar to the way we judge both our own and others' claims in everyday life. However, the difference between everyday life and research is based on the norms of scientific communities that subject findings to communal assessment, and where researchers are willing to change their views if their arguments, from communal assessment, are found to be false, provided that the research community is open to participation by anyone able and willing to participate through communal processes (p. 68). Hammersley notes that not all scientific communities live up to these goals, but so long as they remain a shared aspiration, then the principle of assessing research in terms of its validity remains.

Hammersley suggests that ethnographic thinking has been strongly influenced by naturalism and what he calls naive realism, which is a view of the world in which what you see is what there is – very similar to the discussions of experimental methodology described in earlier chapters. This has led many of its proponents to believe that they reproduce 'the phenomena to which they refer, thereby encouraging neglect of the multiple descriptions possible for any phenomenon' (p. 70). Because of this, 'ethnographers cannot take their task as simply to describe the social world. They, and we as readers, must decide which facts are important, and are therefore worth describing, and which are not' (p. 70).

Hammersley presents several views of the way that ethnography can attempt to achieve relevance through its accounts. The first is the 'engineering' model in which current practice in some area is regarded as having problems based on inadequate knowledge that research might be able to address. This is increasingly common in government-funded research, where ethnographic accounts are often asked to fulfil this role, and so research of this type clearly has to try to make the case for being practitioner-relevant in this way.

The 'emancipatory model' of ethnography, in contrast, aims to show members of oppressed groups their true interests, with ethnographic work not attempting to describe or explain the context of the people studies, but instead to show the effects of ideology upon them. The success of such accounts is therefore judged on their ability to achieve relevance through enlightening and emancipating participants (p. 72). Social research becomes relevant by being a catalyst for transformation. There are clear links here with feminist research programmes, which Hammersley goes on to discuss (pp. 72–73).

Hammersley suggests that both 'engineering' and 'emancipatory' models of relevance are problematic. The engineering view tends to presume that the problems identified by practitioners are automatically the most pressing, and so their accounts are beyond doubt. He suggests, 'Researchers must be free to question practitioner assumptions where this seems necessary' (p. 73). The emancipatory model, in turn, in his view 'suffers from too narrow a conception of the appropriate audience for research' (p. 73) and that the range of topics that are judged important is also too narrow: 'Only those directly related to the task of emancipation (however conceived) are relevant' (p. 73).

In either case, he suggests, participant practice tends to be regarded as being a process of applying scientific knowledge to life, and this is probably mistaken. Practice, Hammersley argues, is 'inevitably contextual' (p. 74), so assessments of the 'appropriate and reasonable' (p. 74) goals of relevance need to be assessed equally contextually. To achieve public relevance researchers 'must be allowed to address issues that are not of immediate concern to practitioners, but which there are reasonable grounds for believing are of relevance to their practice, to address a wide range of practitioner audiences, and to operate a division of labour so that researchers themselves will often serve as the primary audience for research reports' (p. 76).

Hammersley appears to be suggesting, then, that relevance is important to ethnography, but what is meant by 'relevant' has to be considered carefully in each different research context. This doesn't let researchers off the hook in researching whatever area they want, however – they have to be able to explain the relevance of their work as having 'reasonable grounds' for being important in its context and have a responsibility for addressing 'a wide range of practitioner audiences' when they communicate their findings.

As such, for Hammersley, ethnographic research must be both valid and relevant to be of good standard.

What are we to make of all this? As a first reaction, Hammersley makes a great deal of sense. However, what he is suggesting has some difficult implications. If we suggest that the 'engineering' model of ethnography is problematic, then that would cut off one of the major funders of ethnographic work, the government, which usually pays for ethnographic work as a means of trying to understand and solve particular research problems. This puts many researchers (me, for a start!) in a difficult situation – we believe that conducting ethnographies is hugely important, but cutting down the already limited potential funders makes them even more difficult to do. A pragmatic view is that, although we may have reservations about what governments expect us to do with ethnographies, we have to recognise that we have to speak to different audiences in different ways, and so use the language of engineering when applying for government money to conduct ethnographies, and to come up with ways of meeting the agendas it raises, even if we accept Hammersley's concerns about such an approach.

It is also the case, that despite the rigour of Hammersley's conclusions, researchers who already have established academic positions are far more likely to be able to conduct research along the lines he suggests than new researchers, who, having their research topics and agendas driven by governments and research councils that are under pressure to show their work is relevant to both business and wider society, may be deliberately emphasising the engineering approach.

What I'm suggesting is that researchers need to be pragmatic, and to be able to make different arguments about their work to different audiences. It may well be that Hammersley is right (I think he probably is), but that the consequences of him being right for the researcher who want to do ethnographic work would be to make such work extremely difficult to conduct in the future. Research is sometimes a compromise between what we want to do, what we believe is right methodologically to do and what funders are prepared to pay for.

# SIX

## Dealing with qualitative data – or what should I do with all these words?

Just about any study involves dealing with non-numeric data in one form or another. Students are often rather troubled about what to do with data once they have collected it, becoming almost overwhelmed by the volume of material. This chapter aims to give them some guidance in thinking through a range of issues such as: How should students deal with all the textual data they have before them? Is it possible to be rigorous in dealing with non-numeric data? What are the criteria for doing good qualitative analysis?

## Introduction

This chapter deals with one of the least discussed but in many ways central problems of conducting qualitative research – what to do with the data collected on a project. Students often find that the first stages of their research – the process of gaining access to a site, of observing or interviewing – difficult but exhilarating. They are engaging with people, refining their skills in collecting data, working out what additional data to collect next to fill gaps in their study and getting on with the business of being a researcher. They feel that they are genuinely engaging with their chosen problem and finding things out about it. They are able to get some sense of what they think their data is telling them, and so keep collecting more and more data, making notes as they go along, but eventually come to the point where they feel that they want more formally and more comprehensively to analyse their data. And seeing the sheer quantity of it, they wonder what on earth they are going to do.

This problem isn't just restricted to new researchers. Experienced researchers often look at the sheer quantity of qualitative data that projects can accumulate and both worry and wonder how they are going to analyse it in any kind of coherent way.

What follows here is a discussion of some of the methods and techniques that can be useful in dealing with this problem. It is not a complete statement in its own right – it never could be as many of the methods discussed here are elucidated individually across whole texts. But what I can do is give you an overview of the approaches most often used, and explore the benefits and pitfalls of each.

# The aims of qualitative research

## Closeness

A good starting point in thinking about how to treat qualitative data is to go back to the reasons why the researcher adopted a qualitative research process in the first place. Qualitative research gains its legitimacy from being able to claim that its methods produce data that is closer to the research participant and settings than quantitative research is able to provide. It is able to provide the granular detail that quantitative research, which is often concerned with large data sets crossing several sites, cannot provide.

## Description and analysis

We would therefore expect qualitative research to be able to provide additional detail and depth, compared to quantitative data, in answering descriptive research questions (what, when, which, where), as well as having the potential to deal with more analytical questions (how, why). However, this leap from the descriptive to the analytical comes with presuppositions about what is possible on qualitative research programmes and about what makes good research, and is contested territory. Whereas it is probably fair to say that the majority of qualitative researchers would claim to be aiming for analysis as a result of their work, writers such as Latour and Law would be a little incredulous of these claims, suggesting that achieving descriptions that do not come with conceptual baggage is a sufficiently worthy aim in its own right. They would claim that in order to see better the world around us, we should try and cut through hackneyed, clichéd terminology and try to see things afresh and make up our own minds. Moving towards analysis, in this view, introduces value-laden terms and imposes a framework of understanding upon the data that it cannot carry and cannot justify. Description, according to these authors, is sufficient in its own right.

Presenting a view of qualitative data that is both an unclichéd and systematic description is a considerable challenge. It takes us into a world where how things are said is as important as what is being said, with the author taking responsibility for the way that the research is presented, and accepting that any decision taken about what to include or exclude is political as much as driven by the data itself. However, this approach to qualitative research, derived from anthropological understandings of research, whilst being deeply admirable, also comes with problems.

## The problems of descriptive work

It may be that the researcher is unable to complete a research project by promising descriptive research alone, with grant awarders and PhD panels suspicious of such an approach and wondering why the research refuses to engage in analysis. Certainly, researchers working for governmental bodies would routinely expect to have to conduct analysis or evaluation, and were they to promise description only, would probably find themselves unfunded or risking the award of their doctorate. Even though Latour and Law have strong reasons for the epistemological and ontological claims that their research programme implies, they are themselves in a privileged position, already holding academic posts and having existing legitimacy in conducting research according to these tenets. It is far more difficult for a new researcher to behave according to these rules.

So accepting the context in which researchers have to operate, what views of qualitative data interpretation are available?

# Grounded theory, coding and generalisation

Perhaps the most widely cited approach to qualitative research remains that of grounded theory. Grounded theory is an inductive approach to research that encourages researchers to move iteratively between their data and their emergent ideas to build theory that is literally 'grounded' in the research setting or settings in which they find themselves.

Because grounded theory is an inductive research strategy, building theory from the bottom up, it is often taken to be an appropriate strategy for researching new sites or new locations where work has not been done before. There is some truth in this – an inductive research programme attempts to start anew in terms of theory generation and so this will tend to be most conducive in an area where we know very little. However, this need not always be the case. It might be that there are good arguments for trying to visit a well-established research site with fresh eyes and to rebuild ideas about it from the bottom up where research in that field appears to be stagnating or depending upon a limited range of concepts with little new or interesting appearing.

## Existing theory and grounded theory

Equally, grounded theory has the potential to be able to incorporate existing theoretical ideas as well as building new theory from the bottom up. The two founders of grounded theory, Anselm Strauss and Barney Glaser (Glaser and Strauss, 1967), went through something of a falling out over this point in the 1970s and 1980s, with Strauss apparently wanting to preserve grounded theory as an inductive strategy for building new theory only, but with Glaser arguing that it was acceptable to bring in existing concepts and ideas in order to achieve what he called 'theoretical sensitivity' (Glaser, 1978) towards the data. Strauss's approach, with his later collaborator Juliet Corbin, went on to create ever more elaborate systems of coding data to attempt to demonstrate in as transparent a way as possible how the original data linked to the normative and theoretical codes the researcher has come up with, and in turn how the theory generated can link right back down to the original data (Strauss and Corbin, 1998) Glaser, however, seems to have become more pragmatic, suggesting that purely inductive research is neither possible nor necessary, with there being considerable merit in introducing pre-existing theoretical ideas into research where they fit (Glaser, 1992).

## Different approaches to grounded theory

It is worth having some sense of this debate because researchers using grounded theory have to take a position on whether they are trying to achieve understandings of their data that attempt to build from the bottom up and avoid using existing theoretical concepts, or whether they can be incorporated into studies where they can be shown to be appropriate. The first approach would be a version of grounded theory closest to that which Latour and Law would advocate, trying to demand that researchers come up with their own ideas that best describe what is going on, rather than relying upon pre-existing concepts. However, with this choice comes with the price that it becomes difficult to compare the theoretical ideas from new studies conducted in this way with pre-existing ones as the concepts and ideas will not be easily compared. The choice to try and use original terminology and description makes comparisons more difficult, and is based on the idea that qualitative research gains its power from being as close to the research site in all of its originality and specificity. It may well be that adopting the approach of Latour and Law means that comparisons become near impossible to make, as well as arguing against the possibilities of other types of analysis, and this clearly carries implications for the research designs that are possible.

## The mechanics of grounded theory

Grounded theory works by the researcher examining the text (or possibly recorded words) of research participants, as well as their own notes, and coming up with codes that capture and summarise the date.

## Open codes

A first step is to try and come up with open codes that appear to capture in some form or another what is going on in the data. These can be simple descriptions of talk or events, and aim to give the researcher a grasp of the data that allows him or her to begin to look for patterns of similarity and difference in the data. The aim is to conceptualise what is going on in some form or another. The researcher goes through the data, coding text or talk, coming up with new codes or using codes that have already been used, and trying to find concepts that most accurately capture what is going on.

The extent to which the codes in grounded theory should be original to the project, or be based on pre-existing social science ideas, is a contentious area. It can be extremely difficult to come up with concepts that both capture the data and haven't been used before. This in many respects is the issue at dispute between Glaser and Strauss – Glaser thought it was reasonable (and to some extent inevitable) that concepts be re-used where they accurately represent what is going on in the data, but Strauss was more circumspect. Either way, the theoretical coding process tries to find relationships between codes in the data and, through a continuing process of comparison between their instances, develop the theory to show how it applies in different situations for different subjects.

## Comparison and axial coding

Grounded theory suggests that researchers should look at codings to see if what has been coded in a particular way is consistent, and to become aware of how codings might differ from one incident to the next. This comparison (grounded theory was originally based on the idea of 'constant comparison') allows the researcher to continually refine and question their own understanding of the data and to create more and more nuanced understandings of what is going on within it. This is the process of axial coding, where researchers step back from the data to look at the categories of codes and see what dimensions they might have. If a code for 'abuse' was established in a study about family violence, for example, a researcher would then want to try to establish what the dimensions of abuse might be, looking to establish the types, times and places in which abuse occurred. This allows the researcher to revisit their previous codings, so that they might become more sensitive, but also for researchers to look at their designs to see what dimensions of coding appear to be missing from the present research, and ask questions about whether they should be actively sampled for in future observations, meetings, and so on.

The movement between analysis and fieldwork is an important part of grounded theory. This is because, after coding, the researcher might find that some codes are highly populated, with a very fine-grained view of what is going on within them, but others are far more scarcely populated. This can mean that they aren't as important, but the researcher needs to be able to verify that and revisit the field to look for instances where those codes might emerge in order to be able to test that idea. So, in the case where a particular theoretical coding has relatively few instances in the data, the researcher might take the view that they are going to look for sites where they can add additional depth to that data, perhaps asking research subjects specifically for instances where it has occurred or might occur. This going back and forth between the data and the field allows theory to be built iteratively, as well as for theory to be tested to see under what circumstances the relationships suggested by researchers appear to work and when they do not.

## Iteration

This iterative movement between analysis and fieldwork suggests that grounded theory can also be used for theoretical development and theoretical testing, a more deductive approach to qualitative research that attempts to try out existing ideas in the specific context of the fieldwork being conducted. This approach to grounded theory can be seen to be at odds with Glaser and Strauss's original formulation of the approach, but makes sense in that, as long as it adequately takes account of the differing contexts between qualitative settings, research is attempting to test existing theoretical ideas (a deductive approach), by in-depth and close study of the phenomena under investigation. Grounded theory purists might question whether the approach can take account of deductive insights, but have to accept that generating purely inductive categories in research in every new research setting is rather a lot to ask for, and rather unlikely in practice (can we really start afresh every time we conduct fieldwork, and is this even a good idea from the perspective of attempting to develop knowledge?).

## Grounded theory and generalisation

There is a final difficulty in relation to grounded theory that we've already seen applies to ethnographic work more generally – the extent to which it is meant to create generalised theory. Glaser and Strauss's original statement and manifesto for the approach (Glaser and Strauss, 1967) was quite explicit that the approach aimed to produce general theory, with the specific instances of empirical studies to be considered to see what they might contribute to general theory. The creation of general theory was to be the last step in a grounded theory study – asking the question of what the specific area studied could tell us about social theory in the wider sense.

However, if this was a goal of grounded theory, it has been picked up by remarkably few studies adopting the approach. Recent scholarship has suggested that detailed work of the type found in grounded theory is misguided in trying to create general theory (Flyvbjerg, 2001) because social scientific knowledge is likely to be highly context sensitive. This raises the question of whether the purpose of social science is to produce general theory, or whether it is enough to explain or describe particular research contexts. Positivistic views of social science would be appalled at the idea that it cannot generate theory beyond very specific contexts, whereas those nearer the idealist end would be appalled at the prospect of trying to create any kind of generalisable theory, regarding it as an attempt to impose a form of knowledge upon the world that is inextricably associated with an exercise in power.

Grounded theory, then, has the advantage of joining together in-depth fieldwork with theoretical development, and so has the potential to produce rigorous and illuminating work. However, it also has problems in that the role of pre-existing theory in grounded theory studies remains something of a thorny issue, particularly in relation to whether existing theories can be tested using the approach, and whether theories developed by the approach can be generalisable. It remains one of the most popular approaches to analysing textual data, despite the concerns about it. However, it is not the only approach to textual analysis.

# Discourse analysis and its variants

Discourse analysis has become something of an industry in social science over the last forty years, with the advantage that there are now vast quantities of research that comes within this tradition for researchers to explore. The corresponding problem, however, is that it can be extremely difficult to find what all of these studies have in common exactly. Comparing the work of Foucault, Mouffe, Laclau, Wodak, Fairclough and van Dijk can lead a researcher to wondering exactly how such disparate approaches can all claim to be doing discourse analysis.

It is certainly possible to identify several what we might call 'schools' of discourse analysis, with van Dijk's edited multi-volume *Handbook of Discourse Analysis* bringing out the variances in approach and method available, and Wodak and Krzyzanowski's edited collection *Qualitative Discourse Analysis in the Social Sciences* attempting to clarify terms and concepts that exist within the field, especially in Wodak's introductory chapter in that book.

## What is discourse analysis?

So what exactly is discourse analysis? Given the diversity of approaches that label themselves within the field, it isn't easy to come up with a definition everyone doing this kind of work would agree with, but van Dijk's (1990: 164) labelling of it as referring to 'text in context' is as good a starting point as any. It tends to involve an interest in text that is naturally occurring, that is text as used by real language users (as opposed to the invented examples that often dominate linguistic analyses), and focus on larger units of text than individual words or sentences. It also tends to focus on the strategies used in texts to persuade or dissuade (locating rhetorical analysis within discourse analysis), whilst at the same time trying to examine the social contexts within which texts were produced. This inevitably means that political questions get drawn into analysis about how texts preserve or disturb power relationships.

The diversity of approaches taken to discourse analysis makes it a vibrant field of study, but also a frustrating one for a researcher to enter as it can be difficult to get a clear view of what those within it are methodologically. Perhaps the clearest explicator within the field is Norman Fairclough, whose work provides a clear framework for his 'critical discourse analysis' (Fairclough, 1992), showing how it relates to theoretical luminaries such as Foucault, but also providing practical examples of how his analysis was derived and step-by-step procedural guides for how researchers might conduct analysis within this approach (Fairclough, 1989). Fairclough's work has included analyses of the speeches of Tony Blair (Fairclough, 2000) and explorations of the changing language of capitalism (Fairclough, 2002). As such, he provides a rich basis of work for students to draw from.

## Critical discourse analysis

Fairclough's approach is distinctive among discourse theoreticians because he seeks to combine social theory with a rigorous approach to linguistic analysis derived from Halliday's functional grammar. Fairclough's work is therefore rigorous from the perspectives of both social theory and linguistics, and this makes it particularly valuable because it shows not only what textual effects are being deployed in texts, but linguistically how those effects are being achieved. This makes it extremely powerful, but also means that it can be difficult to learn as it requires students to gain a strong understanding not only of social theory, but also of linguistic theory as well.

Within critical discourse analysis more generally, other authors place a smaller emphasis on textual analysis, and tend to follow Foucault in showing how power relations play themselves through texts with reflective and reflexive approaches that attempt to build up analyses from the instances of text and talk researchers find, and to link and locate these within the wider discourses present within society. For example, Czarniawska (1997) showed how stories and narratives in public organisations were used to manage social change in Swedish public organisations.

## Taking a less textual approach

Taking a less linguistic approach to discourse analysis can often make the textual analysis stage closely resemble that of grounded theory, building up interpretation of the text through the use of open and axial coding, and then attempting to explore the strategies used in the text to achieve persuasive, power effects. Accepting the link between the two begins to make fluid the boundaries between the techniques of qualitative textual analysis, and this is an entirely good thing. What is important is not that researchers focus on trying to do the purest form of grounded theory or discourse analysis that they are able to, but instead that they come up with coherent and rigorous approaches to examining their texts that produce interesting results. An interesting question is the extent to which quantitative approaches can be used as supplements (or even replacements) to text analysis.

## Quantitative approaches to textual analysis

Grounded theory gives researchers, in its Strauss formulation at least, a rigorous process for the generation of both normative and theoretical codes, and for generating theory from the data. However, the grounded theory approach is incredibly time consuming, even when computer software such as Nvivo and MAXQDA is used to expedite the process, because of its demands to code and re-code, and to constantly compare findings and systematise results.

Researchers often feel completely lost in the data for a considerable amount of time when conducting grounded theory. If they are researching alone, they may also have doubts that their coding structure represents the data in any kind of comprehensive way, and be concerned that their understanding of it is contestable. Working in data interpretation teams can get around this problem to some extent as it allows for comparison between coding structures and theories, for discussion and the possibility that consensus might be reached (or at least differences in interpretation be made explicit). However, this often isn't possible when the research being conducted is a PhD thesis, or a solo research project.

An alternative approach that might initially appear to be philosophically at odds with qualitative data is to use quantitative techniques in interpreting the data. Many qualitative researchers might throw up their hands in horror at the prospect of introducing numbers into qualitative interpretive processes, but this seems to me to be something of an over-reaction. In an intuitive way, if the same sequence of words or a particular interpretation of a word keep recurring in a text or across texts then that is likely to be of interest to a researcher, and it surely then makes sense to count how many times that usage or interpretation appears. Once you have a count of that instance, it begins to be possible to compare it to counts of other instances and from there a basic quantitative strategy begins to appear.

### Starting points in quantitative textual analysis

Taking a quantitative approach to examining text or texts assumes that frequency is a relevant starting point for describing or analysing it or them. If one thing appears in the text more than another, then it is likely to be worthy of note, not necessarily with the most frequently occurring item being the most important, but begging the question of why some items appear more than others in the text and what this might mean.

When viewed in this way, quantitative analysis of textual data becomes a means of getting a different perspective or finding a starting point for analysis rather than trying to replace the necessity of reading the text carefully and trying to work out what is going on within it. If particular words or phrases occur or recur frequently within the text then a close reading is likely to pick that up, but it can still be a help to analyse a text to see exactly how often that these words or phrases appear, and whether there is a statistical difference between sections or texts in their usage, as this can help generate new insights into those texts. Computer software such as T-lab (http://www.tlab.it/en/default.php) not only allows researchers to examine texts in this way, but also to produce comparisons of how often particular terms appear in different sections of the text through techniques such as correspondence analysis, which produce tables of words that appear 'over' or 'under' used, so raising interesting questions about frequency that can help in interpreting texts. MAXQDA, already mentioned above, can also present word counts of key terms through the use of its MAXDictio add-in.

### Starting points for additional analysis

In addition, even relatively simple techniques can provide interesting starting points for the analysis of texts. If the text can be obtained electronically and loaded into software such as Microsoft Word, then the 'autosummarise' feature can provide a starting point by producing an outline of what the software thinks the text is about, which can highlight relationships that appear between key words in the text. This again provides a starting point for an analysis of what is going on within the text rather than anything definitive in itself – a means for generating interesting questions about the text rather than being an end in itself. Equally, software such as Devonthink for the Mac is capable of examining individual texts and finding others within its database that appear to be structured in a similar kind of way, finding links that the researcher might not have thought of and producing potentially interesting comparisons.

However, as I've emphasised above, these techniques are not a replacement for detailed qualitative research, spending time getting to know the data and for the hard work of coding the data and comparing different instances of concepts and occurrences. What they do, however, is provide a different way of looking at the text that can be a fruitful source of new interpretation of it. The extent to which they will be included is a function of the perspective the researcher has on analysis, and so it is therefore to the problem of exploring what makes a good qualitative analysis that the chapter now turns.

## Analysing documents

Grounded theory, discourse analysis and quantitative techniques can be applied to textual data of all kinds, be they interview transcripts (or recordings), field notes, or documents collected from field sites. However, it is worth exploring the specific issues that documents represent in a little more depth, as they present particular challenges.

Researchers will often find numerous opportunities to collect documents during their studies. The social research area most obviously collecting large amounts of documentary data is history, where visits to archives and other places where records are kept is a central part of the discipline. Debates around method in history are important to social researchers in other disciplines as they discuss the relationship between documentary sources and the accounts that researchers produce of them.

## Debates in history

History has had a vigorous debate in recent years with writers from more traditional historiographical approaches arguing that their methods can be relied upon to produce reliable and objective accounts of the past (Himmelfarb, 2004), whereas those influenced by contemporary social theory have asked questions about what history is trying to achieve, and calling for more theoretically and methodologically robust and explicit ways of dealing with data (Jenkins, 1995). History has researchers who regard the process of doing social research as relatively unproblematic, with archives regarded as important recordings of contemporary events which the historian can write about in an objective and reliable way, and others who regard archives and documentary stores as being partial and fragmentary, ignoring the vast majority of people's experiences in the time periods they were collected and added to, and for historical methods to be dangerously under-informed and unaccountable in terms of the way they report archival work. The view that holds the construction of history to be straightforward has a realist and empiricist view of the world, with documents representing accounts of that world, and an objective approach to the construction of history through narrative methods that are robust through their close relationship to sources (Evans, 2001). The second, more problematic, view may still be realist in that it regards archives as possible sources, but suggests that the partiality of records conceals power relationships in terms of what was worth recording in each time period, and what was not, and views the construction of narrative accounts from such partial records critically, taking a far more idealist approach to that goal.

In these different views of history, documents are viewed as contributing different things to the research project. In the first, more traditional, view they are primary data upon which the narrative accounts of the historian will be built, and are regarded as records around which the historians' narrative must be constructed. Historians at least implicitly rank documents in terms of their perceived reliability. Those that are most trusted are often those best corroborated or which appear to report what are taken to be the facts of the situation by the historian, and form the base of the timeline around which the historian crafts a narrative to link together such sources. In the second view of history, documents are more like hostile witnesses, having to explain themselves as to why their accounts of events and not others were recorded, being more open to bias and being quizzed as to what they are concealing. Narrative accounts are still probably constructed around the documents taken to be the most reliable, but that reliability may be less explicitly realist, and more concerned, in line with idealism, in exploring the subjectivities of those that collected the documents in the first place. Rather than trying to present history as objective narrative truth, history becomes a series of competing claims to legitimacy and the struggle between them.

Researchers examining documents as a part of research projects often treat documents in an unproblematic, empiricist way, producing accounts of them that suggest they are objective presentations of truth that their research design has to incorporate and work around. This is very much taking an unproblematic view of materials that neither view of history described above would subscribe to – even in the traditional historical approach documents are scrutinised for their reliability and authenticity. The question the traditional view of history would ask of documentary analysis is 'How reliable are your sources?' – having a great deal in common with the systematic review approach to literature reviews discussed in Chapter 2 in attempting to assess the quality of research materials before they can be analysed. The second approach to history also asks this question, but also asks others such as 'Why was this document produced?', seeking to draw out how the document might be partial or biased, and 'What view of the world does the document present?', seeking to draw out the subjective understanding of the world that the document contains.

Analysing documents needs researchers to consider what role their analysis is going to play in the research, and what view of the documents they are going to take. Are they to be regarded as accounts of a world that may no longer be with us, but may be more or less reliable, or as clues to the subjectivities of those who wrote them? The different perspectives lead to different roles for documents and for different kinds of knowledge claims.

## What are the criteria for a good qualitative analysis?

Given the diversity of possible approaches to interpreting qualitative data, how do we know if a particular piece of work is a good analysis?

The important thing is that researchers are able to account for what they have done in their analysis, and explain how it meets the demands of their research area and their research topic. Some examples might help clarify this.

### Richness and multi-vocality

If you start from the position that this chapter began with, that of Latour and Law, in claiming that qualitative research should reject realist underpinnings, and instead focus on representing the views of research subjects in as rich and multi-vocal a way as possible, then that brings a range of commitments to the study. It suggests that researchers must be rigorous in recording the views of research subjects, of sharing findings with them and claiming no authorial privilege in the writing up of research, which becomes a more collaborative process than in many other forms of qualitative work, and attempting to capture the complexity of the research site through strategies such as multi-vocal writing, and perhaps innovative use of images, sound and video. If you start from Latour and Law's set of beliefs, and then seek to claim legitimacy for your research because you are able to come up with a definitive interpretation of social reality, then you risk incoherence – a strategy that aims to demonstrate rigorous analysis in that view tends to fall down because of Latour and Law's incredulity towards realism.

Starting from a more realist perspective, however, it becomes possible to conduct analysis that might privilege the researcher's view of the world as getting close to the reality of the situation in a research site, and so attempt to gain legitimacy from demonstrating this through gathering a wide variety of evidence and then synthesising it into an account that attempts to show what life is like there. This account could be descriptive, as in Latour and Law's, but it is less likely to be multi-vocal because of the commitment to realism, and may produce theory because of the possibility of engaging in analysis and using theoretical ideas by allowing the researcher's expertise to be privileged.

## Guba and Lincoln's view

Guba and Lincoln (1989) have attempted to come up with generic criteria for assessing the validity of qualitative research which clearly have some bearing on how it should be analysed. They come up with four quality issues: truth value, applicability, consistency and neutrality. Truth value is concerned with how researchers can establish the truth of inquiry findings for the subjects of the research. Applicability asks how we can determine the extent to which findings apply only the particular site under investigation, or whether they can be useful in other settings as well. Consistency considers whether the findings of an inquiry would be repeated if it were replicated with the same subjects in the same (or similar) contexts. Finally, neutrality considers how we can establish the degree to which findings are determined by the subjects instead of the assumptions, biases or interests of the researcher. Once these criteria have been assembled, it is possible to construct a table (6.1) that links together these quality issues and, according to Guba and Lincoln, compare how they are dealt with in quantitative and qualitative inquiry.

According to Guba and Lincoln, then, qualitative inquiry, which is based on a constructivist epistemology, seeks to establish credibility through methods that involve prolonged engagement and immersion in the field (leading to the

**Table 6.1**   Guba and Lincoln's view of quality

| Quality issues | Quantitative inquiry (positivistic) | Qualitative inquiry (constructivist) |
| --- | --- | --- |
| Truth value | Internal validity | Credibility |
| Applicability | External validity | Transferability |
| Consistency | Reliability | Dependability |
| Neutrality | Objectivity | Confirmability |

claim of expertise based on immersion), observational methods and triangulation between multiple qualitative methods to provide multiple perspectives on the data. Transferability is about achieving thick description, as in anthropology, with explanation now being the primary aim of research. Dependability is achieved through a transparency of research processes through the idea of inquiry audit, in which the notes and materials gathered by research teams are open to scrutiny within teams and potentially outside them. Confirmability is viewed as working in a similar way – if the materials of a research team are open to audit, then the reasoning that researchers used to come to their findings should also be traceable and confirmable by other researchers. In addition, reflexivity is of paramount importance, with field notes and researcher diaries of the development of their thoughts being important elements that other researchers may use as means for confirming earlier studies.

The link to Latour and Law's approach to social inquiry is clear here – any qualitative social research is likely to come up with contested and differing interpretations of events. According to this view, the social researcher should not adjudicate between them, but seek to present them, gaining credibility as a result. Social life is messy, so perhaps our representations of it should be too. However, this isn't much of a guide as to how researchers can go about analysing the material they have gathered. Their books do provide help on these fronts, but their radical epistemological position makes it difficult to come up with any kind of formal process for the analysis of data – the answer in each case is always 'it depends' – this is a view of qualitative analysis as being bound up with the skill of the researcher themselves.

# Truth in social research

To get a sense of how researchers can treat these debates, it is possible to consider at least three versions of 'truth' in social research and then to work out what the criteria for good qualitative research might be in relation to each of them. Social research can be about correspondence to reality, pragmatism or perspective. Each of these gives a different kind of criterion for good qualitative work.

## The correspondence theory of truth

The correspondence view of truth suggests that social research is true if it corresponds to reality. This is a realist ontology, and may embrace an objectivist or interpretivist epistemology. A positivist, objectivist approach would suggest that knowledge is true if it corresponds to reality – with experimental methods being preferred because they allow the testing of hypotheses and application of the scientific method to social research. Qualitative research, in this view, is best regarded where it is conducted as near as possible to the quantitative principles presented by Guba and Lincoln, aiming for rigorous internal validity through rigorous methods, strong external validity through the generation of testable theory (theories that are not testable would be regarded as unscientific and even irrelevant), with social research needing to be reliable in its construction of generalisable laws and objective, where research should be in principle replicable and independent of researcher bias.

A realist but interpretivist view of the correspondence theory of truth would suggest that social research is true if it corresponds to reality, but also that different individuals and groups have different interpretations of the same reality, even though it is external to our ideas about it. The world is independent of us, but we don't all understand it the same way. However, just because we hold different understandings of the world, it doesn't mean that all of them are equally valid. It is the job of qualitative work, in this view, to produce rigorous research that helps us to understand the similarities and differences in interpretations of the world, but also to bear in mind that those understandings are not all equally valid – some will be closer to the facts of the external world than others. It is the job of the social researcher to see which understandings and theories fit best, to 'retroduct' (Danermark et al., 2001) theories about what happened to what we know about the particular research context and see which one fits best.

## A pragmatic theory of truth

The two views above hold to the correspondence theory of truth, but this is not the only one available to social researchers. The pragmatic theory of truth is not based on social research corresponding to an external reality, but instead suggests that something is true if, for us, it 'works'. The most vigorous exponent of social research from this perspective in recent times has been Richard Rorty who at various times has asked what the use of truth even is (Rorty and Engel, 2007), suggesting instead that we should be more concerned about living our lives in an ethical manner that is considerate to others (Rorty, 1999) and treating any grand claims to truth or knowledge with irony. This view of truth suggests that we treat the claims of Latour and Law seriously, that we have no right to judge others' lives and that we lack the understanding to be able to explain them, as realist approaches might attempt to do. The implication of this is that good qualitative social research should try and describe what it finds in as rigorous and transparent way as possible, accepting and celebrating difference. However, as we've noted above, this view of social research may be so far from the positivistic view that new researchers find it difficult to adopt and grant-awarding bodies show suspicions towards it.

However, the pragmatic theory of truth does have a strong appeal for research that is evaluative in areas such as governmental social programmes. In such circumstances, research commissioners may have little interest in whether the social programme's understanding of the world is true (in the correspondence view), but simply whether it appears to be working. Such programmes often employ qualitative social researchers to gather detailed empirical accounts of the programmes 'on the ground', exploring their implementation as closely as possible. This type of social research clearly fits well within the Latour and Law view, but researchers may still face challenges in writing up their findings, as governments may be sceptical of ideas such as multivocality. But the pragmatic view of social research can find a home where detailed accounts of policy interventions or new social programmes are required.

## A perspectival view of truth

The perspectival view of truth has something in common with the pragmatic version, in that it holds that truth is likely to be different for each of us, and that none of us can take a 'God's eye view' that is independent of our own subjectivity to adjudicate between different accounts. But whereas the pragmatic view of truth starts with the question 'what works?', the perspectival view starts with the question 'who's asking?' Perspectival qualitative research takes an explicitly idealist view in suggesting that the existence of a world external to us is actually irrelevant to social research, and that what we need to understand instead is how differing subjectivities construct political identities that can oppress and reinforce power relationships. Good qualitative research is that which show the links between subjectivities, identities and oppression, showing the mechanisms of power and the opportunities for resistance.

Law and Latour would, I suspect, wholeheartedly approve of these research aims, even if they would be concerned about the use of non-descriptive social science ideas like oppression and power. They would argue that description, in itself, is sufficiently political for social research, whereas perspectival social researchers would want to go further in their exposure of practices that prevent others from achieving their potential. Both views of research are idealist, but with differences of what they regard as good social research being based on whether it should document subjective understandings of the world (pragmatism) or scrutinise them (perspectival).

# Conclusion – finding appropriate methods for dealing with your data

This chapter has taken readers through a maze of material that explores the considerations social researchers must have in mind when analysing qualitative data.

I have not made the difference between primary and secondary data made in some texts as different disciplines view the distinction in different ways (what is primary data to an historian is likely to be secondary data to a sociologist, for example). What should be clear is that there is a variety of different ways of treating qualitative data, and that researchers need to have a clear idea not only about how they are going to collect such data, but what they are going to do with it. Very often analytical issues are concealed by researchers writing that they 'analysed in line with the principles of grounded theory' or that they 'conducted a discourse analysis', giving very few clues as to exactly what was done by researchers or how. Sadly, the methods sections of academic papers (and often books) give us few clues as to how research actually progressed, the problems that researchers experienced, the false starts they went through and the ways these problems were overcome. Regardless of what you think of Law's view of social science methodology, it is hard not to agree with his assertion that social research is an intrinsically messy process.

Again, though, what I'd like to argue is that researchers have to be aware of what it is their methods of handling data are meant to achieve in terms of their research project or plan, and to make an argument about which methods fall out from that. Researchers at the interpretivist end of social research will often to be suspicious of any attempt to use quantitative textual techniques, but this seems to me to be a misplaced concern – it is appropriate to count in some circumstances, the key thing being able to justify when and why you are doing it. Equally, even the most hard-bitten content analytical researcher, who believes that claims cannot be made from qualitative data unless interviews, document and questionnaires have been analysed by groups of researchers, cross-checking one another's findings, and that as little room as possible has been allowed for individual researcher interpretation, has to allow room for non-quantitative measures and descriptive accounts in the reporting of their work.

The different methods in dealing with text in particular have their own criteria and understanding of what counts as good practice, and researchers need to look in detail around debates within grounded theory, for example, if that is the approach they decide to take. They must not only understand debates within their research field, but also methodological debates in the treatment and reporting of data within it. This does place heavy demands on researchers, asking them to become experts in a particular research context, and also become knowledgeable about methods, but they stand a much better chance of doing successful research if they have both.

The successful analysis of qualitative data is a contested and difficult area in social research, but it is also an exciting one where innovation and new approaches to exploring data are never far away. By becoming aware of the implicit assumptions contained in particular methods, their perspective on research, their criteria for doing good work and their understanding of truth, researchers can make their own practice more consistent and understand better where there are opportunities for being innovative.

# Five things to remember about this chapter

1 Qualitative research gets its legitimacy from its claim to be close to the data – if you are trying to adopt a research strategy that conceals the basic need for you to know your data inside-out, then you probably aren't doing analysis well.

2 Whereas particular approaches to social research advocate description as its highest goal, it might be difficult for new researchers to achieve much success in publication or grant-raising by pursuing this as a strategy. Method choice needs to be justified, and methods which produce results that might be regarded suspiciously within a wider research community need to be justified at greater length than those that are not – but that doesn't mean they aren't right.

3 Grounded theory and discourse analysis provide an established means for 'doing' textual analysis, but you need to be aware of the debates and differences within the approaches if you are going to attempt to do them. You need to become an expert on method as well as on your subject area.

4 Computerised textual analysis is controversial, but a growing research area that it can be worth engaging in at least as a complement to more established techniques.

5 Be clear where you stand in relation to debates about quality in qualitative research – if you don't know what standard you are trying to achieve, or what you mean by truth in social research (if anything), how are you going to achieve it?

## Example – *The Body Multiple*

Annemarie Mol's book *The Body Multiple* (2002) is remarkable in a number of ways. The first is that, as well as presenting an in-depth ethnography about the treatment of arteriosclerosis, Mol also gives us a running exploration of how she carried out her research, with the pages split in two. As well as being innovative in its presentation, her book is also an important one in understanding contemporary ethnographic ideas.

Mol's main research point is a challenging one – that her findings suggest there is not one arteriosclerosis, but many, and that the tools and techniques used by doctors and nurses to measure the disease(s) actively constitute it (them) as the same time. Mol shows us how different diagnostic techniques interpret the disease in different ways, suggesting that it cannot be easily pinned down to a single condition in the neat categories that medical categories imply. By painstakingly establishing the links between the tools and techniques used to measure arteriosclerosis, the problems that the differences in diagnosis lead to and the experience of the disease(s) from patients, Mol shows us how meanings about disease are established, but often refuse to be pinned down sufficiently to become clear and definite. Instead, patients with no pain appear when the measurements suggest they should not be able to walk, and others with few measurable problems report such pain that they are not able to walk at all.

Mol's claim, then, is that the usual causation we associated with medicine is, in her case at least, backwards. That the techniques and tools associate with the disease do not measure it, but instead construct and constitute it. Our knowledge of the disease does not arise from some external reality to it, but instead actually constitutes the disease itself. This is a claim that has a great deal in common with the approach to social research advocated by Law (2004), who writes of it approvingly.

One of the most interesting aspects of Mol's work is how counter-intuitive it is to most people. Can it really be the case that the means of measuring a condition actually come to define or set the limits on it? Mol's work is impeccably argued, and deeply thoughtful, but for me doesn't quite, in the end, ring true. The problem for me may be as much disciplinary as anything else – the conclusion that our measures often define social problems can lead to us claiming, for example, that there is nothing more to poverty than the measure we apply to it. I am not in any way suggesting that Mol is suggesting such a thing, but I can see how her work could be used in that way. None of us has control of the way our research is picked up and utilised by others, but it seems to me that Mol's conclusions could very easily be manipulated by those, for example, who might want to cut funding for particular diseases or conditions on the grounds that they have no real existence outside doctors' research.

Mol's work is important reading, even if you do not agree with her findings, because of its detailed accounts of the medical sites in which her ethnography was conducted, but also because of her reflections upon the research that run alongside them.

# SEVEN

## Causality in your research – or how deep should ontology go?

### Introduction

The issue of causality in social research has cropped up from time to time throughout the book, so it is time to consider the topic in more depth.

Some approaches to social research have a 'depth' version of causality, suggesting that what is the cause of particular phenomena might be complex and hidden, whereas other versions of social research would suggest that if you cannot empirically measure one thing causing another then you are not entitled to say that causality exists at all. Another branch of social research again argues that the whole debate around causation is mistaken, and that describing events in all their rich detail should be its goal. Understanding the issues that surround these debates is important, not only because it gives social researchers a better understanding of how they stand in relation to the debates within their own field, but also because it gives them a better chance of producing research and research proposals that are informed by a consistent view of the social research and so do not contradict themselves in the relationship between their goals and their methods.

The chapter proceeds as follows. First it considers 'flat' approaches to social explanation, revisiting experiments as an example, and then moving on to actor-network theory, which has had a considerable impact in social studies of science (and beyond). It then compares these 'flat' approaches with each other, as well as with 'depth' approaches that have been advocated by contemporary realist writers who suggest that explaining the social world requires an approach different from both natural science experiments, and the methods used by actor-network writers. It then moves on to consider debates around levels of analysis, considering their significance in relation to social explanation, again contrasting the actor-network and realist approaches in relation to them. Finally, it presents a conclusion that suggests that it is possible to claim that both the actor-network and realist approaches have their place because the world may actually vary in terms of ontological depth at different times and places.

# Ontology and depth

Before we begin to consider the different approaches to social research within this chapter, it is perhaps worth considering the terms it uses again. Ontology, assiduous readers will recall, is the theory of being. When we talk about 'flat' ontologies we are not saying that the world is literally flat, but that what we see is what there is. This claim can be taken at least two ways, as I'll attempt to explain in a moment, but what unites these claims is the idea that claims made about the world that rely upon hidden concepts or mechanisms are inaccurate or just plain wrong because either they can't be measured or are irrelevant in the day-to-day social world. Depth ontologies, on the other hand, suggest that much of what causes day-to-day behaviour is complex and hidden even from the participants of social research themselves. Instead, they suggest, we need to seek out mechanisms that influence behaviour, but may not be empirically obvious – we need to look for deeper explanations often based around ideas such as class or ethnicity or gender. These explanations do not directly cause behaviour, but they provide a profound influence over it.

Causality is often implicit in the selection of approaches or methods that researchers make. It is important, however, to understand the link between cause and effect in different models of social research in order to better design it.

# Science, method and causality

The benchmark used so far in the book is the hypothetico-deductive, experimental method, which has a distinctive model of causality against which other social research perspectives can be compared.

## Experiments

Experimental methods adopt a realist view of the world; they assume that the world is external to the researcher. They are based on researchers generating hypotheses which are tested in relation to that world.

There are two domains of analysis in the experimental model. First, there is the world itself. Then there is science, which is treated as the best available explanation of the world. Implicit in this view is the idea that science is progressive, proceeding by a process of rigorous experimental design that gets us closer and closer to the truth. Truth in this model is based on the correspondence theory of truth – something is true if it corresponds to the way things are in the world.

Thinking back to the split between ontology, epistemology and methodology, experiments collapse epistemology and methodology together because the scientific method is regarded as being the way in which true knowledge is generated, and experiments are an example (perhaps the example) of the scientific method.

This argument is rather circular, but it is hard to argue against the achievements of the scientific method in achieving knowledge about the physical world.

# Constant conjunction

Experiments depend on measuring the effect of phenomena, comparing the results of repeatedly running an experiment over and over until we are confident that a regularity exists – that we can say one thing is (or is not) causing another. This is known as the constant conjunction model – causation occurs where one thing can be empirically seen to cause another over and over again. It is not enough to claim a result based on finding out something from a single experiment – the test has to be repeated until the researcher is certain that the claim they are making is reliable.

However, just because two things co-occur in an experiment, it doesn't necessarily mean that a cause and an effect have been found. Both the phenomena could be caused by some other third thing which precedes them both, or it may be that lags between the two phenomena mean that the cause and the effect are actually the other way around. Equally, correlation is not causality. Two measured variables can appear to be statistically related due to coincidence. We can, however, differentiate to some extent between statistically significant results and substantively significant results because the latter are both rigorous and either prove or disprove specific hypotheses, whereas the former might be the result of statistical fishing expeditions to which researchers can offer no particular explanation.

## Criticisms of the constant conjunction model

The constant conjunction model of causation has been with us for hundreds of years. It does, however, have a range of criticisms that can be made against it. First, it is not really about causation. It is about the presence or absence of a statistical relationship, with the explanation of that relationship often appearing to be a second thought. New statistical techniques such as data mining often make a virtue of attempting to find variables that are 'hidden' in data sets, but which appear to have significant statistical relationships with one another. This approach can lead to some startling findings, as new relationships appear that can help us genuinely understand the world better. Retailers, in particular, want to know which products tend to sell together, and so might want to approach quantitative data in an inductive way, trying not to prove hypotheses but instead trying to look for constant conjunctions in their data, with few concerns as to why they are appearing. This highlights that a constant conjunction does not necessarily tell us anything about cause and effect – it just tells us that two (or more) things tend to occur in a sequence at the same time.

Second, the constant conjunction model has found itself under criticism from both contemporary realists and contemporary idealists. The former camp argue that they have a better explanation of why the scientific approach might work in some areas, but not in others, and what this means in terms of causation. The latter argue that scientists themselves don't adhere to their own methods, and that close studies of laboratory life (Latour and Woolgar, 1986) reveal that the scientific method itself is actually far from scientific, and that we need a better way of describing social reality. It is to these alternatives that we now turn.

# The world is flat

Amongst contemporary idealists one of the most influential groups are the actor-network theorists, who have made significant contributions to the social study of science (Latour, 1988; Mol, 2002), to sociology (Law, 1986) and to organisation studies (Lee and Hassard, 1999). Although actor-network theorists tend to reject labels of all kinds, and so would have a problem being called idealists, their work does show many of the characteristics of that perspective, and so can be fruitfully shown to offer a very different view of causation to that of science.

## Actor-network theory

Actor-network theory (ANT) is explicitly built in a flat ontology, but comes to this conclusion from a very different direction to experiments. ANT has its bases in sociological accounts of scientific practices that showed them to be as contingent and as social as events in the rest of the social world. Its ethnographic studies of laboratory life claim that, rather than the sterile, controlled and scientific places we imagine them to be, in practice they are messy, with experiments going wrong as often as right, and with technicians being very human rather than the white-gown clad pseudo-robots they are often portrayed as in the popular media.

ANT suggests that, far from objectively measuring the social world, scientific methods, technologies and practices actually play a significant role in making it. To revisit the example at the end of Chapter 6, Mol (2002) claims that the condition arteriosclerosis, instead of being a biological phenomenon that is assessed, measured and treated by particular scientific techniques and technologies, is actually *created* by them, with different systems of diagnosing and treating not only often being contradictory, but unable to explain patients' symptoms and pathology.

ANT is important not only because of its distinctive approach to social research but also because it has prompted some of the most interesting writing on social research methods in recent years. Two of its leading writers, John Law (2004) and Bruno Latour (2005), have published methods books that explain the tenets of ANT, and which mount a direct challenge to the way social research is often done.

## Ontological relativism and epistemological realism

Both Law and Latour advocate a position that most research is based on an assumption of ontological realism combined with epistemological relativism. What this means is that social research assumes that the world independent of human conceptions of it (ontological realism), but that our knowledge of it may differ according to the concepts that we use and the technologies that we utilise (epistemological relativism).

Law and Latour, however, want to turn this logic on its head, claiming that social research should be based on exactly the opposite view – a combination of epistemological realism and ontological relativism. Epistemological realism is the view that what we know is what there is – a claim that, as with the experimental method, the world is ontologically flat.

## Experiments and ANT compared

Experiments are based on a view of the world that is ontologically real, and that we are able to access that world through the use of the experimental method. The experimental method therefore produces truth because its results correspond with reality – what we know is what there is because the experimental method gives us access to the truth.

ANT, however, presents a different kind of ontological flatness. It suggests that what we know about the world comes through the concepts, ideas and technologies through which we experience it. This means that ANT is ontological relativist – what we know about the world shapes and determines what the world is like. What we know about the world is all there is to say. Experiments are ontologically flat because the method is held to capture empirical reality, and that is all there is. ANT is ontologically flat because all we can know about reality is contained in our knowledge of it.

## The futility of causation

ANT has a different model of causality to experiments. Instead of causes being the result of constant conjunctions, or generated by hidden mechanisms, it would tend to suggest that causes simply aren't that important. In some accounts of events, from some participants, causes might be given, but in others they may not. ANT would ask why we should privilege one account over another, given that the concepts and ideas present in the accounts were so instrumental in shaping them. If we cannot know the world except through our ideas, then how can we possibly claim one source of knowledge is better than another? How can we say that one thing caused another when someone else could re-describe things in a completely different way? This is a call for mutual tolerance and understanding – that we all have a right to a voice.

ANT's methods usually entail detailed observation of the actors in a research setting, recording in as much detail the everyday events that surround them, and then describing them in as rich account as possible what happened. If you want to understand what is happening in a social situation, you must 'follow the actors' as they go about their business, and describe in as much detail as possible, avoiding social science theory and concepts where at all possible in order to avoid imposing them inappropriately.

# Going deeper

ANT is meant to be a radical approach to research – it seeks to deliberately question existing social research (and indeed scientific) practices. That is one of the things that is exciting about it. However, it also places it a great distance from both experimental approaches and those that advocate depth ontologies. To recap, depth ontologies suggest that it is not enough to deal with the empirical world (as experiments do), as what we can measure is only one part of the social world. The empirical domain, in Bhaskar's terminology (Bhaskar, 1979), is only one of the three domains that research should take into account.

## The empirical, actual and real domains

The empirical domain contains all that is measurable. But in addition to it there is also the actual domain, but which contains all those things that either cannot be measured, or which have not been measured so far. So in a classroom the empirical domain might contain the number of students present if a register has been taken, but not necessarily how many desks there are (the number of desks and chairs in a classroom often seems to be only tangentially related to how many there are supposed to be) or, more obscurely, how many carpet tiles or pens there are. All of these things are measurable, but they probably haven't been measured yet. If you were re-carpeting the room, carpet tiles would be important, and if you were a pen company trying to market to students, the number of students would be – neither is irrelevant data depending on what it is you are trying to measure. However, there may also be a range of other things going on in the room that may not be easily measurable at all. Two or more students might be in a relationship, but we could not really measure how much love there is in the room (which is probably just as well). I can't tell how clever the students are (although I might be able to come up with some approximations) or how happy they feel (although, again, I could come up with some indicators of it). As such, the actual domain is bigger than the empirical – it contains things that are either unmeasurable or unmeasured.

Then we get to the final of Bhaskar's three domains – the real. The real is where generative mechanisms exist that have significant effects upon the actual and the empirical. They may have measurable effects, but they may not be easily measurable or observable themselves. Social class is again a good example – you might be able to measure the effects of social class in terms of particular people from particular classes being able to access highly paid jobs, whereas people from other social groups are unable to, but the precise mechanisms by which this discrimination occurs might be difficult to observe in action, even though there is little doubt it is there. Equally, because society is a radically open system, with lots of factors affecting our everyday lives as we navigate through our worlds, realists would argue that causality is not straightforwardly an empirical matter where one thing leads to another in a neat relationship. Instead, causes tend to be over-determined, influenced by many overlapping factors in complex ways. To understand causality we need to look at it in terms of generative mechanisms – processes that shape behaviour through regularities in complex systems which may not be easy to observe, but profoundly affect our lives and life chances. The work of Pierre Bourdieu fits within this tradition, as he shows how everything from art to careers to education is affected by social actors' accents, posture and other bodily dispositions that allow others to form distinctions about them. Social class in this view is not something that signifies where a person has come from, but is carried with them throughout their life, and can be given away at a moment's notice through an inappropriate gesture or phrase.

## Society as being ontologically prior

Within realism, a key idea is that the path of time matters profoundly. Individuals are able to influence their worlds and change them for the better (or worse), but they have to deal with the inheritance of their social position at every turn. Society is regarded as being ontologically prior to the individual – we are all born into different societal positions, some of which allow greater social chances and social mobility than others. It is possible to achieve more than your social position would initially suggest, but going against the grain of your social class is likely to carry with it opportunity costs in terms of having to make sacrifices (parents paying for their children to attend university or private schooling), and individuals might have to leave their old social backgrounds behind in order to achieve greater mobility and occupy new social spaces. Even though society is ultimately made up of other people, the roles, expectations and resources that they hold form durable structures that persist over time, and mean that different people have different opportunities.

## Regularities and structures

The job of social research within this approach is to identify the regularities of social structures and to investigate them. Quantitative techniques are often useful in finding regularities in the social order that indicate that mechanisms of inequality are in place (consider women's pay, lagging behind men's, for example), and then performing in-depth, qualitative investigations to find out through what mechanisms these differences persist (unequal recruitment practices, unfair promotion strategies, etc.).

## Realism compared to ANT

Realists would argue that actor-network theorists have a naïve view of the world that ignores structural inequalities such as poverty, and that it is unable to deal with the mechanisms that discriminate against people through gender or ethnicity or class. They would argue that a depth ontology is necessary in order to be able to adequately explain these phenomena in society (as does Reed, 1997). Actor-network theorists would argue that realists reify structures that can be changed and challenged in everyday practices, and that as a result of this reification there is a danger of our concepts coming to trap us into accepted patterns of behaviour that can actually be changed.

Realists utilise a generative model of causation that stresses the importance of finding the mechanisms that influence or condition our behaviour, actor-network theorists tend to regard such searches with incredulity, wanting instead to stress the possibilities of change and seek the diversity of social life rather than trying to produce a single, authoritative account of particular events that they believe does not exist.

So experiments use the constant conjunction model of causality – that one thing can be shown to cause another if they tend to co-occur, and if we can explain why the cause leads to the effect. In contrast, ANT has a 'flat' approach to ontology, and this can be compared to the 'depth' approach of realism. In ANT causality is not the central question – the 'how' question is far less important than the 'what' question – the goal of research is to describe. In realism the goal of research is to explain, and so causality has a central role.

Table 7.1 compares the three versions of causation described above.

There are other ways, however, in which social research can be 'flat' or 'deep' – in reference to levels of analysis.

**Table 7.1**  Causation in realism, ANT and experiments

|  | Realism | ANT | Experiments |
|---|---|---|---|
| Model of causation | Generative | Causation not really important | Constant conjunction |
| View of ontology | Deep, real | Flat, relative | Flat, real (empiricism is the truth) |
| View of epistemology | Relativist | Real (what we know is what there is) | Real (what we know is what is the world) |
| View of society | Ontologically prior to the individual | The result of negotiation and interaction | The combination of individuals (see below) |

# Levels of analysis

Another area where there are significant differences between traditions in social research is in the way that they treat levels of analysis. What I mean by 'levels of analysis' in this context is primarily issues of scale. It is the relationship between, for example, individuals, households and society, working upwards. Many social theorists would even argue that the individual is an inappropriate starting point for social analysis as we have multiple identities and these are therefore the best starting point for thinking about scale, but for convenience I'll use individuals in this example.

The most important question when thinking about levels of analysis is how the different levels we can identify interact with one another. Are groups of various kinds simply the result of the interactions between their members, or do they have a different status? Are groups ontologically different from the individuals that make them up? If you look at the literature in many popular science sections of bookshops you will find claims that men and women are sufficiently biologically different to have different developmental paths when children, leading to different behavioural patterns and different career choices (Pinker, 2009), a claim that biological factors can cause influences that affect individuals' behaviours and which can form the basis of societal patterns. This is an argument that goes across three levels of analysis that many sociologists and psychologists would find extraordinary.

## How are levels of analysis conceptualised in terms of the perspectives in this chapter?

In the hypothetico-deductive perspective, levels of analysis tend to be regarded relatively unproblematically as either the constituents of one another, or the aggregate, depending on whether you are starting from the small scale or the large. This is because it is hard to account for the phenomenon of emergence, which is where the aggregate level of analysis might have characteristics that aren't apparent in the constituent elements that make it up. An obvious example of this is consciousness – humans have consciousness, but the constituent physiological elements that make us up do not. At some point physiology combines to create something that has a characteristic that the constituent elements do not.

## Levels of analysis in economics

In economics the debate between levels of analysis has been a contentious one. In that subject there is a split between microeconomics (the behaviour of individuals and firms) and macroeconomics (the behaviour of whole economies). A central tension has been working out what the relationship between the two levels of analysis, micro and macro, should be. Microeconomists have often criticised macroeconomics because, at least in the Keynesian view, it is not based on micro-assumptions – macroeconomics is based on aggregate phenomena such as consumption, savings and investment, rather than being linked explicitly to individual and firm decisions. The central problem is whether the macroeconomy is simply an aggregate of all the decisions made by individuals and firms within an economy, or is an emergent property of all of those decisions. The two are not the same.

Taking an aggregate approach suggests that the macroeconomy is simply the sum of individual and firm decisions, which in a mathematical sense, it is. However, there is another view that says the macroeconomy is the sum of individual and firm decisions, but also of all the complex interrelationships between them, and as such is not irreducible to a simple aggregate. This is because the macroeconomy has causal properties of its own – it provides the context within which individual decisions are made, so is not simply the sum total of all the decisions are made, but also the cause of many of them. If the economy as a whole is shrinking, then it is not just a statistical aggregate, but also a potential cause of further economic decline, as firms, seeing that unemployment is high, may lay off staff themselves because of the poor state of the economy this implies.

## Emergence

The idea of emergence fits best within the realist account of social life of the three perspectives we have compared within this book. Realists present the idea of 'emergent properties' (Archer, 1995) which make levels of analysis potentially different from those above and below them. So a household is not the same as the collection of individuals that make it up, and neither is an institution. A household will have emergent properties that creates particular roles (breadwinner, parent, child, grandparent, etc.) that individuals have to negotiate – roles that come with the context of being in a household, but are not simply the product of the individuals within them. We occupy different roles in each of these social settings that are defined in relation to the social roles occupied by others, and which lead to different patterns of behaviour. None of us have to comply with the expectations that these situations might offer us, although at work it will often be more difficult to not comply than at home because of employment contracts, but these roles create contexts that we have to negotiate, even if we choose to reject them. As such, realists hold that the family or work context that we enter is ontologically prior to us – it can be changed through our interactions with it, but our roles in group settings, the resources we can or cannot occupy in them, and the expectations others have of us in those roles, means that they are ontologically distinct from the individuals that make them up. Institutions are not the sum of the individuals that make them up – they are ontologically separable from them and create emergent properties that individuals have to contend with.

## ANT and enrolment

Again, actor-network theorists are likely to look at the claims of realists in relation to levels of analysis with some bafflement. Some of the most impressive actor-network accounts are about collective phenomena, and the process by which particular actors (or, more recently, 'actants', because they can be human or non-human) 'enrol' others into networks through the use of ideas or technologies and come to 'translate' the way that network subsequently behaves. This has something in common with the realist idea of different levels of analysis having emergent properties and being separable from the individuals that make them up, but whereas realists stress the ontological separation of structures from individuals, actor-network theorists stress that enrolments into networks are always open to negotiation and contingency, that they are the product of interactions between actors, and so can be continually renegotiated and changed at any moment. For realists, society is a durable fact; for actor-network theorists, it is a continuous achievement on that part of those that make it up.

Actor-networks theorists are happy to consider levels of analysis – one of the central parts of the work done within the field has been to consider how technology makes society 'durable' (Latour, 1991), but whereas for realists this means that our families, workplaces and other settings become ontologically prior to us, actor-network theorists would suggest that this is to reify social structures beyond a level that they deserve. The point of levels of analysis for actor-network theorists is to show how they are built up, and can be collapsed again, to demonstrate how they can create power relationships which can be opposed and resisted.

## The ontological status of society

This debate about the ontological status of society is hugely important because it implies very different research strategies and very different ways of seeing the world. Many social theorists will have preferences for one of the two views over the other, but they won't always be made explicit. You yourself will have assumptions that get built into the way you go about your everyday life and research that might favour one approach over the other – do you regard institutions as being fixed and immovable, or do they represent a series of negotiations and encounters for you? When you are putting together a research proposal or project, do you regard individuals as products of their background with all that might entail, or are they skilful players in complex social worlds that carry with them the possibility of change at any moment? Do you regard gender and ethnicity as categories that are relatively fixed, or as labels which are open to negotiation and redefinition? All of these questions will influence the way that research is deigned and conceptualised, but it is important to have thought through these assumptions in terms of the debates presented in this chapter because they also carry with them assumptions in terms of the processes of causality and the purpose of social research itself.

## Conclusion – how deep do you need to go?

This chapter has tried to show how different perspectives in social research have different ways of dealing with causality, and how different views on how to deal

**Table 7.2** Causality and levels of analysis

| | Hypothetico-deductive | Realist | Actor-network theorist |
|---|---|---|---|
| Model of causality | Constant conjunctions | Generative | Narrative or none – not relevant to social phenomena |
| Approach to levels of analysis | Aggregates | Emergent | Micro–macro durability as an expression of power to be resisted |

with levels of analysis also carry with them different presumptions about the way that social phenomena work.

To recap, hypothetico-deductive models present constant conjunction models of causality and tend to regard the claims that different levels of analysis are anything but the sum or components of one another with some scepticism because they involve introducing notions like emergence, which are difficult to account for, and using quantitative methods, which are difficult to model or explain. Realists present generative models of causation, meaning that causes and effects do not have to take place in the same time or space, and are happy with the idea that different levels of analysis might have emergent properties and not simply be aggregates of one another. Actor-network theorists wonder what the point of trying to demonstrate causality is for social phenomena, preferring instead to show how contested and difficult it is to come to any kind of agreement about it, as well as demonstrating how micro-phenomena can be combined to create macro-effects, especially through the use of technology, but also how they can be collapsed and resisted. This is summarised in Table 7.2.

What this amounts to is the claim that adopting a particular perspective on social research has implications for both the way that causality is treated and the way that researchers conceptualise different levels of analysis. The models and approaches are not fixed in stone – it is perfectly possible for realists to make use of constant conjunction models of causality as well as generative ones, and in order to utilise techniques such as correlation in their work this may be a necessity. However, understanding the tendencies of each of the perspectives to view causality and levels of analysis in very different ways has implications for the claims each can make and the justifications that are needed for those claims. If a researcher is making idealist claims about knowledge and then proceeds to run regressions, we have a right to be suspicious and to demand more justification for their approach.

## Five things to remember about this chapter

1   Assigning causes and effects in social research carries with it assumptions about how social research should be carried out, as well as ontological assumptions about the nature of the world.

2   The most prevalent model of causality, the constant conjunction model, isn't really a model of causation at all – it is a statistical measure of association between two relationships. And correlation is not causation.

3  Different approaches to causation range from social researchers who deny that it is important at all (ANT) to those that believe it is hugely important, but depends on mechanisms that are often hidden from us (depth realism), through to the constant conjunctions model that is still the mainstay of scientific research.

4  Different approaches to social research treat the problems of levels of analysis in very different ways. Macro-phenomena can simply be the aggregate of micro-phenomena, or they can be viewed as having a separate status because of the existence, if you believe in it, of emergence.

5  The way that levels of analysis also adjust the way that social research conceptualises society – it can be viewed as something that we are born into, and so have to adjust to (society as ontologically prior), or as a contingent series of associations enrolled into a network which can be challenged (ANT).

## Example – Rogue Traders and financial losses

In the last twenty years there have been several examples of the 'Rogue Trader' phenomenon where individual traders on financial markets generate substantial losses to their employers, sometimes even, as in the case of Nick Leeson at Barings Bank, bringing the bank to collapse in the process (Leeson, 1996; Gapper and Denton, 1997).

In such situations, causality is important. If we blame the individuals, following the narrative of the 'Rogue Trader' we can put together an account in which the individual banker is able to subvert their bank's risk control systems to allow them greater discretion than they should have had, until a point is reached where their losses are discovered, usually because of their sheer size, and the bank has to either accept the losses or is even forced into bankruptcy. This is an actor-based account, one that might be organised around a flat ontology that emphasises the choices involved in generating a financial loss (Greener, 2006).

It is equally possible, however, to construct a 'depth' explanation of the Rogue Trader that presents them as an almost passive figure, where they were only acting the bizarre incentives that their organisations gave them. In such an account, a figure such as Leeson was put under barely any scrutiny, and was able to pursue his fantasy of being a successful trader in a culture where profits and bonuses come before accountability and control, and where Leeson was protected by bosses who did not really understand his actions because of the profits he claimed to be making. This is a depth explanation that asks questions about the way we structure financial trading to incentivise bankers with the promise of huge bonuses and don't require them to be sufficiently accountable for their actions (Sebag-Montefiore, 1996).

Of course, understanding Rogue Traders requires us to understand both narratives, and to be able to balance these accounts to find which seems most accurately to reflect the individual case we are researching. No financial trader ever caused a collapse entirely on their own, and no collapse was entirely caused by a bank having a bonus-driven culture. The job of social research is to apply these ideas to the particular case before us.

DESIGNING SOCIAL RESEARCH

# EIGHT

## Dealing with time and control – or what time period suits my research, and how do I stop the world from interfering in it?

### Introduction

Chapter 7 dealt with the issue of ontological depth in research design, comparing approaches to social research that stress 'flatness' or 'depth', and considering the circumstances when each might be most appropriate. This chapter deals with two other issues – time and control.

Time has already been mentioned in Chapter 7 because of its importance in realism, and that aspect is relevant to this chapter, but the main focus here will be on the selection of the time frame for research, and its implications for the selection of method. Timescales in research can go from considering the present only, through to examining social changes over hundreds of years, and clearly what works for one period will struggle to deal with the other.

The issue of control in social research will then be considered because researchers need to be able to explain how they can make claims about social phenomena that might be influenced by a wide range of factors. Given this problem, how is it possible to conclude anything at all? Clearly this topic links with the discussions around experiments, but needs to be extended to consider how they are used in different contexts in social research and how they deal (or don't deal) with the problem of control outside of a controlled laboratory setting. Both of these elements are key in researchers developing a sense of which methods are appropriate when planning and designing social research.

### How does social research deal with time?

Social research can consider a range of different time spans from trying to account for the immediate and present, through to looking at changes over several decades or even hundreds of years. To consider these differences a contrast can be offered between research that uses the consideration of processes as its starting point and work which is more concerned with showing how events, institutions or even countries have changed over longer periods of time.

# Phenomenology and process philosophy – researching the present

Phenomenology is the tradition in social research that has what might be called the 'thickest' conception of the present. It is usually defined in terms of the study of structures of consciousness experienced from a first-person point of view. This rather dry definition doesn't really capture its contemporary usage, however, in which researchers attempt not only to address the sensations of consciousness, but also their meaning. So Husserl and Merleau-Ponty wrote about the need for pure description of lived experience as a means of exploring experience phenomenologically, and hermeneutical writing has dealt with attempts to explore social and linguistic interpretation within the context with which it occurred. In both there is a general emphasis on the analysis of experience.

## Phenomenology in human geography and organisation studies

In human geography, there has been a phenomenological turn to explore the experience of walking, not only describing the walk as it occurred, but also attempting to capture its richness in terms of its meaning for the author/researcher as it occurred. This results in something approaching a literary form, with the criterion of success of the piece coming through its persuasiveness not in terms of method, but whether it works in capturing the flow of experience the author wishes to communicate.

In organisation studies, Wood (2005) has examined the implications of considering leadership not as an event or the property of a person, but instead as an event. Wood, making use of process philosophy, suggests that instead we should consider leadership as being something that is emergent, requiring the participation of contexts and social actors together. Wood emphasises not the behaviour of leaders or followers, but how events demonstrate the being and becoming of leadership, a focus on presence rather than on the personal qualities of those running businesses.

## The openness of the present

What these approaches lead to is a sense of the present being extraordinarily rich, of being open with possibility and where humans, contexts and processes combine to create processes where little or nothing is pre-determined. There is clearly something in common with actor-network theory on the emphasis on description rather than conceptual elaboration, and this leads to a strong sense of the present and the emergent future being the time frames of most relevance. The present becomes extremely thick as we provide rich descriptions of it, exploring both the experiences of it and the meanings we attach to them. The here and now becomes overwhelming when viewed this way – our senses provide us with more stimulus than we can possibly take in at once.

Most readers of this book will have had moments in their lives where time appears too slow and sensory experience becomes overwhelming. These moments show the subjective nature of time, but also the importance of sensory experience for us in understanding the world. Examining how our consciousness interacts with the world and the processes through which we come to attach meaning remains an ambitious and exciting area of study. However, there are clearly problems with this conception of research when considered from the point of view of time.

## Difficulties

First, how are we to capture periods of time longer than the present when there is such an emphasis on rich descriptions of experience? Does this exclude us from performing research on the past (except perhaps through flights of imagination), and what about phenomena that we may not be able to experience directly ourselves?

Perhaps more seriously, how can phenomenological research gain any critical purchase upon its subject? Examining processes of being and becoming allow space to be created for calls for research to engage with alternative paradigms, but very little room for generalisation or comparison beyond the immediate case's description or meaning. Great stories can be instructive and powerful, and rich phenomenological accounts can provide us with insights into the creation of meaning in similar kinds of ways to the work of an author such as Virginia Woolf, but in a world where research is often required to demonstrate its relevance, and where funders are often reluctant to pay for work that is unable to be comparative or critical, work in this tradition has to work hard in order to demonstrate relevance, no matter how wonderful it might be to read.

# History and political science – researching the past

In direct contrast to phenomenology and process philosophy, history and political science are often about researching longer periods of time in the past, often (although by no means always) in periods when significant changes of one kind or another are taking place. We can learn a great deal by comparing how research is conducted in the two disciplines.

## History and time

As we discussed earlier in the book, historians have often demonstrated a reticence to engage in methodological debates, and a contrast is sometimes made between historical, archive-driven narrative history (Himmelfarb, 2004) and more contemporary, social theory-driven history that attempts to take account of developments in philosophy (especially post-structuralism and postmodernism) (Jenkins, 1995). The 'old' history (to use Himmelfarb's terminology) is based on archival research, and involves historians carefully reading and comparing sources to produce a narrative of events that is as objective and fair as possible. From this perspective a historian's claim to have produced an objective account will be that it is as close as possible to what happened, given the state of our records of it.

The form that historical accounts typically take is that of a narrative, telling the story of events in sequence, or arranged according to various dimensions or themes that were present. As such, history is often viewed as a humanity rather than a social science, with accounts being assessed on the basis of how rigorously the archival records appear to have been researched, how persuasively the narrative accounts for the events recorded within the archives, and whether the account is able to shed any new light upon the past by finding a new source or a new interpretation of events. Good history is not like a novel, but may be as well written, giving a shape and a flow to events as they appear. In history, objectivity and fairness are about being true to sources and fair to those from the past.

## Political science and the past

Political science, where it considers issues such as continuity and change in government policy, often covers significant periods of time (thirty to fifty years and more), examining how institutions became established and went on to change (Hall, 1993). The methods used may have something in common with history in getting access to primary data (although this will tend to be in the form of interviews rather than archives, although it may involve both), but will tend to consider time periods that are more recent than the historian (although there are more contemporary histories as well), but usually with an eye to developing a theoretical perspective rather than producing a narrative account for its own sake.

New institutional writers in political science examine historical events to show how actions in those periods became constrained or enabled by choices of institutional design that contemporary or previous actors have made (Steinmo et al., 1992). History matters profoundly in such accounts because it influences the present, creating institutions that interact with individuals to provide rules, roles and resources that are not equally distributed. Think of the differences between the UK's approach to health policy, where a National Health Service was established in 1948 to provide free care to its population, and health policy in the US where a far more expensive system exists based on decisions made in the 1960s (and before), and which, until very recently, has been remarkably resistant to attempts to reform it.

New institutional writers would argue that the difference between the two countries, and the reason why the US puts up with having 40 million people without health insurance until the Obama reforms are implemented, is that interest groups in the US have prevented change to protect their positions in healthcare there. In the UK, in contrast, the private health system was reformed rather earlier, moving to a more publicly funded system which managed to overrule established interest groups as a result of the experience of wartime and because of the election of a socialist government after it. The very different political systems produced different political outcomes and different institutions for dealing with healthcare, but the choices made one or two generations ago have significant implications for those in the two countries today and have proven remarkably difficult to change or reform (think of the experience of the Obama and Clinton governments in trying to change US healthcare).

## History and political science compared

The problem both history and political science have is the opposite, in many respects, to that of phenomenology. There is a danger of getting so lost in the narrative of the *longue durée* in each case that the specifics get lost. This can be a particular problem in political science or historical sociology where the empirical case might be primarily about demonstrating the effectiveness of a particular theory rather than being expected to stand up to scrutiny in its own right. Marxist-influenced accounts of history have a tendency to make everything boil down to class-struggle, losing a great amount of empirical detail and richness as a result. Navarro's (1978) book on the creation and establishment of the UK National Health Service, for example, is a wonderful achievement, but bears so little resemblance to other work in the field (Honigsbaum, 1989; Klein, 2006; Greener, 2008) that it is difficult to take all of its claims seriously. Archer's work exploring the relationship between social theory and history sets up a rich and complex framework for the examination of periods of continuity and change, but its empirical examples based on the evolution of education policy do not do it justice; they are far too brief and appear over-generalised, reducing the credibility of one the most significant achievements in social theory in recent years (Archer, 1995).

# What time frame fits your research, and how does time affect what you can say?

Phenomenology and political science (or historical institutionalism at least) represent poles on a spectrum that deals with time in social research. At the one end are rich and thick explanations of the present; at the other, time appears rather thin and perhaps even subservient as an empirical tool for illustrating a theory that runs through and across time. In the first instance, the present becomes overwhelming; in the second, decades can shoot by as we are carried along by a narrative that is usually seeking to explain events through the use of narrative or theory.

## What time period fits your research programme?

This leads to two questions. First, what time period fits a particular research programme? This is an important question that often gets overlooked when putting together proposals to carry out research programmes. How long a period does case-study-type research require before it becomes credible? How long a period does a narrative have to work over before it becomes history? How short a period before it becomes phenomenology? Deciding on a time period that research will be carried out over involves not only a choice about time, but also about the tradition of social research that best fits that time period, and alongside that the methods that particular tradition will favour. Examining the staging and experience of a particular event takes us to one extreme and can produce important research that shows how corporations choose to present themselves (Clark and Mangham, 2004), and so have considerable relevance beyond the immediate narrative of the tale told. Working through historical records to produce accounts of how organisational theory or political policy-making tends to end up reproducing what appear to be the same patterns over and over again necessarily requires a much longer time period, to different traditions of research, and to different criteria for judging the success of such work.

Neither of these traditions is going to be to everyone's taste. Researchers who wish to emphasise the possibilities of the present will find work that covers several decades or time periods prone to superficiality and over-generalisation; researchers who want to seek patterns in human behaviour will often regard phenomenological approaches as subject to over-description and lacking in any kind of critical stance because of the lack of comparison or theory. The important thing to note, however, is that these differences are often rooted in the very different time periods examined by each tradition, and in the differences in methods that result.

## To what extent does the time frame chosen in your research limit what you can say?

The second question that time particularly raises is the extent to which the time frame chosen in a study limits what the researcher can say about the results of the research. This is, in many respects, the flipside of the last question. If there is a focus on the present, on what is happening immediately to an individual through their experience, then claims about the generalisability of that research have to be limited – and this will lead to a knowledge that will present a specific spatio-temporal claim. Moving beyond that specific claim, however, will require a considerable degree of ingenuity and thought. The opposite case comes from taking a far longer time period – there is a loss of specificity. What appears as a pattern or regularity across a long time period may not have relevance to a specific case within that time period in the same way that an average may bear little or no resemblance to one of the data points that were combined to calculate it. Abstracted knowledge may not be of any use in a specific case.

It is therefore important to consider how time affects research both in terms of method choice, but also in terms of the phenomena under investigation. Researchers therefore need to think through this issue carefully. Equally, they need to think through the next issue – the degree of openness that their system under investigation can be said to have.

# The openness (and closedness) of systems

## Science and research

One of the reasons why natural scientific research has had such an impact upon our world is because it is able to find causes to particular phenomena, and make use of them in a way that is able to stabilise and harness them to our advantage. We are surrounded by the practical applications of scientific breakthroughs every day from the moment our digital alarm clocks wake us up through to heating milk in our microwave for our bedtime drink before turning in for the night. Science does some pretty wonderful things for us. It is so successful because it allows technologies to reproduce mechanisms to specific ends in what are mostly closed systems.

## Closed systems

Closed systems are technically completely isolated from their environment. They aren't a very useful concept in social research because they aren't social at all. When we are talking about closed systems in social research, we are usually talking about degree, with relatively closed systems being those that are able to control their relationship with their environment to be able to assess the effects of specific interventions into them. In systems theory the example often given of a single-loop heating system works in this category in that it shows how a single variable (temperature) is measured in a system (by a thermostat), compared to a standard (the required temperature), heating applied if it is too cold, turned off if it is too hot and new measurements taken. The system is open in the sense that it interfaces with the environment, but it is able to control its activities in the sense that this is a single-loop mechanism that takes account of only one variable at a time.

Now the thermostat example is a useful one because a considerable amount of social research is still conceptualised in this way. The idea is that there is a system into which an intervention is introduced, we measure the effect of the intervention and determine what happened as a result. What has to follow for this to be the case? For this model of social research to work, the system which is being studied has to be such that we are able to measure its initial state accurately, then we must be able to control the system so that it remains in that measured state, and to an extent that, when the intervention arrives, it is the only intervention that the system has to be able to deal with. We must, then, again, be able to measure the system to see what effect the intervention has had, taking into account a suitable time period between the intervention and the result in order to be able to adequately measure the effect. There is a lot to control here, and a lot of careful measurement involved.

The model of causality present in a closed system does not necessarily have to be that of the constant conjunction, as we might have a gap between intervention and effect specified through some other mechanism, but it is likely to be because of the sheer difficulty of keeping a system under control for any length of time. Effectively, what this boils down to is that we need to be able to keep a system closed *except for the intervention whose effect we are attempting to measure*. If anything else crops up, then we will be unable to say for sure if the effect was down to our intervention or whatever else managed to creep into our research.

## How closed is the system being researched?

The problem is, then, how closed is the specific area that you are trying to research? The more closed the system, the better the chance of finding out the result of a specific intervention or change; the less closed, the more difficult it will be to isolate the effect of anything specific. However, it is not even that simple as soon as human beings get involved. This is because it is possible to create highly closed situations and introduce human beings into them to measure the effects of particular interventions upon them, but they are likely to wonder what on earth is going on if put in what will seem to them to be such an artificial situation, and so this has considerable potential to cause problems even for social research designed to find ways of removing possible distractions other than the specific intervention being tested for. On this account, the idea of the social experiment seems pretty philosophically doomed. Some methods writers (see Byrne, 2003, for example) argue that they are a dead-end for social research.

Recent work in science and technology studies has muddied the work even further. Latour and Woolgar (1986) suggested that 'laboratory life', the work of scientists, which should surely represent the epitome of science in practice through the hard-headed application of experimental methodology, in fact is far more contingent that this, with processes often not working as they ought to, with results having to be more selectively reported than the method would suggest, and with human error having a rather more central part in the process than the very dry account presented in journals would suggest. If even natural science experiments don't appear to conform to the methodological idea, what hope is there in the social realm?

## Control and experiments

The crucial aspect of experimental methodology is the ability to control a variable or process to be able to compare that result with what would have happened in its absence. Ideally, then, there needs to be at least an experimental group, where something is changed as the result of an intervention, and a control group, where it is not. We can then compare results. In natural science a single comparison would be nowhere near enough, and in disciplines such as psychology the experiment would be repeated until researchers were confident that the result obtained was due to the intervention. In other social science, however, it may be that having an adequate control is extremely difficult, or even unethical.

## Experiments in social policy

The use of experiments in social policy, for example, would imply that some people receive a new intervention of some kind, and some do not (the control group). If the intervention is being introduced on the assumption that it might make people's lives better (a new welfare payment, or a new way of administering an existing payment), and it is only being introduced to one group of people, this would seem to raise an ethical issue – whether the state should be actively intervening in people's lives on a differential basis. One of the central tenets of social policy is that, where interventions are applied, they should be applied to everyone equally on the grounds of fairness. If this is not the case, then the spectre of inequity appears. This can be got around by claiming that the new intervention is untried, and so won't definitely improve things, but this is, in itself, rather worrying as it still means that differences (both good and bad) might emerge – some people might receive life-changing interventions whilst others don't.

## Experiments in organisation studies

In organisation studies, opportunities often arise where interventions can be introduced in some areas of a particular business or public-sector institution, but not in others. So a change in management programme might be introduced in a particular geographic area by a company but not in another, and the results compared. In the US, different states often have different approaches to the way that they run the public sector, allowing comparisons to be made where new ideas are introduced in some localities but not in others. Indeed, this is, in many respects, an argument for allowing experiments in social policy areas in a country such as the US – because states are already doing different things then the complaint that changing things in some areas and not others on fairness grounds doesn't apply because states are already so different. Perhaps the governmental system in the US allows for a wide range of 'natural' experiments to exist because of the diversity of governmental approaches within states?

## Can you have an experiment if you can't control one variable at a time?

However, the main problem with the idea of a 'natural' experiment, as is argued in the US between states and increasingly in the UK as its constituent countries try out different approaches to government as a result of devolution, is that the intervention you are comparing may well be different, but there is no guarantee that the context into which that intervention is made isn't also different, or that the causal mechanisms that seem to arise from the research weren't due to another factor intervening that was entirely outside the bounds of the experimental methodology.

At a philosophical level it is just about impossible to claim that two (or more) social systems, involving an experimental intervention and a control, differ because of the experimental intervention. This is because any number of other things could have intervened in the experimental case to create a different result. Equally, any number of things could also have intervened in the control to prevent (or cause) alternative things to happen. Because social systems are open systems, subject to all manner of influences, and because people aren't going to behave in the same way to the same intervention, either in different social systems or even consistently to the same interventions at different time periods, then experiments seem to be rather difficult to justify. From a philosophical perspective, social experiments seem to be of no use.

## But experiments do work ...

However, the problem with this view, that social experiments can't work on logical grounds, would also seem to be unsustainable because there are a good number of them that have been amongst the most ingenious and influential pieces of social research conducted. Stanley Milgram's work on obedience to authority (Milgram and Bruner, 2005) is amongst the most influential and thought-provoking research ever produced, and although it would be extremely difficult to conduct such research today because of the ethical issues it raised (or perhaps walked all over) it remains a central canon of social science. More recently, Dan Ariely's work (Ariely, 2008) in the field of experimental economics is both methodologically brilliant in terms of its ability to overcome the difficulties with the experimental method and profound in the way it explores the flaws in human decision-making. Milgram's and Ariely's work suggests that, even with the many problems of the experimental method, wonderful work can be produced using it, and so it is a worthy part of the social science canon. The difficulty comes in finding ingenious ways of overcoming these problems to tap into the power of the method.

# A way around the problem of the experimental method – scale and sampling

In the passage above we noted one of the difficulties of carrying out a social experiment is that a comparison between a control group and an intervention group is not really sustainable because of the potential for intervention of other factors in open social systems. One way of trying to get around this is to carry out trials on a very large scale so as to try and make the argument that, if a definite pattern emerges in the control group that is different from the experimental or intervention group, then we can't definitively say that it was because of the intervention because the research was carried out in a social system. However, we can say that an interesting statistical regularity exists that is worthy of further investigation. For this approach to have credence, issues of both scale and sampling need to be taken into account.

Issues of scale arise because enough trials need to be carried out to show that the difference in results between the control and experimental group is down to the intervention. This raises issues of statistical significance. It is beyond the scope of this book to go through these processes step-by-step, but there are plenty of texts that will take students through the process of ensuring results can be subjected to a test of statistical significance.

## Statistical and substantive significance

What is important here, however, is that there is a difference between statistical significance and substantive significance. This split was made by McCloskey (1998), and raises the issue of whether numbers, in themselves, actually tell us anything important. Statistical significance measures how likely a given result is to have occurred by random, assuming that the data as whole resembles a normal distribution (or 'bell' curve). If the result is very unlikely (either less than 5 per cent or 1 per cent, depending on the confidence level applied) then this would seem to suggest that we are onto something. Substantive significance, on the other hand, is where results are examined to see if they are actually meaningful in explaining something. So we might find a statistically significant relationship that seems to have no importance for anyone because the data is rather obscure, or, more importantly, a statistically significant relationship that we cannot explain through the use of existing theory or logic. This split between statistical and substantive significance is important because it reminds us that, just because we seem to have produced some interesting numerical results, it doesn't mean we have answered any research problems.

Equally, just because a relationship is found to exist on a large-scale study, that doesn't mean it will exist in a single case within the study. If, say, we find that a particular change management programme produces results on average across a large number of settings into which it has been introduced, that doesn't mean that it will work for us, in our organisation, here and now. A new welfare benefit system might help people on average, but that doesn't mean it will help any particular individual.

## Sampling

As well as issues of scale, experiments push issues of sampling to the fore. There are many different ways of sampling, but two related strategies are significant here: random sampling and stratified sampling. Random sampling might be appropriate where there are a large number of both control and experimental groups to be included, and where there is a large population of potential participants or sites for the work to take place in. Random sampling, when combined with scale, increases the possibility of any difference in pattern between the control and experimental groups that emerges being down to the intervention rather than other factors as the pattern must have emerged in a variety of different contexts and situations. However, where large numbers of cases cannot be examined, then randomness, in itself, is not a virtue. It can result in cases or individuals being chosen that have a shared characteristic that skews the results of the process. Checks can be put in place to allow for this, but this seems to make the whole idea of random sampling rather pointless – if you are having to correct it, then it is no longer random.

An alternative, but related, method to random sampling is stratified sampling, where researchers deliberately look for cases or individuals with particular characteristics and select their sample based upon these characteristics. Once the population has been divided up into these characteristics, then random sampling can proceed within these characteristics to get the list of research participants.

So, to continue with the example of a new welfare benefit, we might consider that postcode or zip code, type of family, working status, existing benefits received, age and ethnicity might all be relevant in some way in whether a new benefit might help people or not. We can then sample on the basis of these factors to try to make sure that we either have people of all types, or whether we can group people according to patterns between these factors, to make sure that we can produce comparisons later on that have taken these factors, things we have decided are important, into account. Factors might be decided upon based upon what we know about welfare benefit systems, or be based on more general theory, but the important thing is that stratified sampling goes about the process in a very different way to random sampling because it is trying to produce comparisons based on factors systematically or theoretically, rather than suggesting that an intervention is context independent. This is an important difference – stratified sampling attempts to take account of differences in cases or individuals in a way to allow for them, whereas random sampling tries to get over differences by having large-scale sampling that seeks to remove those differences on average. Which is more appropriate is not a simple technical choice, but also carries with it assumptions about the world.

## What are case studies for – an aid to generalisation or an analysis of power and expertise?

The issues outlined above tend to crystallise around case studies. Case studies are a commonly used tool in a variety of social science research areas from social policy through to law. Case studies can be single- or multiple-case designs, but with considerable variation between authors as to what constitutes good multiple-case design. Multiple-case research often seems to be carried out to emphasise or explore different facets of the phenomena that the case represents through a process of stratified sampling (see above). So we might examine the take-up of a welfare benefit by sampling different groups that might be expected to take it up, and looking for differences between them. This carries with it an assumption that exploring the differences between cases is the best way of generating theory. An alternative, however, would be to sample on a logic of replicating cases as much as possible so as to compare the same group in order to look for regularities rather than for differences. The difficulty with the stratified approach is that, in an open system, you can never be sure that differences are down to differences in the group or mechanism that the research aims to pick up – they might be down to other factors. However, this problem equally applies in trying to sample on the basis of replication – how are you going to find two sites which are similar enough to be able to make the claim of similarity?

### Yin and case studies

An alternative is to suggest, as Yin (2008) does, that the purpose of case studies is to contribute to theory rather than to represent a population, but to differentiate between cases according to whether they are exploratory, explanatory or descriptive. Exploratory case studies occur where fieldwork and data collection have to be undertaken prior to the research question – where an inductive approach is required. Explanatory cases, however, are where researchers are aiming to explain causality through pattern matching techniques. The approach taken here can be quantitative, through the application of tools such as regression to the data, or qualitative where hypotheses might be generated and theories tested using other approaches. Finally, descriptive cases require that the research begins with a descriptive theory, which is then used to design the research to cover the required depth and scope of the project. Yin's suggestion is that case studies are to generate theory, and that method should be clearer about what kind of contribution they might make on these terms rather than suggesting that they might stand up as a narrative in their own right (except perhaps at the explanatory level).

## Flyvbjerg and case studies

However, a very different approach is taken by Flyvbjerg who suggests that there are five misunderstandings about case study research (Flyvbjerg, 2007); that general theoretical knowledge is more valuable than concrete practical knowledge; that one cannot generalise on the basis of an individual case; that the case study is most useful for generating hypotheses; that the case study contains a bias towards verification; and that it is often difficult to summarise and develop general propositions from specific case studies (p. 391). Instead, Flyvbjerg argues that it is possible to generalise from a single case (if it is chosen well), that formal generalisation is overvalued and the 'force of example' is underestimated (p. 395). He suggests that case studies should seek 'critical' cases that either falsify what we know, or which are paradigmatic cases that highlight the 'general character' of a culture or society more generally (p. 397). He argues that knowledge is always situated, and that expert knowledge is therefore located within a specific context – that only an in-depth method such as the case study can provide. Finally, he suggests that the power of a good narrative is far greater than that of a statistical, generalised analysis – narratives are instructional to us as we are story-telling creatures, and so narrative case studies can be extremely important in understanding the world. A strong narrative may resonate with us and have a greater potential to provoke action or change than the most carefully crafted science.

As such, case studies represent an example of a research method where the contradictions and difficulties of generalisation come right to the fore. Do we research cases because we want to try and improve theory, or because we want to gain in-depth knowledge that may be symbolic of additional issues, but are primarily about generating in-depth, expert knowledge in a specific area? The approach to generalisation is therefore very different – and you must make your argument carefully. Do you want to argue for generalisation through theory on the basis of stratified sampling, or instead that the specific phenomenon is best understood by selecting a single critical case that illustrates the problem under investigation and allows a far greater in-depth understanding to occur? Mixing up the two logics is possible, but can create the impression that the research is trying to achieve both breadth and depth, and this can appear incoherent.

# Conclusion – time and control in social research

Time and control can both appear to be taken-for-granted aspects of social research. However, we can take different perspectives on them both which have considerable implications in research.

Time is perhaps the least discussed of the two elements in the social research literature. But decisions about what time frame to incorporate into research fundamentally affects the way that research is designed. A phenomenologist approach to time focuses us down onto short periods of it because of their focus on the experience of the present. Phenomenology is associated with idealism because of its emphasis on subjective experience, and therefore with the description of that experience.

Historians often deal with the production of their narratives in an unproblematic way, almost describing their research processes in a positivistic way, as if there can be no alternative to the accounts they produce because they are based on facts. What goes on in historical accounts is far more complex than this though – in fact it is often closer to the way we have described realism in this book. This is because historians establish, to the best of their ability, facts about an external reality that they accept exist, and then present interpretations and explanations of those facts. History as a discipline is objective in the sense that it accepts the existence of an external reality that is recorded in archives, the records of which can be corroborated by other sources to produce, as near as we are able, observer-independent facts about the social world, such as dates of birth, dates of events, sequences of events on particular days (as near as we are able), dates when figures died, and so on. The interpretive bit is working out what we can say in explaining or interpreting those facts.

Both history and political science have to decide what time frame suits the account the author(s) wish to tell. This is not an objective, technical decision, as the time period the author(s) choose will provide limits on the account, necessarily shaping it. The time point chosen at the start of the narrative will clearly influence the shape of the account, as will the end point, structuring the narrative between by shaping how much material will have to appear in between.

The ontology of the subject area chosen for research will also have considerable implications for the way research progresses in it. A system that is nearer to being closed will tend to be better suited to experimental methods as controls can be put in place to make comparisons relatively straightforward. In these circumstances positivistic methods can produce generalisable findings that can show validity by their potential to be repeated by other researchers. Where closedness is a problem, it is for researchers who wish to utilise positivistic methods to show that they have robust means of dealing with the lack of control that this may result in. Experimental economists and psychologists have often found ingenious ways of dealing with this problem, but research in those areas is also subject to considerable contestation (Levitt and Gubner, 2009, Chapter 3) that would appear to suggest that the scientific rigour aspired to in the approach is not being entirely achieved.

As research systems become more open different ways of dealing with openness in design come to the fore. This asks difficult questions about sampling, asking whether random sampling is the most appropriate means, or whether a sample is supposed to achieve representativeness empirically, in which case the relevant dimensions of the population have to be reproduced in the sample, or theoretically, in which case a different approach might be taken in order to try and explore the dimensions of the theory to be tested instead. We might also want to utilise case studies in research, in which case there are decisions to be made as to whether such work is designed to meet representative criteria, or whether a 'critical' approach to sampling might be more appropriate.

What is important, again, is that researchers make informed choices, aware that they carry with them implications about the way that their research will proceed. Decisions made about time periods, and the degree of closedness that can be achieved within them, will affect the research design in very significant ways, and are subject to debate and contestation. It is important that researchers have an opinion on these issues, treating them carefully and thoughtfully, and be able to justify the choices that they make.

## Five things to remember about this chapter

1   The time period chosen in a social research design has significant consequences for the way that research will progress and the way it will be written up afterwards.
2   Approaches to social research that focus very much on the present often produce remarkable and dramatic accounts of the social world, but tend to be weaker on theory and often are so detailed that they appear unique. They are therefore different to generalise from, or compare to.
3   The more a social system can be regarded as an open system, the more difficult it is to successfully conduct an experiment because of the lack of control social researchers are able to exert over it.
4   One way of overcoming the problems of open systems, at least to some extent, is through sampling strategies that compensate through stratified strategies that attempt to produce comparisons and to work with the diversity of systems rather than work against it.
5   Case studies can be viewed in a number of different ways, with very different assumptions about the role of social research and of the social researcher. Understanding these differences allows researchers to say what kind of case studies they want to do, as well as the very different assumptions underlying them.

## Example – accounts of the financial crisis

The financial crisis of 2008 has already produced a large literature. Two genres within it show the difference between presenting an account of the crisis as it happened, from the perspective of those involved in its events, and those who try and take a detached view of it.

Two accounts taking a near first-person perspective are William Cohan's *House of Cards* and Andrew Ross Sorkin's *Too Big To Fail* (Cohan, 2009; Sorkin, 2009). These books aim to present a version of the crisis that unfolds in front of the reader, and are important because of the way they are able to provide an almost overwhelming amount of detail about actors and events. Unless the reader has an encyclopaedic knowledge of the crisis, it is almost impossible not to be swept along by the twistings and turnings of events. The accounts are almost phenomenological in trying to capture the key moments and the dilemmas faced by bankers and regulators during the crisis.

Using time in a different way are accounts of the crisis that spend little time on its specifics, but which attempt to locate it in terms of capital systems or previous economic policy. In Gamble's *The Spectre at the Feast* the crisis is presented in its historical context, linking it to far bigger changes such as globalisation, and so giving the reader an entirely different perspective on the events. Equally, books by Bootle and Cassidy (Bootle, 2009; Cassidy, 2009) include accounts of the financial crisis written in such a way as to present them in a highly summarised form and pre-interpreted to incorporate theoretical ideas from the authors to illustrate how the crisis was a particularly calamitous market failure.

Time is treated entirely differently in these accounts – in Cohan's and Sorkin's books, time is experienced as unfolding before the reader, giving a sense of suspense and emotion but with little attempt to provide any general points about the crisis that might explain it in terms of other crises or to make theoretical points. Gamble, Bootle and Cassidy, however, give far shorter versions of the crisis which they explain in theoretical terms, so allowing comparison and theory to be built or explored, but at the expense of historical detail – they are therefore forced to abstract far more from the specific details of the events and to combine larger swathes of time as a result.

What this illustrates is that the authors have adopted very different strategies in attempting to present the crisis, giving the reader very different understandings of the events as a result. Some books (e.g. Mason, 2009) even combine both, attempting to provide details about events before generalising and providing theory. But these strategies are conscious choices – the time span you settle on to present your research should be carefully considered.

---

# NINE

## Ethics – or what practices are appropriate in my research?

The lecture on ethics in research courses has a tendency to be where students take a reading week and switch off. This is often because it can be an area which seems terribly dull to them, and which imposes a number of rules and regulations that they can perceive to be a barrier to doing interesting work. This is often not helped by research bodies producing terribly generic statements of good ethical practice that don't always help students deal with the practical problems they encounter during their research. This chapter aims to deal with ethics through the lens of the logic of appropriateness to make it an integral part of student practice and embrace recent scholarship that produces a more critical and reflexive approach to ethical practice than often appears in research textbooks.

## Introduction

The area of ethics in social research is rather paradoxical. On the one hand, it is now, because of the widespread use of ethical codes and regulations, one of the most codified, predictable and mundane areas of social research. It is an area where there are clearly established rules and codes of conduct that have to be met, and so where there is the smallest room for reflexivity and discretion. However, on the other hand, ethics is an area where considerable debate and conflict still exist, especially in the applied areas of social research. Debates rage as to whether ethical codes of conduct that attempt to universalise particular principles might lead to funders being able to prevent particular types of research taking place, and whether ethical codes remove or conceal the wider responsibilities of researchers to society as a whole. This chapter considers these debates, asking readers to try to work out their own position in relation to them, whilst at the same time considering the implications of the fact that researchers who apply for, and receive, external funding are likely to be bound by ethical guidelines from those funders.

# The importance of ethics in research

Even though debates rage as how to best deal with ethics in social research, what is significant is that there is very little debate that ethics are important within it. The majority of social research has some kind of ethical impact, be it upon the participants of research, the funders of the research or the participants within it. To explore these impacts, we need first to define what we mean by ethics and then to give some practical examples of what kinds of impact ethics can have on social research.

## The Social Research Association

What is apparent, when reading through different ethical codes of practice published by research bodies, is that there isn't particularly a common view of what ethics might mean. The Social Research Association (SRA) (Social Research Association, 2003) define ethics in terms of core principles and obligations, emphasising that the aim of the document is to attempt to get social researchers, from the bottom-up, to make informed decisions and judgements about how to deal with the dilemmas that can come from doing social research.

## The Economic and Social Research Council

The Economic and Social Research Council (ESRC) (ESRC, 2005) suggests there is less room for debate, giving six principles which they suggest need to be addressed. There is a caveat that these principles need to be considered 'where applicable' (p. 1), but there is a clear sense that there is less room for discussion about those principles than there is in the SRA statement. Part of this comes from the ESRC being one of the major funders of social research in the UK, and so having the dual duty of not only giving guidelines for research, but also making sure that those guidelines are followed for grant-holders.

## The American Sociological Association

The American Sociological Association's (ASA) code of ethics (American Sociological Association, 1999) puts forward what it describes as 'enforceable' (p. 3) rules of conduct that represent a 'common set of values' for sociologists. A range of general principles (ranging from Professional Competence, Integrity, Responsibility and Respect for People's Rights, Dignity and Diversity) are listed, followed by a list of ethical standards linked to these principles. There are clear processes described for the enforcement of the code, the process of investigation and the sanctions that can be imposed upon ASA members as a result. As such, there is a third approach to ethics that is perhaps more like that of a professional body, with the possible sanction of expulsion from membership for sociologists who have been found not to comply with the rules.

As such, the SRA's approach to ethics appears to be to try and help social researchers navigate their way through ethical problems and dilemmas, giving some room for discussion and debate within the framework of ideas offered. The ESRC also offers a framework for researchers to consider problems they may come across, but there appears to be less room for discretion, and with the ESRC being a major funder of social research, there is the clear sanction that failing to conform could result in losing a very valuable source of research income. The ASA's approach is more like a professional organisation, offering what appears to be a set of rules that researchers must conform to or risk losing their right to be members of the Association. The degree to which researchers take this potential sanction seriously depends on how important they regard their membership to be. The SRA is therefore offering ethical guidelines to educate and guide researchers; the ESRC is offering an ethical framework to guide researchers generally, but with the clear sanction that funding will not be offered to researchers who breach it; and the ASA is offering a code of ethics that again offers strong guidance, but which members must follow or face expulsion from the Association. There is a range of positions from ethics as education and guidance, to ethics as guidance and condition of funding, to ethics as rules of conduct for membership. The three approaches therefore offer different, but related, frameworks for dealing with ethics. These frameworks are summarised in Table 9.1.

**Table 9.1** Different approaches to ethics

| SRA | ESRC | ASA |
| --- | --- | --- |
| Stress on obligations | Stress on key principles | Stress on the application of general principles in determining ethical courses of action |
| Obligations to society | Research should be designed, reviewed and undertaken to ensure integrity and quality | Professional competence – recognise limits of expertise, undertake only tasks for which they are qualified |
| Obligations to funders and employers | Research staff and subjects must be informed fully about the purpose, methods and intended possible use of research | Integrity – be honest, fair and respectful of others in their professional activities |
| Obligations to colleagues | The confidentiality of information supplied by research subjects and the anonymity of respondents must be respected | Professional and scientific responsibility – adhere to the highest possible scientific and professional standards and accept responsibility for their work. Show respect for other sociologists with whom they disagree, and be collegial to them |
| Obligations to subjects | Research participants must participate in a voluntary way, free from any coercion | Respect for people's rights, dignity and diversity. Eliminate bias in professional activities, sensitive to cultural, individual and role differences |
| | Harm to research participants must be avoided | Social responsibility. Apply and make public knowledge in order to contribute to the public good |
| | The independence of research must be clear, and any conflicts of interest or partiality must be explicit | |

We can therefore consider ethics in the context of social research to be about offering principles and guidance, conditions of funding (or ethical approval for a project), and rules of membership, with each of the three bodies taking a different stance in relation to these issues. Ethics are therefore important because social researchers are likely to confront difficult problems in their work, and so require guidance and help; because they must show that they are complying with particular principles and rules in order to achieve funding for their work; and because they may have to comply with particular rules in order to be a member of their professional body.

# The official line – what bodies such as the ESRC have to say

The passages above have given some idea of what research bodies have to say about ethics, but it is worth exploring some key ideas in more depth in order to bring out the tensions and difficulties that can arise in social research, and to give some practical examples of how ethics can be important. I will use the ESRC's framework as a source for discussion as it tends to be most clear about the principles it believes are core to social research, but most of the major principles are articulated in some form or other in other major social research bodies' statements.

The ESRC's principles of social research are articulated most clearly on pages 23–26 of their Research Ethics Framework. The six principles are presented in full below:

1 Research should be designed, reviewed and undertaken to ensure integrity and quality.
2 Research staff and subjects must be informed fully about the purpose, methods and intended possible uses of the research, what their participation in the research entails and what risks, if any, are involved. Some variation is allowed in very specific and exceptional research contexts.
3 The confidentiality of information supplied by research subjects and the anonymity of respondents must be respected.
4 Research participants must participate in a voluntary way, free from any coercion.
5 Harm to research participants must be avoided.
6 The independence of research must be clear and any conflicts of interest or partiality must be explicit.

## The principles in more detail

Principle 1 is described as a 'commitment to research of the highest quality' and is regarded as needing 'little further elaboration' (p. 23).

## Consent

Principle 2 is in many respects the cornerstone of the framework. It is organised around the principle of 'informed consent', which entails 'giving as much information as possible about the research so that prospective participants can make an informed decision on their possible involvement' (p. 24). The Framework suggests that, ideally, this consent should be sought in written form, signed off by the research subject, based on the objective of conducting 'research without deception', with research without consent only being sanctioned as a 'last resort where no other approach is possible' (p. 24).

The Framework goes on to explore informed consent in the context of cultural difference, and then considers cases where children, older persons or adults with learning difficulties might be involved, and how proxies might have to be incorporated into research where subjects are not considered to be competent to give their assent. Finally, it discusses the medical situations where tissue or blood samples have been given, and the rights of subjects in these situations.

Informed consent is the most discussed of the ESRC's Framework, and is arguably its centrepiece. I will discuss the problems that can sometimes come up when dealing with informed consent below, but for the moment suggest that, as a principle, it is, on the surface, rather difficult to argue against the idea that, when conducting research, those who participate should do so with their knowledge. If we accept the moral principle that we should 'do as we would be done by' then most of us would expect to be asked before we participate in research, and pre-informed of what the research is about, so we can make an informed judgement of whether we wish to be involved or not.

## Confidentiality and anonymity

The third ESRC principle is about confidentiality and anonymity, and is only covered briefly in the Framework. The ESRC write that researchers must 'take steps to ensure that research data and its sources remain confidential unless participants have consented to their disclosure, and in this latter case ensure that plans have been made for their storage and access to them' (p. 25). In practice what this tends to mean is that researchers have to be organised in the way that they store data – making sure that it is stored safely (which in an age of laptops and data keys can require a great deal of thought and organisation), but also making sure that, when it is being reported, the data preserves the anonymity of its research subjects. If researchers have guaranteed anonymity, they must make sure that reported quotes and incidents are not directly traceable to particular individuals, either by those outside the research context, or by those within it, with the latter often proving a particular challenge.

## Voluntary participation

The fourth ESRC principle is that research participants must participate in a voluntary way, free from coercion. This means that 'researchers should inform subjects of their right to refuse to participate or withdraw from the investigation whenever and for whatever they wish' (p. 25). Covert research, which involves deception, 'should only be used in a research setting where open and transparent research is impossible, whether because of the risks it might create for the researcher or participant, or in work where consent can be secured without providing the participant with full information about the project to avoid jeopardising its performance' (p. 25). As such, voluntary, non-coercive research is the norm, with the researcher being required to provide a strong case along the lines suggested where they wish to diverge from this. The extent to which research will diverge from this in practice varies tremendously between disciplines. There is a well-established tradition, for example, of psychologists having to mislead research participants about the nature of the research being conducted in order to investigate topics which, were participants told exactly what was going on, would severely reduce the potential for doing the research. Telling participants you are investigating under what circumstances they are likely to lie, for example, is likely to considerably alter subject behaviour, and so there would be room in the Framework for misleading subjects in order to gain their participation by telling them the research is about something else on the 'performance' grounds in the statement above, but subsequently offering them the right for their data to be withdrawn from the project after the research has been completed, at which time the nature of the research would have to be disclosed.

## Avoidance of harm

The fifth ESRC principle is that harm must be avoided. What this means is that participants' 'interests or well-being should not be damaged as a result of their participation in the research' and that 'no group should be unreasonably excluded from the research' (p. 25). Research must therefore take account of harm to the immediate subjects, but also to their wider communities, and research designs must 'consider potential harm to respondents' organisations or businesses as a result of the work' (p. 25). It is stressed that this is a matter of 'balance' with 'no simple rule' being applicable. As a result of this, the Framework also includes a lengthy discussion of risk in social research (pp. 21–22) which can help act as a guide. The reporting of research is especially considered in this light where 'results could be misconstrued and subsequently used by third parties against the interests of the research participants or the researchers themselves' (p. 25).

## Independence and impartiality

The sixth and final ESRC principle is that 'The independence and impartiality of researchers must be clear, and any conflicts of interest or partiality must be explicit' (p. 25). This means that the contribution of colleagues and collaborators must be acknowledged in the reporting of the research, and that there are no undeclared conflicts of interest (be they personal, academic or commercial) in the proposed work, and that 'the relation between the sources of funding and researchers' control over results is made clear' (p. 25). Researchers must also attempt to 'ensure that media coverage does not compromise research participants, co-researchers or funding bodies or breach confidentiality' (p. 26).

The idea of a conflict of interest can occur in a range of circumstances, be it concerned with personal relationships, relationships with work colleagues inside or outside academia, or in relation to commercial involvement in the research. The principle here is that such conflicts must be made clear and transparent so that they can be dealt with in the open, rather than suggesting they can be avoided completely. We might treat differently a proposal that offers to investigate a major public organisation by researchers already receiving large grants from that organisation, from one where researchers have few or no ties to it. Both are possible, but one is clearly more potentially complex than the other.

## Questioning the official line – or is it even possible to follow all these ethical principles?

Codes of ethics serve a valuable purpose in that they provide guidance and direction for researchers when having to think about the complex situations in which they often find themselves. However, they also pose a number of practical problems for researchers when the guidelines, frameworks and rules are interpreted in a literal way. This is because ethical principles, although entirely appropriate as a means of getting researchers to think about their practice, have to be applied in a reflexive rather than literal way. Applying ethical principles in a literal way runs the risk of the principles themselves becoming internally incoherent and the tensions and contradictions that run through them are shown to crash into one another. A few examples will illustrate this.

The ESRC's principles promote and support research that is conducted to achieve both integrity and quality, ensuring subjects' informed consent, confidentiality, anonymity, voluntary participation and harm avoidance, while maintaining independence and clearly declaring any conflicts of interest. In themselves, there is little to argue with here – all are statements of good sense.

### Contradictions

However, these statements, in many research contexts, can become somewhat contradictory. In situations where researchers are dealing with vulnerable groups, most of the principles will apply. Those who are unable or who find it difficult to speak for themselves must be protected, and researchers must be supremely mindful of their right not to participate or to withdraw their participation from research if they wish. But not all research falls into this category. Researchers will often be conducting research inside organisations, particularly public organisations, where many of those working are fully functioning adults who have their salaries paid for from public money and may even occupy managerial (or even senior managerial) roles in such organisations. Is it sensible to suggest that a senior public manager earning hundreds of thousands of pounds of money a year paid for by the public purse has the same ethical rights as a child who has little comprehension of the research process which is being carried out around them?

It is also the case that gaining consent in the manner suggested by the ESRC might have strong consequences for the way that the research proceeds. If, at the beginning of every interview a researcher carried out, they had to give a full briefing of the aims of the research and get participants to sign a consent form, it would be likely to result in it taking a great deal of time before any research could be carried out (affecting the quality of the research) but also would significantly affect the way that interview would be likely to proceed. If it has taken ten minutes to gain consent in an interview, it will likely take at least as long again before the participant relaxes into giving any kind of sensible answers because of the concerns and confusions that are likely to have arisen from being fully briefed and being asked to sign a piece of paper. Equally, again, this procedure makes little difference between participants – gaining consent is much more of an issue when dealing with vulnerable groups than with those in responsible positions holding a great deal of authority and power.

Social researchers may also find themselves in situations where, in order to carry out their research effectively, they need to, in the words of C. Wright Mills and Aaron Wildavsky, 'Speak truth to power'. The findings of social research may not always please policy-makers or funders (who may be the same people in the context of government-funded research), in which case an immediate contradiction might appear between quality and consent. If research indicates that there are serious problems in a particular area, but the funder does not want to hear this message, to what extent does the duty to a funder override the duty to society at large and with the researcher's duty to be independent?

Finally, there may well be a case for carrying out research that is covert, and which aims to expose particular societal problems that mean breaching both anonymity and confidentiality as well. Where research finds abuses of power, law-breaking and violence, then does the researcher still have to respect the individual rights of the research subjects, or are there other priorities which are more important? These are not flippant questions – because of the nature of social research, difficult issues and complex dilemmas arise that can make ethical guidelines appear as if they are fine in the abstract, but rather difficult to deal with in practice.

## A middle way?

It seems sensible to suggest that a middle way between regarding ethical guidelines as inviolable laws that can never be broken, on the one hand, and as abstract well-meaning statements that have little application in the real world, on the other, is to think of them as being the beginning of series of conversations that researchers have to be able to work their way through in terms of their particular research context. This takes us back again to the idea of a logic of appropriateness – we must be accountable for the choices that we make, and to show that we have reflexively engaged with guidelines and principles to come to a reasoned conclusion as to why we have made the ethical choices that we have. As a starting point, ethical guidelines provide a valuable means of beginning this discussion, but when interpreted literally, and without a particular research context in mind, they are in danger of becoming a mindless checklist of what researchers have to demonstrate before they are allowed to begin their work. Ethics should be regarded as a reflexive process of designing and conducting research rather than a necessary evil that must be overcome before research is carried out.

## The importance of balance and appropriateness in ethics

What this points to is the need for balance when thinking about research ethics. Instead of being something that needs to be approved before research is carried out, ethics needs to be an ongoing concern for researchers engaged in projects. Some examples will again hopefully illustrate this.

### Case one

A researcher is investigating managerial failure at a hospital. Upon beginning interviews with a range of nurses, it seems that the experience of being employed at the hospital over the last year has been so traumatic that several of them burst into tears in interviews when discussing what has happened at the hospital.

In this situation, should the researcher stop interviewing nurses, so jeopardising the research by excluding a key group, or should they instead carry on at the risk of apparently causing harm by asking nurses to relive events that they are clearly struggling with?

### Case two

A researcher wants to investigate how business leaders behave at conferences. If she goes along as an academic, she knows that business leaders will immediately make their excuses and talk to other people rather than her. To try to get around this, she books herself into the conference as a senior manager of her university (which she is not) and dresses appropriately to convey the impression of being a business leader. She makes the promise that if she is directly asked if she is conducting research, she will admit to it, but will behave as a participant at the conference for the rest of the time, taking notes between and after sessions as she is able.

Is this behaviour justifiable? Is the researcher able to take a weaker view of consent as she is dealing with senior business managers? Would your answer change if the conference was for newly qualified manager graduates instead, and the researcher were to go along and attempt to present herself as one of these? Is it acceptable to declare you are carrying out research only if closely questioned, and leave those that do not ask with a misleading impression?

# Different perspectives on ethics

As with all the other areas discussed in this book, ethics can be explored from different perspectives depending on the assumptions researchers hold about the world and of social research within it.

## Positivism and ethics

Taking a positivistic approach to research ethics tends to lead to one of two positions. The first is to follow the idea that the external world can be examined and interpreted relatively unproblematically, which leads to a similarly unproblematic view of research ethics. Ethical codes, in this view, are followed as being straightforward presentations of the rules of research. Researchers are required, in this view, to attempt to gain consent in whatever form is prescribed by the funder or the body to which researchers belong, and a rule-driven approach in which to follow the rules is to take an ethical approach to research. Much medical research tends to be conducted in this way, with ethical research being viewed as research that follows ethical guidelines.

A second positivistic approach appears in disciplines such as psychology where a complex approach needs to be taken as researchers and research designs acknowledge that, if participants are made fully aware of what the research they are participating in is actually about, it will not be possible to conduct it. Psychological experiments often deliberately mislead participants about the nature of the research being conducted. Now this is clearly a form of covert research, and one that would tend to be regarded as suspicious in other disciplines, but is generally allowed in psychology because so much research in that area would not be possible without some allowance of covert work. People are more likely to behave naturalistically, so the theory goes, if told they are being examined on their mathematical skills than if they are told that what is really being tested is their honesty in marking their own mathematical tests. Consent, in these situations, is often sought after the experiment has been conducted, where participants are fully briefed and have the right to withdraw their data from the experiment if they wish.

This second positivistic approach to ethics supposes that the social world has a more problematic relationship to the concepts we use to understand it, suggesting that, if told what is being researched, that will affect the way that participants behave. As such, a more complex approach to ethics is needed. This approach still takes place within a positivistic method, the experiment, but takes a more pragmatic approach to ethics in that it suggests that participants' understanding of the world (in particular the experiment before them) directly shapes the way that they perceive it. The mix of positivism in design and pragmatism in ethics is a mix that requires care from researchers and clear accountability from them when conducting research in this manner. It also asks difficult philosophical questions of experiments – if the concepts that participants use to understand them can affect designs so radically, how can we ever be sure that adequate controls are being put in place to use experiments in social research? However, the success of the design in a range of subjects from psychology itself through to contemporary economics suggests that, despite these difficulties, extremely valuable work can still be done.

## A realist approach to ethics

A realistic approach to ethics has something in common with the second positivistic perspective outlined above. Realists are looking for generative mechanisms in their work, mechanisms that are often concealed and which have complex relationships with outcomes. Realists accept interpretivism in that participants can have very different understandings of the world, but still point out that these different interpretations are still of an external world that constrains possible interpretations because it is ontologically prior to our understanding of it. What this points to is that the particular research context the researcher is in has to be significantly taken into account when thinking about its ethics. In a context where participants are vulnerable, great care has to be taken in achieving consent because the researcher will be in a privileged and even powerful position. However, where the researcher is investigating powerful public figures, the situation is very different, according to many realists. There, a researcher has an obligation to wider society to make powerful figures accountable to the public, and that obligation may be more important than the need to gain consent. Realism requires the research to reflexively engage with the particular context, and where powerful figures may want to conceal or not participate in research, then there may be an ethical obligation to conduct research without consent (Spicker, 2007).

The implication of a realistic approach to ethics is that codes of ethics can never be more than guides on how researchers should conduct themselves in general – the particular demands of the specific context will tend to overrule them. This points to a virtue ethics perspective in which individual researchers must be accountable for the choices that they make, rather than being held to a tightly defined code. There is a significant danger here of researchers attempting to justify any position they may hold in relation to ethics, and doing whatever kind of research they like. This is not what realists advocate, but arguing from a realist position certainly asks the question of how this problem can be avoided in practice. It suggests a professional role for researchers, and perhaps even a need for professional accreditation that might be withdrawn should researchers transgress ethics in their work. We are still an awfully long way from this – even when bodies such as the ASA suggest that they might expel members who do not comply with their ethical guidelines.

## Interpretivism and ethics

An interpretivist perspective on ethics, finally, emphasises the need to protect the least powerful in society, and because of its nature in exploring inter-subjectivity, places a strong role on the need to achieve consent and to treat data in the most careful way possible. In this view, ethics does not end when consent has been given, but as well as this, participants might be asked to comment on the way their data is used when writing up research in order to make sure that their views have not been misrepresented, and research might go further again in asking participants to co-produce research through incorporating their own ideas into the way it is reported through the use of visual representations or inclusion in presentations. Ethics are regarded as the cornerstone of research, with everything in the researcher's power being done to make sure that different viewpoints are incorporated and that participants' words and ideas are presented fairly in the research.

Interpretivism as a way of dealing with ethics implies a number of obligations on the researcher, that some researchers regard as a need to incorporate participants fully in decisions not only about their data, but also about the way the research should progress, with processes coming close to action research in some areas, with a levelling of researcher and participant roles where the two become difficult to distinguish. This raises ethical questions about the demands placed on participants through such work, but can be extremely valuable in settings where excluded voices are empowered, such as where communities become engaged to make decisions about their environment. It is also very apparent that this approach to ethics is also implied in Flyvbjerg's (2001) approach to case studies, where expertise is achieved through the co-production and involvement of both researchers and participants in social settings.

# Conclusion – doing what's right and doing what's ethical

Ethical guidelines are a good starting point for thinking about the dilemmas of conducting social research and for making sure that the most vulnerable are protected when research is being carried out. However, they should not become checklists by which researchers have to get approval for their work before a project begins; instead ethical principles should be what Clegg (1989) calls 'obligatory passage points' that researchers are required to navigate through in order to do their work. The contexts of social research makes a very significant difference to how the principles and frameworks put forward in ethical frameworks can be applied. We should be encouraging social researchers to be thinking about how they are engaging with ethics, not just at the beginning of their projects but all the way through them.

By no means should we be saying that ethical frameworks are infinitely variable on every point, depending on where and when the research is being carried out. They should reflect the best advice that professional bodies, funders and associations are able to offer to their members and researchers. But they also need to accept that there will be an inevitable need for flexibility around the principles and for the principles to be subject to discussion, criticism and debate.

The worst of all possible worlds is one in which ethical frameworks come to be regarded as meaningless checklists that can be cast aside once research approval has been granted, and where what's right for the researcher to do comes to be seen as separate from what the ethical guidelines appear to be saying. The dilemmas brought out in this chapter give some indications of situations where this might happen. Researchers need to be engaging with ethical principles all the way through their research, not just at the beginning, when they are seeking approval, and at the end, when they are trying to write it up.

It is also clear that the assumptions researchers hold about the context of their research, and the participants within it, have strong implications for the way that they will deal with ethics. Realists tend to regard those in power as potentially requiring less ethical consideration than those that are vulnerable because of their wider duties to conduct research for societal good. Interpretivists often take on a range of additional ethical responsibilities because they are working with vulnerable groups and often advocating an approach to their work that comes close to action research. These views, at the extremes, can result in very different approaches and views to ethics. It is important to understand the differences and what underpins them both to be able to explore the implications of ethical debate, but also to inform our own practices as researchers.

## Five things to remember about this chapter

1   If you want to apply to a funding body, you have to know what their ethics statements say, as breaching them in your proposal means you won't get any money.
2   Ethical research can be regarded as complying with a predefined code, or as a basis for research practice that is somewhat wider than codes are able to specify.
3   Different ethical codes appear to be designed with different purposes in mind and often carry very different ideas about social research.
4   The core principle of many ethical codes is that of informed consent, but there are arguments against even this principle. Understanding these arguments is important because it asks bigger questions about the role of social research.
5   The particular context a researcher is within will directly affect their relationship to research ethics principles. Researchers working primarily with the vulnerable often

have to comply with far tighter rules, which have to be factored in when designing research. Doing secondary research, however, is far less likely to encounter ethical problems and so is often favoured by researchers in fields where access to primary sites is difficult.

## Example – 'Teenagers telling sectarian stories'

Madeleine Leonard's (2006) 'Teenagers telling sectarian stories' is a fascinating article in terms of topic. It explores story-telling amongst teenagers in North Belfast, Northern Ireland, where the locality is still very much divided into Catholic and Protestant areas. The main method was focus-group research, and Leonard presents her results in terms of types of stories about the 'us' and 'them' divide that teenagers use in their story-telling in exploring both real and imagined memories. This work is extremely valuable in terms of what it reveals about growing up in a sectarian environment with a considerable history of violence.

What I'd like to focus on here, however, is what Leonard says about the way she conducted her research. She writes:

> Twenty pupils from four schools participated in the research. The schools reflected the religious, gender and class composition of teenagers in the area. All the teenagers were working class and attended schools segregated on the basis of gender and religion. Hence, the four schools comprised a Catholic boys' and girls' school and a Protestant boys' and girls' school. While at times the researcher acted as a facilitator during focus groups, the key intention of the research was to create an environment whereby teenagers would discuss in general terms what they would define as the good and not so good aspects of growing up in North Belfast. The researcher presented herself as a mother who lived in a different area of Belfast and who had a teenage son or daughter and was considering moving to North Belfast and wanted their advice on what it was like to live in the area. Teenagers produced complementary and conflicting accounts of the nice and not so nice aspects of growing up in their respective localities and a key aspect of their stories concerned placing themselves in opposition to the other community. In recalling events to support their stories or refute the stories of others, teenagers recounted events that happened to them or to others. (p. 1120)

Leonard, then, was conducting a kind of covert research in that she did not tell her participants that she was an academic researcher, but instead 'presented herself as a mother … who had a teenage son or daughter and was considering moving to North Belfast and wanted their advice on what it was like to live in the area'. Looking at the research from an ethical perspective, the obvious question is on what grounds covert research was carried out. There are a number of potential answers.

First, Leonard might argue that she was more likely to get school children to speak openly to a mother than to an academic researcher, and so it was necessary on those grounds to present herself in that light. However, at least in terms of her presentation in this piece, we are left to make this assumption ourselves. It would have added to the piece if the researcher had made this explicit. Regardless, it does ask questions of the research process that participants found themselves in focus group research with someone describing themselves as a parent, rather than a researcher.

Second, Leonard might have argued that the sensitive nature of the topic of the research made it necessary for research to be covert – the participants might have engaged in illegal or at least dangerous activities in the events they constructed their stories around, and that if they felt they were reporting these stories to someone in any kind of authority, especially from outside their community, that they would not participate authentically. This is clearly a related point to the first one.

In both cases, the issue of informed consent appears, and when dealing with children is particularly important. Researchers clearly need to do the type of research Leonard conducts – we need to understand the experiences of growing up in different communities, and we need to capture the voices of children in those situations as authentically as we can. However, from an ethical perspective the question is whether Leonard needed to conduct her research covertly, and we are left hanging somewhat on this point because of her lack of reporting of her reasons. This is a shame, as exploring how the issue of informed consent was dealt with in this work could have been particularly illuminating on the problems discussed in this chapter. Students to whom I have shown this piece since its publication have often reported to me that they find the explanation of the methods section presented above to be rather 'jarring' – opening up a number of questions about consent and researcher representation in fieldwork that they find challenging.

# TEN

## Writing up your research – or what can I say I've found?

### Introduction

Once you have navigated your way through the minefield of planning, designing and conducting social research, you still have what, for many people, is the most intimidating stage remaining – that of writing it up, either in terms of a report for a funder, a dissertation or thesis for an academic qualification, or a paper or book for publication. Each of these different forms has its own rules – funders are likely to have a highly prescribed report format you have to comply with, dissertations and theses will have conventional structures that you are usually wise to follow, and academic papers are usually structured in particular ways with particular word lengths (books may offer more flexibility, but are based on a proposal the author him- or herself makes, so to some extent the structure can vary). In all the cases, though, there are a range of issues that the author would be sensible to think about in order to minimise problems during the writing process and hostile comments later on during peer reviews. This chapter explores these issues, offering suggestions that I hope readers might find helpful, as well as getting them to think about how the way the research has been carried out links to the way it can be written about.

### The differences between description, analysis and argument

A good starting point is to go back to your original research proposal or plan, and to the method or methods involved in that. Methods carry with them ontological and epistemological commitments that also colour the way you can subsequently write about your research. If you have claimed to be testing hypotheses that will require you to write about the research in a different way than if you have promised to describe what is going on in a particular research setting. A couple of examples should again help to illustrate this.

## A realist view

A research proposal will tend to have promised to find causes for particular social phenomena. Realists treat social categories such as class and ethnicity as having causal properties that are independent of individual agents acting in social situations, and which may also be ontologically prior to them – that is, these categories pre-exist individuals which have to then adapt to and work around them. Our ethnicity pre-exists us for a realist, but we may interpret that ethnicity in a variety of ways depending upon social convention, history, our position in relation to other ethnicities, social class and a variety of other factors. However, for realists, ethnicity is a 'real' category with real causal properties. As such, an investigation into ethnicity will be trying to find out how ethnicity matters in particular social settings and contexts, and to demonstrate the causal mechanisms by which it exerts its effects.

## Realism and theory

Realists will usually have promised to find causes for social phenomena in their researcher proposals, and so must now find a way of communicating their research that shows how these causal mechanisms play themselves out. Realists will often be testing pre-existing theories, comparing their data to them, and attempting to work out which theory fits the data best, or elaborating on existing theory to show how it can be improved to better explain data. They will be happy to abstract from the data collected to try and generalise how the data collected might apply to other social contexts and situations – indeed they will regard it as a key part of the research process to try to achieve exactly that.

The realist position is analytical in that it is attempting to break the social world down into causal mechanisms, the results of which can be examined. This does not necessarily mean that the realist programme is reductionist, wishing to reduce the world to a few key variables. Complexity theory has a great deal in common with realism (Byrne, 1997), and the complex interactions between mechanisms are also a central part of the realist agenda. However, realists wish to make a theoretical contribution through their work, and this will involve trying to capture the most significant elements of particular social phenomena and attempting to explore how, when and where they work.

## Actor-network theory and description

In contrast, social researchers that find a greater inspiration in anthropological methods and accounts will tend towards the view covered earlier in the book that actor-network theorists prefer. In this view, the world does not pre-exist us in any way except through our own concepts. Even what we might regard as relatively mundane descriptive categories, such as mountains and hills, are human concepts that do not capture nature in some kind of neutral manner, but instead impose ideas upon it.[1] As such, the best we can do in these circumstances is to try and describe the social world in all the rich detail we find within it, adopting multiple perspectives and, unlike the realist, not adjudicating between them. The world is 'messy', and we must try and capture that mess through a careful description of it rather than attempting to break it down.

## Theory and actor-network theory

Actor-network theorists will regard pre-existing theories about a situation as concepts that actors in that situation may or may not be aware of using to understand the world, but will seek to reflexively challenge their own preconceptions of a situation in order to try and see it as freshly as possible. Pre-existing ideas and theories have no particular precedence over new ones, as the aim of the social research is description not theory generation. Researchers writing from this viewpoint are not really interested in attempting to find causal mechanisms, but in finding out how actors within social situations form relationships, and how ideas and theories become transformed and translated between them as a result. The agenda is explicitly anti-reductionist in that the accounts should be as detailed and rich as possible, with little or no claim that anything found in a particular social situation can be generalised to any other.

## Comparing writing agendas

As such, a realist writing agenda would be far closer to the idea most lay-people would have of what social research might look like. It would explore existing theories and ideas in a review, conduct either a fieldwork or secondary review to find causal mechanisms, test what has been found in that fieldwork or secondary review against pre-existing theories, modifying and synthesising them as was required to improve them, and then produce conclusions that show what has been found. The actual sequence and form of a report written in this way can vary, but most of these elements will probably be present at some point or another.

An actor-network writing approach would, in contrast, attempt to provide a description that made as little use of existing concepts and theories as possible (unless they were a central part of the discourse of research subjects themselves), and to show how the social world was constructed by the actors (both human and non-human) through careful description. There would be little attempt at theory

---

[1] Watch the film *The Englishman Who Went Up a Hill and Came Down a Mountain* to see how even categories we can treat as 'natural' can be problematised and can become political.

generation, but the work could still be political by giving voice to excluded actors and showing sources of resistance and possible change to dominant discourses.

The important thing, then, is that the approach a researcher has taken in conducting research has an influence in the way that the research is going to be written up. It is possible to produce work that is original, attempting to impose realist expectations upon an anthropological account, for example, but these will require a great deal more justification and care than writing in the form that 'fits' the research process more closely.

As such, we might present three research writing strategies – analysis (scientific, realist), description (analytical, interpretivist) and argumentation, which is probably generic to all writing at least to some extent, and to which the vast majority of writing depends upon in some form or another. It is therefore to argument that this chapter turns next.


## Making an argument – what have you found out?

One of the most common criticisms that academics make of student work is that it 'contains no argument'. Now there is a view that, within the actor-network approach, there is no need for an argument, as description is the only goal of the research. This appears to me to be a little disingenuous though – what we describe and how we describe it have significant implications for any description we produce, but as well as that, how we choose to structure, order and take the reader through the description all matter profoundly. Even descriptions have arguments, whether the author intends them to or not. Humans cannot escape from attempting to impose order on what they find, even when there is actually no pattern there at all (Taleb, 2008). Being aware of argumentation is important for all social researchers, even if they are trying to avoid doing it as much as possible!


## The bases of good arguments

The differences between an argument (which is what most academics want students to produce) and the way that many students structure their pieces is that an argument takes the reader through a set of reasons why the author should be believed about a particular point or claim that they wish to make, whereas what most students sometimes produce is a list of not obviously related points that may or may not be reasons and which may or may not be supported by evidence or example or anything else. The key question you should be asking yourself is to ask why your reader should believe you every time you make a point or present a piece of evidence.

An argument, then, is not an attempt to *have* an argument in the sense of a disputation or row (although it can be that too). Neither is it an attempt to state a particular viewpoint – that isn't enough. An argument is an attempt to support a particular view with reasons why it should be believed by others. In order to break down an argument it is useful to introduce some terms that can help a researcher think about the way they make claims when they write.

A conclusion is, as the name implies, the statement which you are attempting to convey, and for which you are going to give the reader reasons to believe. The reasons you give the reader for believing your conclusion are called premises.

## An example

An example should try and make this clear. The American Physiological Society makes the following argument:

> Animals make good research subjects for a variety of reasons. Animals are biologically similar to humans. They are susceptible to many of the same health problems, and they have short life-cycles so they can easily be studied throughout their whole life-span or across several generations. (http://the-aps.org/pa/animals/quest1.html)

So the conclusion is that 'animals make good research subjects' (we might also include 'for a variety of reasons' in that conclusion as well). The premises, or points made to support the conclusion, are that animals are biologically similar to humans, that they are susceptible to many of the same health problems and that they have short life-cycles (which allows them to be studied across their whole life span or across several generations). Now, when assessing that argument, the reader needs to look to see if the premises provide adequate support for the conclusion. There are a number of ways that the writer could try to achieve this.

# Supporting a conclusion

## Support by authority

First, the writer can try to achieve support by authority – that is, they can cite studies in support of the individual premise that they are trying to make. A common mistake here is looking for studies that support all of the premises a researcher is trying to make – this is possible, but leaves writers open to the criticism of misreading authors who might have more finely grained views that this approach might suggest, or of bunching their argument together rather than exploring it point by point. Support by authority is clearly common in academic writing, and if there are key studies in the field that the writer is working, reviewers will often expect them to be cited to show that the writer is aware of them, and so can claim to know the field (not least if the reader has written extensively within it and so might expect to be cited!).

So in the case above, an argument by authority would attempt to find studies, particularly studies that are authoritative (in terms of the number of times they have been cited, or centrality within the field, or importance of the arguments made), and to cite them when the writer presents the particular premise. So, there might be studies showing the extent to which animals are similar to humans, and someone wanting to make the same argument as the APS would be showing support for authority by citing them next to that claim.

## Support by example

A second way of making an argument is supporting it by example, and is perhaps most often made by moving from the specific to the general, and occurs frequently in everyday speech. It is, however, an approach we have to be careful of when writing (especially for academic audiences). This type of argument by example might go as follows:

> Nobody I know would vote for Barack Obama, so he can't possibly win another term as President.

If we break this argument down into a conclusion and premises, you'll see that I reversed the order they appear from the earlier example (just seeing if you are still awake) – the premises are ahead of the conclusion rather than following it. The conclusion is that 'Barack Obama can't possibly win another term as President' and the premise is that 'Nobody I know would vote for Barack Obama'. This argument attempts to persuade us through the example that 'nobody I know' would do something, so it won't happen. Now this may or may not be a weak argument. If I know the majority of everyone who is eligible to vote in the United States, then the argument stands up pretty well. If I know only a tiny proportion of people in that category, it's not a good argument unless I can show that the people I do know are representative of the population at large, which will require an additional premise (and the people I know are representative of the people of America) and evidence of some kind that this is the case. We would then have to assess the extended version of this argument and make our minds up as to whether this is the case or not.

Argument by example is that it is widespread in our everyday lives and a great deal of opinion is formed using it (Weston, 2000). The point of reflexive social research is to understand argument by example, but to be able to see other viewpoints and to be actively questioning and challenging to it. In general, argument by example is a much weaker way of making an argument than argument by authority unless there is additional supporting premises and evidence.

## Support from empirical research

Another kind of argument by example comes when researchers give examples from their empirical research to support their argument. You might make the point that research subjects in a certain context tend to talk about managers of their organisations, using examples from them that describe or present them as incompetent (and when you see examples being presented this is a sure sign that an argument by example is taking place). These examples might be also be illustrated by the managers failing to be able to deal with a particular incident.

This form of argument by example is a very common occurrence in any kind of qualitative social research, which as we know from earlier in the book, is often justified on the grounds that it aims to get close to research participants and demonstrate expertise by immersion in a particular social context for research. To demonstrate this expertise, researchers use quotations and examples.

The problem this form of argument by example has is that researchers must show (or be trusted in showing) that the examples or quotations that they provide are both credible and that they support their arguments (that they provide good premises for the conclusion they are trying to show). This can be extremely difficult to achieve in a short academic paper as researchers will usually have far more data than they are able to include, and, as noted earlier in the book, they may also have only limited room to report their methods so that they can be assessed. This gives researchers a range of choices.

Should researchers show one or two participants' data only, to show their responses throughout the paper or report and so offer consistency in that they give an in-depth insight into those participants? This works if the researcher can show that the participants chosen are representative of the group included, or if they are particularly illuminatory in some way – being an extreme example of a particular viewpoint perhaps. This strategy runs the risk of reviewers claiming that insufficient data has been presented to make the case for this reflecting the research site as a whole, but gains in terms of offering readers data that may have a greater coherence as it comes from just a few participants. Alternatively, the researcher might want to show as wide a range of participants as possible in his or her data, but this runs the risks of making the data appear extremely fragmentary, and of accusations being made by reviewers that they are just mixing and matching data they have collected to support whatever points they wish to make.

As such, using quotations and examples from the field appears to be the most obvious way of using argument by example, but carries with it problems however researchers choose to do it. The most important thing is for the researcher to be up-front and clear about how they have chosen to write their piece, to provide justification for it and to provide evidence that what they are claiming is in fact the case. So using only one or two subjects' data on the grounds that they are representative requires evidence to be produced that this is the case. Equally, producing evidence from a range of recipients requires researchers to demonstrate that the multiple fragments of data do cohere into some kind of story that they wish to present, rather than being just a range of isolated things that subjects happened to say or do.

## Argument by analogy

A third way of making an argument is by analogy. Social science has a lot of these, as has everyday life. Every song that tries to explain that 'love is like… [something or other]' is trying to make an argument by analogy. In organisation studies Gareth Morgan (1986) produced one of the most influential books in recent times that is explicitly based on providing analogies for organisational life. Morgan's argument is that by breaking free of the metaphors that abound in organisation life (cultures, organisms, brains, political systems, psychic prisons, etc.) managers can do a better job of understanding what is going on around them. Karl Marx was also a thinker who made significant use of analogy, including the following:

> Capital is dead labour, which, vampire-like, lives only by sucking living labour, and lives the more, the more labour it sucks. (*Capital*, Volume 1, Chapter 10)

So capitalism is like an undead creature here, because it lives only by exploiting 'living labour'. The point about analogy is that is requires, in order to be persuasive, an example that is both relevant and similar. What is interesting in Marx's example is that you will tend to find vampires both relevant and similar to capital (and to some capitalists too) if you regard capitalism to be an economic system that exploits the many in favour of the few and where the very rich get richer on the back of the poor (even in writing that sentence notice the analogy 'on the back' and think about its connotations). However, supporters of capitalism will tend to regard this argument by analogy as silly and unsupported. Analogies can be very powerful – their use in everyday life is pervasive. But they won't work if others don't think your analogy is either relevant or appropriate. Again, then, they have a place in academic writing but an argument by analogy will usually not be regarded as being as strong as an argument by authority.

So arguments are most commonly based on authority, example or analogy, and in academic writing arguments by authority are usually regarded as the most credible (so long as the authorities they cite are also credible). Arguments by example are common when writing up field notes, but authors have choices to make about how they present their data. Examples by analogy surround us all the time, but care must be taken not to isolate readers who are confused by or disagree with the analogies chosen, in case this undermines the claims that the researcher is trying to make.

## Other concerns with arguments

There are two other main interrelated areas worth discussing in relation to the way that researchers write up their arguments; arguments about causes and the underlying differences between deductive or inductive arguments.

## Arguments about causes

In many approaches to social research, coming up with the causes of a particular phenomena are regarded as being key to the research agenda. However, we have seen in earlier chapters that causation is a complicated issue, with there being at least three approaches to it: the constant conjunction model; the generative mechanism model; and the model that stresses that causes aren't terribly important in social research. Each of these approaches to research requires that research be written up in a way that is compatible with the assumptions underlying the way the research was conducted.

## Constant conjunctions and argument

A constant conjunction model, one that attempts to bring causes and effects together by showing that they always co-occur, has to show that the cause and the effect are inextricably linked with one another, or at least that they are inextricably linked within a particular research context or space or time. Within economics and finance this is often achieved through statistical testing, particularly through the use of correlation and regression. This approach has a range of well-established tests for demonstrating that the causes authors are showing form a statistically valid relationship with one another. However, of course, a statistically significant relationship is not the same as a substantively significant one – correlated events do not necessarily cause one another. The world is full of coincidences, and we have to be sure that just because data seems to indicate a causal relationship that one is actually occurring. Equally, a correlation doesn't tell us which variable is the cause and which is the effect – just that two things appear to be statistically related and many correlated events can have a single cause. We therefore have to be careful in ascribing the sequence of events as well as claiming that a relationship exists.

A constant conjunction model will be further supported if not only can a relationship be shown, but the researcher can explain how it is meant to be occurring. The researcher might use pre-existing theory here, or be able to give a persuasive new theory about the relationship he or she has found. One of the most contentious writers in recent times is Stephen Levitt whose work was popularised in the book *Freakonomics* (Levitt and Gubner, 2007). Levitt's work claims that falling crime rates in the 1990s are related to changes in abortion law decades earlier, and that the reduction in crime in the latter period had little to do with policies about 'zero tolerance' as is often claimed, but simply that many of those who would have been disruptive criminals in the latter period were simply not born. So Levitt has both a theory and a statistical model that he argues supports it. Whatever you think of this argument, and whether you think the data presented by Levitt supports it, it is clearly a provocative one that provides a model for social research of this type.

## Generative causation and argument

A generative model of causation requires researchers to be able to show that the 'deep' causes they have identified in their work are actually related to the particular effects that they claim to have empirical evidence for. Again, correlation can help in this task by showing that there is at least a statistical relationship between two variables, but those in favour of generative causation tend to favour the construction of models to try and show how relationships work as well as demonstrating that they exist. Generative models of causation can be solely quantitative, but often incorporate approaches that include both quantitative and qualitative data, accepting that in order to explore how generative mechanisms manifest themselves in specific locations it is necessary to explore them in depth in a way that quantitative methods may not be able to achieve. Generative models are often about testing or elaborating particular theories, and showing which ones fit the data best – about showing which mechanisms seem to be having the most effect. As such, writing up a generative model requires the researcher to make the links between the mechanisms specified and the effects they cause, even if they are not immediately related to one another in terms of time or space.

So if you are making the argument that social class is an important factor in deciding the educational attainment of individuals, realists would want, not only to show strong statistical evidence of a link (probably including variables that might have considerable lags), but also to explain exactly how social class affects educational achievement through the use of detailed case studies that demonstrate in detail how the effects found in the quantitative analysis play themselves out.


## Making an argument where causation isn't important

Finally, there is the argument that causation isn't important. This has been most associated with the actor-network approach within this book. What is important here is that researchers relying upon an epistemological stance that is based on actor-network theory don't start building elaborate theories about the social world and don't claim to have found causes and effects beyond the local. If the aim of this research programme is descriptive, researchers have to find ways of writing up their research that complies with this goal, but also allows them to produce work that is sufficiently robust to be accepted by reviewers. This can be a considerable challenge as the accusation that research is just 'telling stories' can be made. However, Latour's work shows that research within this tradition can be vital and political (Latour, 2005), and this is an aspiration that work of this type can aspire to as a means of answering the 'so what?' question reviewers can sometimes ask of it.

This kind of argument is also likely to lend itself to unconventional presentations of findings. We have already described Mol's attempt to present her ethnographic results alongside her reflections on the research process. Attempting to present the results of research that provide as rich a picture as possible might include the use of images, film, interactive media or anything that can get across something about the case being explored in the research. Here, argument by analogy might be the explicit aim – to try to change readers' (or observers') minds by presenting research in a form that deliberately challenges their preconceptions.

# Deductive and inductive arguments

In earlier chapters deductive and inductive research strategies have been discussed. Equally, arguments can be deductive and inductive, and it is worth spending a few moments to show how this is the case.

## Deductive arguments

Deductive arguments are those for which, if the premises are true, then the arguments must be true as well. There are two forms of this that are commonly found. The first is where an argument is structured as follows:

1   If (p) then (q)
2   p
3   Therefore q

So, we can say that:

1   If there are millions of habitable planets in the universe, then intelligent life must exist on more than one of them
2   There are millions of habitable planets in the universe
3   Therefore, intelligent life must exist on more than one of them

Now, in order for this argument to work, you would have to be able to demonstrate that the first statement is the case (that the 'if' leads to the 'then') and that the second statement is also the case (which is an empirical claim that could need justification). Only then would the third statement be deductively true and the argument be made.

A second form of deductive argument is in many ways the opposite:

1   If (p) then (q)
2   Not q
3   Therefore, not p

So:

1   If social class was important, then we would all still talk about it
2   We don't talk about social class
3   Therefore, social class isn't important

So for this argument to work, we have to demonstrate again that there is a link between the 'if' and the 'then' in statement one, and empirically demonstrate that statement two is also empirically the case. Only if both of those are the case is statement three deductively true.

## Adding several steps

Deductive arguments can of course build chains of reasoning along the lines of:

1  If (p) then (q)
2  If (q) then (r)
3  (p), therefore (r)

Or they can be expressed in terms of a choice:

1  (p) or (q)
2  Not (p)
3  Therefore (q)

What is important is not the many forms of deductive arguments that can be made, but rather that researchers are aware of what form *their* argument is making, and whether there is sufficient grounds to support it. Is the argument you are making based on logic (claiming that one thing must lead to another because of its form) or empirical (that one thing always seems to lead to another)? If you are structuring your argument in the form of a choice (as above) is it a genuine choice you are presenting, or are you presenting a false one (as in 'Either you must be a racist or stupid, you're not a racist so you must be stupid').

## Inductive arguments

A deductive argument is certain, provided that the premises can be shown to be true. This is because the conclusion is actually contained in the premises. An inductive argument, on the other hand, is one where the conclusion is probably true, provided that the premises are also true. This is because the conclusion goes *beyond* the premises. The classic example of an inductive argument is that, because the sun has risen every day of my life so far, it will rise tomorrow. So the conclusion is that the sun will rise tomorrow, and the premise is that it has risen every day of my life so far. Now the problem with this sort of argument is that, as we noted above, the conclusion goes beyond the premises.

An inductive argument has much in common with the discussion on argument by example above – they are much the same thing. An argument by induction depends on three things:

1   Whether the previous observations are accurate, how frequent they are and how comprehensive they are. This question asks whether we can show that the observations of the past seem to have been accurately recorded, how many times we have recorded them and how many times these observations have been recorded in relation to the total number of times the phenomenon has occurred.
2   Whether the causal link between the two events seems to be persuasive and strong. This question asks whether the writer has explained how the two events are linked and asks whether that explanation is credible or not.
3   Whether the situation the inductive argument is now being applied to is similar or the same as the context in which it was generated. This question asks whether the case the author is attempting to show is relevant to the argument and in turn is relevant to the previous cases.

So in the case of the sun rising, there is a pretty good case for it rising tomorrow in terms of question (1) in that not only has the sun risen every day in my life, but also every day in every human being's life in recorded history. In terms of question (2), it is pretty dicey though – we have provided no explanation why the sun should rise tomorrow, and perhaps need to work on this. In terms of question (3), we also have a strong argument however – unless something occurs to make tomorrow significantly unlike today (nuclear war, for example), then it seems reasonable to assume that it will be much the same, especially given the answer to question (1).

Assessing an inductive argument therefore depends on assessing evidence carefully, as well as looking at the logic of what the writer is claiming – with the logic being especially important in relation to question (2).

# Structuring a piece of writing to bring out your argument

Now that we've looked at the ways that arguments can be structured, we can address how they can be written up to bring out what you are trying to say.

## Audience

The first thing to bear in mind is that you need to have an idea of who your audience is, and to be able to find an approach and structure that fits for them. In the case of research reports this will often be prescribed, so you will have few choices. However, it is still a good idea to get hold of a report that the funder or commissioning body regards as being a good example in order to get a sense of what is expected of you. In the case of writing a journal article, then, you need to look at the past few years of that journal in order to make sure that you are citing relevant research (remember, journals send papers to authors who have published with them for review), but also to get a sense of what the house style is. Journals usually have pretty comprehensive instructions for authors available, but there is no substitute for spending time looking at pieces that the journal has already published. For student essays and assignments, again ask to see examples of work that was highly regarded in order to get a sense of what is expected of you.

Once you've spent some time looking at work that is already out there, there are some general guidelines you can bear in mind that can help to make your argument persuasive.

## Your contribution

It is useful, for both yourself and your readers, to make clear, as soon as possible in your piece, what the contribution your piece makes to our understanding. Doing this will remind you to make sure that you cover what you promise and it will give your readers a reason for reading your work.

## Balance

First, unless you are specifically trying to publish a polemic, you need to show that you are being even-handed in your treatment of both previous work and any new empirical material you have collected. When reviewing others' work, generosity is likely to provoke a more favourable response from reviewers than hostility, with the latter also requiring more space and time to justify adequately. Not only is it polite to treat others' work with respect, it is also probably more efficient in terms of the space that is available. It is perfectly reasonable to disagree with what others have said, but there is a world of difference between doing this in an aggressive and dismissive way, and doing it thoughtfully and carefully.

Examining others' arguments can be done in exactly the same way as I have suggested above for looking at your own. What are the conclusions other authors have drawn? What are their premises? Which premises seem to be supported and which do not, and how might this lead to you to revise the conclusions that authors have so far drawn? Do the premises that are supported lead you to new conclusions, or to the ones that previous research has led to?

## Your research question

When designing your research, ideally you will have found a question that your work is aiming to address. This question might be something you have identified as a gap in current research – something that simply has not been covered (or covered in much depth), in which case you still need to show that your question is important – but just because your question is novel is doesn't mean it is important.

You might want to apply a finding from others' research to a new context to see if it applies there as well, in which case you need to explain why that finding is important, and why it might be transferable to the new context (in effect, you are attempting to establish an inductive argument). Whatever you are trying to address, you need ideally to be able to show that it arises in some way from previous work (which shows reviewers that you are an expert in the field, and so are qualified to conduct research), even if you are arguing that it arises from its absence, as in the case of identifying a 'gap' in the research.

Once you have come up with the question that you are attempting to answer, and have explained why it is important, you can then proceed to explain how you went about answering it. This is the tricky methods section.

## The methods section

One of the most important things to bear in mind when writing up a methods section is to be able to explain, even if in terms of a brief outline, how the research was conducted, which will often bring with it the researcher's commitment to a particular approach to social research, at least in terms of its attendant epistemology. When writing up methods sections, then, be clear about what you are communicating to reviewers not only in terms of how you did the research (in terms of the nuts and bolts of the process, how many subjects there were, what the specific tools and techniques you used were) but also showing how those methods were the most appropriate in answering the question that you asked and what kind of knowledge you expected to produce as a result. If you were attempting to prove or disprove a hypothesis, this carries with it an approach to research that carries through how it will have been conducted and what kind of results a reviewer will expect to find. If you claim to be testing a hypothesis, then you need to show how it is going to be tested, how you know whether it will have been proved or disproved, and to be able to draw conclusions that clearly link to the findings you have found in the research. This is a different way of writing about social research compared to someone conducting an ethnography, which might lead instead to largely inductive arguments based on harnessing what they have found in terms of their subjects' responses to open questions, and with no attempt to test hypotheses or show causes.

## Arguments

When writing up your research, you need to make sure that whenever you make a claim, the premises supporting it are adequate to do the job. You need to be making the link between your conclusions and premises as clear as possible and showing how the two relate. You need to make sure that each premise is adequately supported by either logical or empirical evidence, and to make sure you have considered how your arguments might be interpreted differently by someone else. What other explanations might there be for what you have found? What objections might someone else offer?

Finally, there is a tendency for researchers to want to try and make a grand, eye-catching claim. If you have found something novel and important, congratulations and well done. However, most research, although it makes a contribution to the academic world, doesn't achieve that. Don't over-claim – specifically don't claim more than you have shown. Doing this gives reviewers an opportunity to discredit your work, undoing the good work you have done up to this point. Be clear about what you think the contribution your work makes – in fact put this in the opening of your paper or proposal. But don't over-claim – the bigger the claim you make, the more supporting evidence you are going to need to be persuasive.

## Conclusion – writing up research so that it is clear to you (and to everyone else)

In conclusion, then, you increase your chances of successfully writing up your research if you keep in mind a few principles that, in themselves, aren't that complicated to suggest in theory, but are rather more difficult to keep to in practice. Very few pieces of published research are perfect in the sense that they get everything right – that they are entirely clearly written, they are argued perfectly and they manage to achieve all of the research goals. However, you will be more successful in your writing by following a few simple ideas.

First, you need to know who you are writing for. Find out about the readership, be it a research council, an academic journal or a periodical of some other kind. Look to see what kind of research they seem to like, even if it means that you end up having to look for funding elsewhere or for a different outlet for your work.

Second, become more aware of the kind of arguments you tend to make. When writing, do you adopt inductive or deductive forms? Look at the conclusions you are trying to come to and the premises that support them. Are the premises based on logic or empirical information? Does the logic stack up? Is there sufficient empirical data to support the point you are trying to make with it? Are your arguments based on citing authorities that you can depend upon and which will be trusted by others, or are they less than authoritative? Do the sources you claim for authority actually support what you are trying to say, or are there differences that might be spotted by reviewers and which might undermine your argument?

Third, when reviewing others' work, be generous rather than hostile. However, do look to see what kind of arguments they are making and whether the premises support them. If there are gaps in the literature, are they there because those topics aren't that interesting, or are they genuinely new avenues for research?

Finally, make clear when you are writing exactly what your contribution is – make clear to reviewers and to readers what it is they can get from your work that they can't get elsewhere. Then make sure you live up to that. Don't claim more than you can deliver, and don't conceal your contribution to such an extent that a reader has to go through page after page before finding out what it is that you think your paper or report is all about.

## Five things to remember about this chapter

1   The way that you conduct your research places limitations in the way you can write it up. If you've conducted an experiment, there are definite expectations in the way you have to write it up. The same thing applies to other methods – find a good example in the published literature of the type of work you've done and see how it might provide you with a template.
2   Making an argument is a key part of presenting your work. Think on what basis you are making your arguments and make sure they are adequately supported.
3   You need to make sure that the way you argue about cause and effect is compatible with your research strategy – be clear what your assumptions are.
4   Think carefully who your audience is, make sure that you present your work in a balanced way (unless you are trying to write a polemic) and be clear what your contribution is – give your readers a reason to look at your work.
5   When reviewing others' work, bear in mind that they are human beings too. If you are going to be critical, do so in a generous spirit. It is fine to criticise others' work, but in doing so, you don't have to be rude.

# ELEVEN

## Writing up reviews and putting together proposals – or can you provide some examples of all of this?

## Introduction

Having provided a grounding in the conceptual issues involved in thinking about research and generic advice in how to write it up, this chapter gives hands-on advice for how students can deal with two practical problems they often have to face. It covers how to write up a literature review and how to make a research proposal.

Chapter 10 covered writing, especially focusing on how to make the kind of argument researchers need to make consistent with the type of research they are carrying out. The approach taken there was generic, but perhaps applied most to the writing of papers of one kind or another. This chapter, because it is focused on particular aspects of writing, incorporates what was said in Chapters 2 and 10 in a more 'nuts and bolts' way to make the approach advocated here as clear as possible.

## Putting together a literature review

Most researchers, at some point or another, will have to write a literature review. For many researchers this is the most tedious part of their job – the thing that keeps them from the field, and which involves instead trawling through electronic and paper-based sources, visits to libraries and the sheer hard work of going through the research that has already been conducted in a specific area.

Many of these aspects aren't the most exciting part of doing research. However, the process of putting together a literature review can be interesting, challenging and rewarding, if you think about it in a particular way and so long as you are prepared to organise it properly.

# The role of the literature review

A good place to start is to ask exactly what the purpose of a literature review is. The short answer, of course, is that there are several. A literature review should show the reader that the researcher knows what they are talking about – that they understand previous research in the area and are able to demonstrate mastery of it.

## Exercise

Imagine that you are reviewing someone's literature review. How would you be able to tell if they were an expert in the field? What would you be looking for? What would indicate to you that they hadn't mastered the area?

I think some key indications of whether someone has mastered a field are as follows (and these, again, are the sort of things that reviewers tend to be looking for):

1   The researcher cites key sources in their review. There are some sources that are so inextricably associated with particular topics that you have to include them in your review, or you risk making it appear that you don't know about them. These sources have been central in shaping debate in the field, so even if you're not going to talk about them, you probably need to provide a good reason why. When you are conducting your review, these are the sources that will come up again and again, and will therefore be amongst the most-cited papers in the area in databases such as Web of Knowledge or Google Scholar.

2   The researcher doesn't simply reiterate what authors have said, but is able to relate their views to one another, exploring similarities and differences. What this amounts to is the researcher having an argument about the existing literature – having something to say about what it covers (and what it doesn't), about how the authors agree and what about, and about potential gaps in what has been researched so far. A researcher should be conducting a review to have something to say about it, not simply to report, blow by blow, on what others have said. If you aren't adding value to the existing research by exploring the debates thematically in some kind of way, rather than simply repeating what authors say, then what is the point of the review?

3   The researcher is able to come to a conclusion about the existing literature, based on clear and supported premises, that set up the rest of the study. What this means is that the literature review must serve a purpose beyond simply showing that the researcher is an authority – it must link in to other parts of the paper or book or report that is being put together and do some work within it. The review might end by showing there is a need for research of a particular type that the researcher is now going to provide, or it might provide a new synthesis of the research that combines it and reinterprets it in a new light. It might include previously overlooked sources that illuminate what we know about the field. What it must do is add value in some way to sources that it is citing, either through combination, or through synthesis, or through debate, or by showing that the present field has gaps.

How can you achieve this? What follows is a step-by-step guide to carrying out a literature review. This necessarily involves a little repetition of the material presented in Chapter 2, but presented in a different form (as a 'how to' guide) rather than a critical discussion.

# Doing a literature review

## 1 Working out what your topic is

The first problem researchers face in putting together a review is to work out exactly what it is they are looking for. This isn't as obvious as it may seem because it can be quite difficult to come up with a summary of the key words of your topic that can be used to enter into a research database, or to be able to pick out relevant articles from paper-based journals from looking at their titles or abstracts alone. Ironically, it is hard to come up with what your topic is about until you already know all about it, and so you can't expect to come up with the key terms you are searching for until you've done some reading and research.

Most importantly, perhaps, you must expect the process of defining your topic to be an iterative one that will take several attempts and cycles of reading, thinking, searching and more reading, thinking and searching until you are confident that you've covered the ground you need to.

An example of this might help to illustrate the problem. A few years ago I was involved in a project that was investigating what the existing literature said about the decentralisation of health service organisation. Now, on the surface of it, decentralisation is a pretty obvious term to be looking for as a starting point. However, there are also several terms that are often used instead of decentralisation in the literature, but refer to relevant research, including devolution and delegation. As well as that, the literature on centralisation, on centre–local relations and localism were all highly relevant. Only by careful and thoughtful searching do these other terms come out and help the research become more complete.

## 2 Working out where you are going to look for your topic

Once you have some idea of the 'what', there is the 'where' question – where are you going to look? When I began research, the answer was usually 'the library' – going through journal stacks and book catalogues (sometimes on card indexes) trying to find relevant research. Now searches are far more likely to be done electronically, making it far more directed and covering a potentially far wider range of sources, but perhaps reducing the chance of a serendipitous find that is outside the present search criteria, but very relevant, in the process.

The precise database you search will depend on your topic, the country you are searching from and the facilities you have access to. Electronic databases are great in that they can provide you with a wide range of apparently relevant sources very quickly. However, accessing the papers or reports themselves can be frustrating as your library may or may not subscribe to them, and because the database you are searching may find the article, but it may only be available in full (or even in abstract form) on another one.

Perhaps the most important thing is to be catholic in which databases you search on. Using only one is likely to result in the anachronisms of that database limiting what you can find. Some databases deal better with wild cards in searches better than others (where you might search for 'decentralis*' instead of decentralisation in order to include 'decentralising' as well, for example) and some may be rather 'deeper' than others (looking at particular journals over a longer time period).

In general, I think it is best to define the discipline of your topic as widely as possible and to search across several databases. It is better to have too many sources to choose from and to have to work out a process of excluding some from the study, rather than only finding a few and compromising the search by missing out a range of relevant sources as a result.

## 3 Working out which of the sources you find are relevant to what you're looking for

The next step, once you've performed such searches and got the results back, is to try and decide which papers or reports are relevant to what you are doing and which are not. The importance of defining your research area clearly comes into focus here – you need to know what you are looking for in order to be able to find it. Even if you have to modify the range of the search as your research progresses, with it becoming wider or narrower, you need to know when you are evaluating sources which research fits your criteria for inclusion and which doesn't.

Broadly, there are two schools of thought as to how the process should proceed. Both are clear about the first – you need to pick which sources are relevant to your current research project. Rather than reading all of the papers you have found in your research, as there are likely to be a large number for most topics in the first instance, a sensible compromise is to look at the abstracts for the pieces you have found and include or exclude them on the impression that they give. This isn't a perfect process, but is more time-effective than trying to assess whole pieces when you may have found literally hundreds of sources in your initial search. So the first process of excluding papers is on the grounds of their apparent relevance to your study, and that will depend on how clearly you have defined your topic.

## Exclusion and systematic review

The second process of exclusion can be done at least two ways. The first of these, following the methodology of medical science and evidence-based medicine, attempts to discriminate between papers on the grounds of scientific quality. In systematic reviews of clinical work, papers which followed the randomised controlled-trial methodology will be included, but those that use methods which are not regarded as being robust, including trials which are not double-blind (with neither participants nor those administering trials knowing which subjects are subject to an intervention or not), or those where adequate control groups were not set up, will be seen as inferior and so subject to being weighted as less important or even excluded completely.

This approach to exclusion requires a checklist of the qualities of a good research paper in the field being drawn up (which might include methods, sample size, robustness of findings, quality of evidence and argument, and so on) and papers which have passed the relevance test being scored, with only those above a defined threshold being included in the study. These papers are then examined to see their potential for synthesis (which is easier in the case of quantitative data, as numerical data is more easily combinable than qualitative data) or for commonalities and differences in findings. We might term this approach to summarising research as the 'systematic review' method.

The problem with this approach is that it assumes that knowledge and evidence in each social research field is the same or similar to knowledge and evidence in medicine. It may well be that for some fields, especially an area such as clinical psychology, this is an aspiration, and so there is a consensus amongst many researchers in the field that the approach is appropriate. This depends, however, on researchers being able to demonstrate that they are producing knowledge of a similar kind to medical knowledge which is subject to synthesis, where published work has an established structure which allows judgements about quality to be read off from it, and where a strong consensus exists in that discipline that particular methods, results and their presentation are agreed upon.

In other disciplines, such as sociology, politics or organisation studies, there may be far less consensus. In these circumstances the quality of a piece of research might be contested, with some researchers regarding pieces that make extensive use of ethnography to be vague, unscientific and unrepresentative, and others stressing their importance because of the rich detail they bring, their multi-vocality and their specificity. Where there is considerable debate about the criteria of quality in a field, it surely makes little sense to pretend that there is, and to impose contentious criteria upon a search. This involves reviewing more from a 'realist review' perspective.

## Exclusion and realist review

An alternative method for conducting a review has been advocated by Ray Pawson and his collaborators (Pawson and Tilley, 1997; Pawson et al., 2005; Pawson, 2006b). Pawson's approach has been widely applied in the field of evaluation studies, and he has recently considered how it might be used in reviews of evidence for social policy, but it also has strong implications for the way literature reviews could be conducted.

Pawson suggests that we should look at the evaluation of evidence in a different way to that of a clinical trial because the social world is fundamentally an open system, with the context of where the research was carried out being far more important than it is in clinical research because it significantly affects the outcome of research. Even where it is possible to insert identical interventions into a research setting (and that itself is remarkably difficult), then outcomes will vary because researching human beings is not the same thing as researching a vaccination for measles. Human beings don't always conform to the rules, or do what is expected of them, so attempting to come up with any kind of law about their behaviour is unlikely to work.

Pawson's approach leads to a method of reviewing where, instead of trying to judge the scientific quality of research, we should be trying to try and identify a range of contexts, mechanisms and outcomes for research, and to explore their interrelationships. The mechanisms for research might be a particular social phenomenon, such as social class, ethnicity or, in the example above, the decentralisation of health services. We should then look to assemble a range of papers that examine that mechanism in as wide a range of contexts as possible – different countries, regions, cities, areas, times – anything which varies what might affect our mechanism. We should then try to see how different contexts and mechanisms come together to create different outcomes, or results, and so see if there are patterns – do certain circumstances lead to social class having a stronger effect on education than others, for example? Or does the decentralisation of health services lead to more responsive health services in urban areas than rural ones?

So instead of assessing work in terms of its scientific quality, we should be looking to see what it adds to an emerging theory, or explanation, of how what we are investigating (the mechanism) varies in different social contexts, to produce different outcomes. Now it might well be that the research we find all points to the same pattern – in which case there is a strong consensus in the field. Once we get research that does not fit with an emerging pattern, however, we have to look at it to see what is different about the context of the research, the way that the mechanisms occurred or the way the outcome was measured, that led to this different pattern, and this allows us to elaborate on our theory of what the research seems to be telling us.

Pawson's approach does not explicitly attempt to measure the quality of published research, but instead asks a different question – how significant is the paper given the research already examined? Pawson goes as far as suggesting that 'bad' research can be significant for a project where it offers something novel or different (Pawson, 2006a). So the measure of whether a paper should be included in a research project for detailed reading is about its contribution to the project, measured in terms of what it offers the emerging theory the researcher is constructing about the literature under review.

As such, Pawson's approach is explicitly about building theory from the existing literature, of constructing a theory about what the existing literature says, of how it is similar and how it is different, and of accounting for differences between what other researchers have said. It is adding value to existing research by synthesising it, whilst at the same time treating it in a rigorous way.

## 4 Taking notes on what you've found

Once a researcher has worked out what they are looking for, where they are looking for it, and how they wish to include and exclude studies from the review, then they need to begin to read through the materials to be included in the study or examined in depth and to take notes on them.

In the case of books, taking notes on the paper itself is a good start, but can make them difficult to find later on. Even if you are using ebooks, because of the volume of material to be covered, it makes sense for you to be trying to actively summarise what the author has said so you have a sense of what you believe the main arguments to be. It is a time-consuming process summarising other researchers' work, but is worth it as you will be left with your own description and analysis of it that will be far more readily incorporated into your review than the original book.

With articles, you may wish to initially take notes onto the paper or electronic copy of the article (taking notes electronically can be done with some pdf readers, with 'preview' on the Apple Mac particularly suited to this). However, even if you do this, you still need ideally to produce a summary of the article as it will make you express the author's ideas in your own words. If you are using the systematic review approach described above, these accounts will provide you with a basis for comparing accounts and for synthesis. In this approach, cover sheets for articles are often created providing the summary at a glance. In the Pawsonian approach, these summaries allow articles to be sorted into piles of those with similar patterns between contexts, mechanisms and outcomes, and for the researcher to begin to generate ideas about why some patterns emerge more than others and why some are different.

Either way, I'm afraid, taking notes is a central part of the review process. It is time-consuming, but it avoids a lot of heartache later on, removing the need for the researcher to remember what each piece of research says from the original source and creating a record that the review has been carried out – which is especially important where the work is being done as part of a funded project or in a research team (or both).

## 5 Finding more sources based on what you've found and refining your search

Once you begin to work your way through the papers you've included in your study, you'll see sources you haven't presently included being cited. Where these citations keep coming up then you need to look at that original paper, as it is clearly important in your field, even if it didn't come up in your search. This is the argument for searching for further sources based on frequency – if a citation comes up a lot in your field, and you don't know about it, you probably need to.

There are at least two other reasons why you might need to refine your search, effectively going back to stage 1 described above. First, you might find that there is a body of related literature that your original research didn't pick up. Second, you might find that the research makes use of a particular theoretical perspective or method that you don't know very much about and, in order to understand it, require you to find out about that.

In the first case, where you identify a new body of research that you need to include, you need to be brave and just get on with it. It is always easier to try and ignore it when a whole range of new material appears, especially when you might have thought you were getting to the end of the review process. However, it can also be exciting to find a new academic area you were unaware of, and it is best to think of your new discovery as something to be celebrated rather than as a barrier to you finishing. It's better to do the job properly rather than have a reviewer tell you you've missed something important later on.

In the second case, again, I'm afraid you are just going to have to get up to speed with the new theoretical perspective in order to understand the new research you've found. If you're not very fond of theory this can be a daunting proposition, but under these circumstances it's helpful to try and think of the new material as presenting a challenge to your own understanding from which you might benefit as a researcher, and to approach it in as open-minded a fashion as you can until you are in a position to compare it to the research tradition you know more about.

## 6 Organising what you've found

Once you've read through the papers and reports you've included in the study and taken notes on them, researchers can often get intimidated by the sheer volume of work they have in front of them. What on earth are they supposed to do with it all?

Summarising research as you read through it certainly helps with this process. It at least means that the pile of what you have to organise is smaller and more manageable. Summary also helps you to get to the core of what the existing research is saying so you can see the elements that need to be incorporated into your explanation of what it says.

The central point of organising others' research is to find a scheme or format or framework that structures it in a way that allows you to develop an argument about it. Developing an argument, as you'll recall, is about drawing a conclusion based on premises. In this case, it is capturing what an author has said, based on the argument, evidence and logic they have themselves presented. Some material is easier to summarise in this way than others – dealing with research that examines the decentralisation of healthcare is more straightforward than that which critiques the social theory of Deleuze and Guattari. However, the same principles do apply, and can often be illuminating in capturing what the research's importance, and the author's contribution, is.

If you are working in the systematic review format, you will need to summarise statistical evidence in many cases, in which case you will need a sound knowledge of how to do this. You'll need to look at the practice of summarising quantitative evidence to make sure you don't fall into the many errors that can be made in combining statistical studies. If you are summarising qualitative research using this method, you will need to find ways of synthesising findings, perhaps in terms of their frequency of occurrence, or perhaps in terms of mapping their similarities and differences in some kind of other rigorous way. Taking the systematic approach means that the measure of success you apply to the review is likely to involve some numeric measure of occurrence because of the roots of this method.

When utilising a Pawsonian approach, the work is organised according to its relationship with other pieces in the context, mechanism and outcome framework. Work which produces similar patterns can be clustered together and work which produces different patterns compared. This immediately creates a framework for organising your work, forcing you into thinking about others' research in this way.

## 7 Writing about what you've found and making it work for you

Finally, then, after going through the other six stages, possibly iteratively if you have found sources that needed to be included that were not in your original search (and you almost certainly will), you come to the stage of writing up what you've found.

First, it is important to document how the review was carried out, which is especially important if it is being conducted as a part of a PhD, funded research project, or for a journal article. What you need to do is to show that the review method was robust and rigorous, and can be shown to have picked up all of the sources to your study. You then need to show that you have conducted the research in a way consistent with that method, and that you have reported the review according to those principles as well. You also need to be aware of any requirements that the journal, funder or reader has put on the format of the review, including referencing style, word length or structure.

If you have conducted a systematic review you will need to show how you conducted your search, what databases or other search methods were included, how you included or excluded relevant papers, and then report your findings from the data in a format that is consistent with the way the original research was presented. If you are summarising and synthesising quantitative data you need to show that you have adopted appropriate techniques and tests, and to present these elements accordingly, and if summarising qualitative data, you will still need to include statistics such as occurrences and counts, or come up with some method for showing that your method was robust and defendable in terms of the process it went through. In other words, you need to show that your summary is objective in the sense that you have managed to minimise partiality. What this boils down to is the idea that, were someone else to repeat your review, they would come up with the same, or at least very similar, findings – a key part to the claim to knowledge of the systematic review is that of producing objective knowledge.

If you have followed a more Pawsonian approach you will need to come up with a way of exploring the relationships between contexts, mechanisms and outcomes, organising research around the different patterns you have found, perhaps under thematic headings. Again, you will have to explain the approach taken to the review, justifying it in terms of the area being researched or the type of papers being reviewed, and to show that you have met the criteria for success for this type of review. This requires you to bring out the relationships between contexts, mechanisms and outcomes for the relevant research, and to provide some kind of explanation for the similarities and differences between the patterns found. However, the distinctiveness of this approach is not its claim to objectivity, but instead the success of the review will be based on its ability to generate a theory that illuminates our understanding of the literature. Pawson's best example of this has already been explained in this book – his review of naming and shaming that shows how the approach works in some contexts but not in others.

Regardless of the approach you have taken to writing your review, you will have to go through something of an exercise in humility in writing it. You are not going to get it right first time. In fact, a leading social scientist in his guide for writers specifically suggests that you should be aiming to just get on with writing and produce several drafts of anything you write (Becker, 2008). There is a great deal to be said for this approach – blank sheets of paper or an empty screen can be extremely intimidating when you are trying to get your ideas down, and the earlier you start the process of writing, even if what you produce is very much a draft and will require a great deal of revision later on, the earlier you take pressure off yourself by having at least written something. Don't expect to get your writing even remotely right first time, but be pleasantly surprised should it happen. Be honest about what you've written and get used to having to produce several drafts of it before you get to the finished version.

## Putting together a research proposal

Much of the advice above also applies when putting together a research proposal to a funder of some kind. However, there are different emphases on what you need to concentrate on, so what follows is an attempt to work through these.

## 1 Finding out what it is they want (and sticking to it)

The first point when putting together a research proposal is for you to make sure that you know what your potential funder wants. Read through the call for bids or funding specification carefully, taking notes of key words, requirements and deadlines as you do so. Then read it again. No, really. The most important thing you need to get in your head when beginning to bid for funds is what the funder wants. I have been on bid-assessment panels where over 50 per cent of the fully worked-out bids that have been received have been rejected immediately on the grounds that they don't meet the criteria specified in the call for proposals. This is a huge waste of time for everyone concerned – for the researchers trying to get funds, for the organisations trying to get research funded, for the reviewers of the bids, and for all the support services and favours that researchers will have utilised in getting the bid in. So make sure that before you start writing a bid you understand what the funder wants and that what you have in mind for your proposal will meet it.

It may well be that the document issued by the potential funder will have ambiguities, or you won't be sure, even having read through it carefully several times, of whether the research you want to do fits with the call. In those circumstances it is perfectly reasonable to contact the funder to seek clarification. Major funding bodies will have specific contacts or academic leads available to answer questions such as these, and will include them on the call. But do make sure that your question is not covered in the document before you get in touch with them, or again, you are potentially wasting both your own, and other people's time. Equally, don't pester funders with lots of tiny queries that aren't particularly important in terms of understanding the call or writing your bid. You don't want to get a reputation for sending lots of trivial queries.

## 2 Getting organised

Once you have decided that the call for proposals fits with something that you want to do, you then need to get yourself organised. Most application forms will have guidance notes that you need to make sure you have a copy of, and which you have read through carefully in order to know exactly what is required of you. This will mean that you avoid spending time writing up sections of a proposal that subsequently turn out to be incorrect in some way, leading to you having to do them again.

A number of funding bodies now require proposals to be submitted fully electronically using a web-based system of some kind or another. This is good in the sense that it makes for an efficient submission system (as opposed to having to copy and submit 25 or more copies of a paper-based application, as might have been the case in the past). However, it does mean that, if you rely on the application system itself, you won't be able to work on the application form while you are off-line. In addition, it can be difficult to work with collaborators, if you have them, in an online form where it is not clear what changes each of you have made.

As such, a good answer is for you to make a word-processor document in the format of the application form, making a careful note of the acceptable length of each section under the relevant headings. Using a document in this fashion allows you to add material to the bid on the order you feel comfortable with, to see how the bid as a whole is progressing and how sections fit together for consistency and style, and to see (using tools such as track changes) what changes other members of the bidding team have made (if there are any). You can also save the document in new versions frequently, giving yourself a back-up of previous versions in case you end up regretting a change that you make – something again that an online application system won't be able to provide you with.

In addition to organising the application form, you also need to work out what additional support you are going to need. If the funders require financial statements of one kind or another you will need to find out who is responsible for putting these together and give them as much notice as possible that the bid is going ahead. You also need to find out what deadlines might apply for finance forms – they quite often have to be produced weeks before the final submission date for the bid in order to get institutional approvals of one kind or another, and you need to know what those additional deadlines might be.

Equally, a number of application forms require you to offer potential referees to funders. You need to seek the permission of referees before putting them down on your application, so will need to contact them as soon as possible to make sure you have this. There are two good reasons for this – first, because it is polite and you will need your referees to support your proposal; second, because referees are likely to be busy people and so it is only fair to ask them in advance if you are going to cause them the extra work of potentially reviewing what you have written.

In all, then, you need to have the application form in a medium that you can access easily, edit and review, and it may well be that using an online system might not work for you in achieving these goals. Equally, you need to organise yourself in terms of gaining institutional approvals for bids and for getting permission from referees. Bids may have additional requirements, in which case you need to know what they are, and it is a good idea to work out a timeline for yourself, starting with the deadline for the bid and other fixed dates (such as institutional approval times), and then work back to the present date, giving yourself an idea of when you are going to get the various sections completed and so giving yourself an idea of how much work the bid is going to be.

## 3 Getting on with the writing

The writing part of the bid is likely to be highly prescribed by the potential funder. There is likely to be a series of headings with which you must comply, and you should get as clear an idea as possible as to what is required of you in each. Getting a look at successful bids from the past will help with this, and it may well be that you can get access to these from either your own institution or through your collaborators, networks or friends. Some general principles do apply though.

In 'background' sections you need to show that you have a strong understanding of the field in which the research is being conducted, citing key sources to show that you know what they are, and setting up the research problem that you want to address in your study within it. This section has much in common with a miniature literature review. If yourself or the bidding team have publications in this area, it is a good idea to cite them to show how your work fits in with the field as a whole, but don't get too carried away with this – reading an application where the author believes themselves to be the only authority in the field doesn't reflect terribly well on them. If you are applying for a grant or bursary for a PhD this is unlikely to be the case though, but you should still consider citing your prospective supervisors if possible as it will show funders that their expertise is relevant and important within the field. Equally, it won't do you any harm to look at names of the funding panel, if they are available, and citing their work where it is relevant. As with a literature review, it helps if, by the end of the background section, you've managed to show that the research you are proposing is either a gap in the present work or something that needs urgently addressing for some reason.

At some point in your proposal you are going to have to say what the aims of your research are, what your research questions are, or specify in some other way exactly what it is you are trying to achieve. What makes a good research question is a topic for a book in itself (I recommend White, 2009), and can be divided up into whether you are attempting to achieve descriptive or explanatory research (broadly, answering 'how' or 'why' questions respectively), or whether you are adopting an inductive or deductive research strategy (with the former tending to more open questions and the latter towards more tightly worded hypotheses or propositions). There is some additional guidance on research questions in Chapter 2, but the key point is that your research questions should be linked to your research aims, that they are themselves clear and understandable, both to yourself and to the audience assessing your proposal, and that the questions you ask can be answered with the methods and programme of research that you propose.

In 'methods' sections you need to be as clear as possible about what it is you are going to do, showing expertise in both the methodological literature (generally) and the way that those methods have been applied in the field you are working in (specifically). Be as clear as possible about what you are proposing. Say exactly how big samples will be (don't just say 'about'), show that you've thought about how you will go about recruiting subjects into your study, where they will be drawn from and how they will be chosen. Be consistent between the language you use in your methods and the type of research you are proposing – if you going to test hypotheses show exactly how they will be tested. It can help dividing up your proposed research into sections or phases, clearly explaining how you are going to do the work in each (so phase one might be a review, phase two fieldwork and so on).

Make sure that you know what each section of the proposal requires of you, and that you present a persuasive argument in each. Justify which methods you are going to use. Be clear about the potential contribution of the research, as funders will want to know why they should give you the money and not someone else.

Above all, make sure of two things. First, that what you are proposing will appear to reviewers to be viable within the time and budget that is available. Funders are extremely hesitant about giving money to a project that is over-ambitious in case it isn't completed. This doesn't mean that you can't deal with big social problems, but it does mean that you need to come up with a proposal that looks like it will be viable to address them. Second, you need to show that your proposal addresses the funder's requirements and that it is clear in doing so. Look at the language the funders use in their call and reproduce key words in your proposal. Make sure you understand any technical terms or specific methods they include in their call and make sure that you incorporate them into your study, or give a specific reason why you have not.

## 4 Linking together sections (even when they might not appear to be linked)

Good proposals find ways of linking together the various sections of the proposal. Presenting a coherent plan for research means showing how the proposed project arises out of existing research, how the methods you are adopting are appropriate to that project, and how the results you will achieve flow naturally from those methods to address the research problem that arose from the existing literature.

It can be easy, when writing a proposal, to concentrate on it one section at a time. This can lead to a number of problems. First, you can end up writing in a different style in each section, making the proposal appear fragmented. This is especially a problem when writing directly into an online system, where you may only be able to see one section of the proposal, the one currently being edited, at a time. This problem can be a particularly difficult one where you are trying to write the proposal in a team, and have assigned different people to write different sections. In these circumstances it is important for one member of the team, most often the lead applicant of the bid, to take editorial responsibility for the final form of the bid, making sure that it appears even in style throughout.

Writing in separate sections can also lead to mistakes that can undermine the credibility of your bid. Saying you are going to include 30 people as subjects in one section, and then changing your mind and decreasing it to 20 later on is fine (so long as you can justify the sample size), but every time you make such a change you have to make sure that the document as a whole is still consistent. A surprising number of bids appear in funders' offices with these sorts of inconsistencies, making it harder for reviewers to assess them and reducing the credibility of the bidder. Having to make changes throughout the document to keep the bid consistent is also a good reason to have as much as possible of the bid in one document to make this easier, rather than having to call up separate sections one by one on an online application form.

Overall, then, make sure that your bid is written in a style that is consistent between sections, with one bidder taking responsibility for this, and every time you make a change to the bid, make sure that all relevant sections are updated to reflect it.

## 5 Being innovative and interesting without scaring people

In many respects the most tricky bit of writing a bid is to show that you are doing something new, innovative and interesting, but not anything that is so far outside the scope of present work that it is unviable and unachievable. You need to be able to show that the roots of what you want to achieve are within the present research and, although you are doing something new, you have a clear plan for how it will be done and how it will be achieved. Showing mastery of existing research and presenting clear methods and timetables for your proposed research will help you to achieve this.

## 6 Losing hostages to fortune

'Hostages to fortune' are statements in your proposal that are likely to raise hostile questions in the reviewers' minds. You need to read through your proposal to make sure that your arguments have adequate premises, that they are adequately supported by both logic and empirical evidence. If your argument has holes in it, the chances are a competent team of reviewers will spot it, and so it is important that you try to anticipate possible objections to your proposal and address them in advance. Be careful about the claims you make about current research (in case the researchers you discuss end up as reviewers of your bid), and make sure that your bid doesn't depend upon claims that you aren't able to support.

## 7 Getting it peer-reviewed

Once you are getting to the stage where you have a full draft, then you really need to get someone else to look at your bid. Be careful to explain to them what stage you are at – if you think you are near the end of the process you will be asking for a different kind of peer review than if you have completed the first draft and want someone to say whether they think your ideas are sensible or not.

Getting a review of your bid is instrumental to its success. Until you have a lot of experience (perhaps even if you have a lot of experience) then getting a fresh pair of eyes to look at what you have put together can lead to you getting a new perspective on what you've put together, to bring up potential objectives and other points that you might not have thought of, and to offer suggestions for how the bid or proposal needs to be improved further.

Once you have feedback, preferably from at least one reviewer, you then need to decide how you are going to deal with it. You need ideally to set aside the proposal for a couple of days to create a little emotional and intellectual distance from it, and to approach it as freshly as possible, in order to see which of the criticism and comments made by reviewers seem to you to be correct or not. If you are the lead bidder, then it is up to you whether you think that changes others are suggesting need to be improved, but you do need to bear in mind that your reviewers wouldn't have made those suggestions unless they thought they should be incorporated. Have a debate with yourself, or a dialogue with the peer reviewer if possible, to work through each of the points they have raised and make sure that they are adequately dealt with in the next draft of the bid.

## 8 Being realistic in your expectations

Once you have the whole bid together, submitted on time and to the best of your ability, you should be pleased with yourself. Getting a project together and seeing it through the whole proposal is no mean achievement. However, you do need to be realistic about its potential for success. Bidding for research funds is a competitive process and requires you to have a thick skin.

Ideally, your bid will be considered carefully by a qualified team of reviewers, compared to other bids, and will stand or fall on its merits. Most good funders do their best to achieve this goal. Even a very good bid can be unsuccessful because it appeared at a time when an even better bid happened to come in. There is nothing you can do now, so it is important to get on with the rest of your life and not get too obsessed about the result of an attempt to get funding. It may well be that the work you've done on the bid can be incorporated into writing a paper, and if this is the case, it's not a bad idea to get on with this while the material is fresh in your mind.

Once you do get a decision from the funder, it will tend to come with some feedback. This feedback can be useful in working out why your bid was successful or not, and good funders again will make some attempt at explaining this. However, again, I'm afraid you can't expect a great deal of explanation from many funders in respect of this. Funding calls often lead to very large numbers of applicants, and so it is extremely difficult to give comprehensive feedback to everyone. Try and get the best sense you can of why your bid was successful or not, and learn what you can from it. If you were unsuccessful, it might make the difference for your next application. Above all, if your bid was seen to have merits, don't just file it away – think of other funding bodies where you might be able to send it (with appropriate modifications).

# Conclusion – the skills of being a practising researcher

Being a practising researcher means that you will have to write for publication and that you will have to apply for funding. Universities require research-active staff to do both, and so both are skills you will have to acquire.

Writing up others' work can be a demanding and time-consuming process, but can be made more interesting by following the advice above. Think of the process of reviewing literature not as a tedious slog you have to go through (as some researchers express it), but rather as a process of discovery of ideas and as a way of finding your own research projects.

Writing research bids and bidding for funding is a process that is also extremely time-consuming, and the competitive nature of trying to get grants can be demoralising, especially when funders are often not able to say much about why bids are unsuccessful. However, it is important to develop a thick skin, to learn what you can from each bidding process, and to make sure that the learning you get from bidding is incorporated into future bids and incorporated into writing papers on the subject of your bid.

## Five things to remember about this chapter

1   Writing papers or proposals is a skill. You'll get better at it as you do more of it. So practise. Pay attention to the feedback you get and look to improve.

2   There are two distinct approaches to writing a literature review. Be clear about which one you are trying to achieve, and be consistent in the way you go about the review and the way you write about it.

3   Don't expect writing a review or a proposal to work out right first time. It may take many attempts. But if you bear in mind that you are developing a skill, and learn from the process, then you'll be better at it next time.

4   Many research proposals fail because they don't adequately address the brief. Make sure you know what it says and don't end up writing a proposal that answers a problem you have invented.

5   It is a good idea to get your work, be it a review or a proposal, reviewed by your peers before you send them off. Find trustworthy people you have been successful in what you are trying to achieve, and ask them if they'll have a look. It is better to get suggestions for improvement before you submit than after it has been rejected.

# TWELVE

## Conclusion – or getting on with social research

This book now reaches its conclusion by summarising its argument and encouraging students to work through the issues of their research in a systematic, justifiable way, and work out what methods are most appropriate for them to incorporate into their research design.

## Introduction

What I have tried to advocate in this book is what amounts to a pragmatic view of research. I believe that there is no one right answer for doing good research, but that you are likely to substantially improve your chances of doing good research if you have some idea of the philosophical issues involved in creating and justifying knowledge, if you think carefully about research as you do it and that you are sensitive to how the methods you use in your research impact upon the context where it is being carried out. None of these statements, I think, is particularly ground-breaking, but they do require researchers to be generous to their peers by accepting that there is more than one way to do good work, but to be aware of those differences and aware of the debates that underpin them in order to make informed choices about which way they wish their own work to proceed. It requires researchers to be reflexive in dealing with the problems that come up as a part of any social research and to be thinking about ethics not just at the beginning of the project. It requires researchers to be able to justify their methodological choices not just in terms of what is conventional in their discipline or subject area, but to be able to explain why their methods are appropriate in dealing with the subject matter that they wish to address.

Most of these topics have been covered in depth in the chapters through this book, and what follows here can only therefore be a short summary of some of the most important points I've raised. However, I hope it will be useful in refreshing readers' minds about these points.

# Others' claims as a basis for your own work

First of all, it is difficult to claim that you are a researcher in a field until you have a mastery of the existing research in your subject area. You need to know what researchers have already done in your field, to know how they conducted their research by understanding its methods and to know what results they managed to achieve. Until you understand existing research, you can't know what further research needs doing, or whether what you think you would like to do has already been done.

## Reading through others' research

This is part of your duty to your peers as a researcher, but also offers you opportunities. As you read through existing research, you should be looking for points of agreement and disagreement both between researchers and between yourself and the research. Disagreements offer sources of contention that further research might help with. Equally, you should be looking for gaps in the literature, areas that aren't covered by it and thinking whether you might be interested in doing research in them. Reading in this way turns others' work into sources of opportunity as well as knowledge and information.

Unless you're regularly reading research in your field, you don't really have the grounds to claim that you should be conducting research in it. Work out which journals, authors, publishers and websites regularly publish research that you are interested in and make sure that you visit them frequently to remain on top of your subject area. See what debates seem to be current and think what you might be able to contribute to them. Look for special editions of journals in your research area, conferences that are discussing your field and new books from authors whose work you enjoy.

# Defining the job at hand

Once you have identified a research topic you want to investigate, either from previous literature, papers at a conference you have been to, a funding call or just sitting in the bath and having a good idea, then you need to get on with developing it.

A key part of developing your research idea is to define exactly what it is you want to do. Are you trying to answer a specific question and, if so, what is it? Are you trying to produce a speculative piece of work to address a problem rather than answer a precise question? Do you have a range of aims for your research, in which case do you have a list of questions that directly relate to those aims and which you can go about answering? What is the contribution that you believe this research will make to your field? The important thing here is to achieve as much clarity as you can in defining the scope of what it is you want to do. This is especially important when putting together a research proposal that someone else will have to assess, but is good practice even if you are working on your own, unfunded research.

Finally, don't expect to be able to define your project clearly first time. It will often take several attempts at defining things, at looking at methods, sources of data, possible sites where studies might be carried out, potential subjects and the project's viability, before you manage to find a project that is interesting enough for you to want to do (and possibly for someone to fund!) but is practically viable, so that you might be able to complete it.

## Designing research that is appropriate for the job at hand

Once you know what it is you want to do, then you need to come up with a research design that addresses the problem you want to deal with. Look at the aims of your research and the research questions you have come up with, and try to come up with what seems to you to be the best ways of addressing them. Think about your methods reflexively – have you just come up with your twentieth proposal in a row suggesting that interviews are the best tool for the job, in which case are you just putting forward what you feel most comfortable with, rather than what might be the most appropriate method?

### Think about what legitimacy you are trying to achieve for your research

Is your research distinctive because of it's closeness to the research subjects, representativeness, volume, theoretical novelty, empirical uniqueness or something else? Given this, what methods best give this legitimacy, and what are the objectives that researchers from other backgrounds might make and how might you counter them? Given that what you are trying to claim is going to be your research's contribution, what is the best way to go about demonstrating that you can achieve it? Are you looking to make a theoretical contribution, an empirical one, both, or something else? What does this mean in terms of designing and delivering your research?

As I have said above, I don't personally think there is one right answer to any social research problem. But it is up to you to make the case for the methods or methods that you have chosen, and for showing how those methods link to the problem and will produce the results that you are claiming you will be able to show.

## Mixing methods

Many research projects try and demonstrate comprehensiveness or epistemological plurality by being explicitly mixed methods. There is no problem in principle with mixing methods, but researchers are often extremely vague in proposals and papers as to why they have decided upon a mixed-methods strategy.

There are several grounds for mixing methods in a research project. The important thing is to have a reason for using mixed methods and to be able to provide an epistemological justification for doing them.

A first possible justification is where research aims to achieve both breadth, which justifies the use of quantitative methods, and depth or closeness, which justifies the use of qualitative methods. So we might have a large-scale survey to look for patterns within a large sample, and then a detailed ethnography to look at a particular incidence or case within the sample in detail.

However, that can't be all there is to the story of mixing methods to achieve breadth and depth. As well as this, researchers need to be able to show rigour in their sampling by justifying what kind of sample they have chosen and relating that to their topic and to the research context in which it is being conducted. Equally, they will need to provide a justification for the choice of site for the detailed ethnographic work. This brings in a range of additional questions about the sequencing of mixed-methods research.

Should quantitative work go before qualitative work, justified on the grounds of looking for patterns of variables that are worth investigating in a wider sample, and so aiding the choice of qualitative site, or should the qualitative research be conducted first, with the quantitative research then showing how widespread the findings from the qualitative research are? The first strategy would be justified in situations where there is little previous research, and it is necessary to find out what particular aspects of a social phenomenon need investigating in depth before proceeding. The second strategy, where the qualitative work comes before the quantitative work, might be relevant where previous research already gives us strong clues as to what we might be looking for, but after investigating it we might want to conduct quantitative work to find out how widespread the findings of the particular study we have conducted are.

Of course, it is equally possible to do quantitative and qualitative work at the same time. We might, for example, send everyone in an organisation in the research setting a questionnaire, whilst at the same time conducting interviews and doing observant-participation work. In this case, we will be looking for one research process to inform the other and comparing findings to find out more about the quantitative findings through appropriate qualitative work, and looking to see how widespread the findings from the qualitative work are in the survey. If we are conducting a survey at the beginning and end in a research design, the two can genuinely inform one another in a way that has the potential to be mutually reinforcing.

We can also mix methods, however, by using two methods of the same broad type. We might, for example, perform statistical analysis of data from an organisational setting, such as numbers of operations, mortality or morbidity from a hospital, and combine them with a questionnaire about surgery practice. This would give us two quantitative studies, but provide different perspectives on the same process – that of surgery. This might inform us, for example, how safe particular surgeons appear to be based on their outcomes, compared to how safe they (and their peer perhaps) believe them to be. The two quantitative methods combine to create an interesting study.

Qualitative methods can also be combined. In fact, any ethnography is likely to make use of a range of individual methods, using interviews, observation, documentary analysis and just about anything else that is available in order to build up as rich a picture of life in a research setting as possible. The goal is to create as full a picture of the research site as possible, but of course faces the risk of producing contradictory findings. This may or may not be a problem. If you are conducting research within a realist epistemology, there may be a need to adjudicate between competing accounts to get, as near as possible, to the truth of a situation based on its correspondence to what might have happened in reality. Taking a more anthropological stance, however, would mean that contradiction is an inevitable part of the research process, stressing the perspectival nature of knowledge, with the researcher having no right to impose their own view of subjects' accounts.

A third view of mixed-methods research is that it is a means of gaining greater validity for research. In other words, mixed-methods work is there to cross-check between methods. As such, this can be a process for comparing the findings of very different methods, mixing quantitative with qualitative work, or for comparing research within the same tradition to give it greater validity. When researchers write about validating findings through 'triangulation' this is often what they mean by the use of that term.

This approach to research is underpinned by a realistic conception of the social world – that different methods, rather than constituting different realities through their different tools, techniques and measurements, measure an objective reality independent of the methods themselves. It is important to recognise this, as adopting subjectivist research strategies, such as auto-ethnography, and attempting to mix them with objectivist approaches in the name of achieving validity, would seem to be a rather contradictory position to adopt, unless you can offer a compelling reason for doing research that way. This highlights the importance of having a clear reason for mixing methods, and understanding whether the methods being combined come from different research traditions, with different assumptions about knowledge creation, and what this means for their combination.

I would argue that, where you get different results from different methods, this, in itself, is an interesting finding. If your survey is indicating everything in a setting is going well, but your ethnography is showing conflict, tension and tears, that doesn't mean that you have failed to triangulate, but it does mean that you need to have a hard think about why your results appear so contradictory. That should lead to a deeper understanding of your research site rather than being a threat to your research. It might mean that one of your means of data collection hasn't been designed well, or it might mean that they are measuring different things. Writers such as Law and Latour would probably just shrug and say that life is like that – we shouldn't expect consistency. More realist researchers would want to try and find whether different generative mechanisms are at work to create different results. However, if as a positivistic researcher you believe that your findings are based on a close relationship between an objective social world and objective methods to measure it, then contradictory findings present you with rather more of a problem.

A fourth reason for mixing methods brings the methods themselves into focus. It asks whether different methods do produce different findings in the same research setting. This is an under-researched area, and one that clearly needs more work. If the argument that I have offered, that different research contexts require different methods, and that researchers need to be pragmatic and careful in their method selection, then it may well be the case that different methods do produce different results. It therefore makes sense to find out whether this is so and if there are systematic differences between methods. Do quantitative methods privilege particular results that qualitative methods tend to underplay? Does this vary by research setting? Do computer-mediated approaches to analysing data produce different results from methods that make greater use of older technologies? These are interesting questions that we know surprisingly little about.

A fifth reason for using mixed methods is a pragmatic one. The researchers recognise that research in a particular field tends to be done in a particular way, and they wish to continue with that approach. But they also want to try something new to see if that generates novel findings of some kind. So a research proposal might recognise that discourse analysis is often dominated by approaches that attempt to look at power relationships and the meanings of words using interpretive techniques, and seek to continue that tradition. But it might also propose attempting to use computer software that allows key terms to be highlighted statistically by exploring the relationships between words and their frequencies. Equally, using the auto-summary feature available on some computer packages allows texts to be boiled down to their bare bones with often interesting results. This use of computer software does not illuminate the need for the careful discourse analysis, but it can sharpen researchers' minds and expose them to new ideas during the research that can provide a fresh perspective on their analysis. Trying new things, where there is a sensible reason for doing so, has the potential to lead to new understandings of the social world. I think researchers have a duty not to get used to doing their work one way only – when we stop learning we are no longer learning, and for a researcher that seems to me to be a really bad idea.

## Being careful with data and with ethics

Another aspect of doing social research is reflexively engaging with ethical issues as the research progresses. What I've tried to suggest is that researchers don't regard ethical clearance at the beginning of the project as being an end to this, but instead to regard ethics as being something that they must engage with at every stage of their research. Researchers should try to be 'good' by considering what their research requires of them, and to behave in a professional manner to achieve this. Researchers must engage with the contexts that their research demands, and to be justifying, if only to themselves, the choices that they make in their engagements with subjects, the way that they store and treat their data, the way that they report their data and the way their results are subsequently reported.

Ethical principles and guidelines from research organisations are crucial touchstones for researchers to engage with, but just about any principle of research requires reflexive engagement in order to understand how it applies in a particular context and to understand what to do when guidelines appear to offer contradictions – as when, for example, the researcher's duty to society appears to clash with their duty to the funder or their duty to minimise harm to their research subjects. There are no easy answers to these questions – the best we can hope for is for researchers to be thinking carefully about these issues and to be behaving in a thoughtful and careful way.

## Writing it all up

Finally, there is the need for researchers to report their findings. This is part of a researcher's ethical duty – if you have carried out research that you have carefully planned and implemented, it surely makes sense for you to want to tell others about it as well, and if it is good research, then there will be a ready audience waiting to hear about it. Not writing up good research means that the world doesn't get to find out what your results were, and researchers should surely look to avoid that.

One of the interesting questions researchers have to ask themselves is where they want their research to be reported. The stock answer in the academic world is in high-quality, peer-reviewed journals, which leads to credibility for them and creates a reputation within their field. However, increasingly, academics are being asked to engage with other readerships as well – to publish in popular journals that might exist within their field and which attempt to reach a wider readership, in professional journals, as well as in newspapers and magazines.

Different outlets for research require very different writing styles. Reports are often inflexible and quite formal, whereas trying to put together a short piece for a newspaper requires a different writing style where researchers have to find ways of simplifying what they have found without making it trivial or banal. As the need for researchers to demonstrate not only that they are doing good research, but also making sure that research has an impact within their field and beyond, the skill of writing for different readerships becomes more important, but it is still one that few researchers have.

Writing publications, as with research proposal writing, requires researchers to develop thick skins. If you haven't had a paper rejected by a journal, then you're probably not trying to get into journals of sufficient quality. As with research grants, it is important to learn from journal rejections, to read the reports of reviewers and editors, to learn what their criticisms of their works are and to try to improve. Nobody gets all of their work accepted for publication all of the time. Writing is a craft that requires a long time to get anywhere near good at.

## Conclusion – doing research well

Getting to do research is a hugely rewarding way of earning a living. It requires researchers to develop a range of skills in terms of what the particular methods they favour require of them, to manage themselves during long and often complex projects where it may feel like the data they've collected is too complicated to ever be summarised or systematised, and to develop the craft of writing up what they've found for a range of potential audiences.

There is a great deal to be learned, and few researchers have mastered all of the skills required. But that's a reason for doing research well to become a lifelong goal. I can't think of anything I'd rather do with my working life.

## Example – Ladbroke Grove

The Ladbroke Grove train crash in 1999 was an appalling event. In his section on the tragedy in Chapter 5 of his book *After Method: Mess in Social Science Research* (2004), John Law says: 'On 5 October 1999, a three-carriage Thames Train diesel unit ("165") collided with a First Great Western High Speed Train ("HST") at Ladbroke Grove, two miles outside London's Paddington railway station. The result was devastation' (p. 93).

The collision was a disaster for those involved, as well as for all those that knew them. It also had repercussions across the British rail system: 'There was widespread belief that things had gone horribly wrong, not just at Ladbroke Grove, but also, and much more generally, for the railways as a whole' (p. 94). There was a public inquiry that took two years to report, gathering hundreds of witnesses in the process as well as carrying out forensic investigation of trains and track.

Law suggests that 'The Ladbroke Grove collision can be understood as a bundle of relations and entities. Some are brought together in the terrible scene of the accident itself' (p. 94). Further:

there are two ways of doing this, of treating it as an allegory. The first is to go into it in the form of words and make a consistent linguistic account. This is what happened at the public inquiry, and in the report issued at the end of that inquiry. The report crafts and represents a reality in the form of the circumstances that led to the accident. The second is to try and apprehend the wreckage and the horror without attempting to build a single discursive account. Both are allegorical strategies. Both are possible. Indeed, both are important. But it is obvious they work in different ways. (p. 94)

In the first case, the conditions of inquiry of the report were constituted by the Health and Safety Executive's terms of reference, and required to produce a coherent account: 'There will be many contributory causes to the accident. But they will be drawn together and mapped. The railway reality will, so to speak, cohere in its incoherence. The accident was caused by a determinate set of circumstances. The issue is to determine their character' (p. 96). This is how we constitute public inquiries, but it is also the way that we often envisage social research – as a means of making reality coherent. This carries with it a series of assumptions about that reality – that it is external to ourselves, and that we can achieve an objective perspective upon it from which to create a coherent narrative.

However, it is not the only way of portraying the accident. Law continues:

What happens if we treat this more directly as allegory ... To treat it as a moment, a dreadful enactment of presence written not in texts and statements, but in steel and flesh and fuel and fire. Written as impact, collapse, inferno, agonising pain, terrible burns, grief, panic, and death ... This is the stuff of nightmare ... I don't think it stretches commonsense to say that the collision crafts and depicts the non-coherences that produced it, the ramifications of a messy organisational and technical hinterland. Or refracts this non-coherence. Or condenses and articulates it. Terribly, in the bodies, the injuries and the wreckage. Pain, let us allow, is indeed a witness. (p. 97)

Law is suggesting that

what is at stake is not the creation of horror. Rather it is about how to think about it and what to do when it happens. To read it as enacted by a single set of causal circumstances. That is one possibility – an option followed in the inquiry. To acknowledge a set of non-coherent realities that escape a single narrative – that is an alternative. The making of pain, broken lives, lost partners, parents and children, these are the kinds of realities we apprehend if we read the wreckage more directly. (p. 97)

Law's passage is challenging – he is suggesting that social research can have goals other than those of realist inquiry – in fact he is demanding that it does. This is because, he argues, a realist inquiry misses out so much of what it is to be human, and these omissions are magnified by the horror of situations such as those of Ladbroke Grove. When there is a disaster, we want to know why it happened, but the danger of public inquiries is that they are constrained by their terms of reference and that they are required to produce a linear narrative that cannot do justice to the complexities, the sheer mess, that led to the disaster being investigated.

What we need, Law suggests, is to understand such events from multiple perspectives; the linear, public inquiry narrative can be one, but equally there are other views of the world that must be incorporated as well. We must be conscious of what we are missing out as well as what we are including; we must be able to present incoherence as well as coherence, or we risk simplifying the world to a point where it no longer bears much resemblance to our experiences of it.

Law is in no way treating the events of Ladbroke Grove in a trivial manner. In fact – it may well be the opposite. Any events, when singular, simple narratives are constructed of them, lose their distinctiveness and detail, the markers of what made them unique. Losing these elements in a railway disaster means that we are able to rationalise them and try to find ways of avoiding the mistakes that were made again. However, it also desensitises us to the extent of the tragedy that has occurred. Social research has more than one function – Law makes us question not only what its function should be, but also makes us consider, if we are to take account of the messy and incoherent state of the world, how we can go about social research.

However, Law's claims also appear in a specific context. The assumptions underlying the way that we inquire into disasters such as Ladbroke Grove mean that there is little scope for understanding them from multiple perspectives – inquiries are supposed to come up with a definitive single reason for the event. We have a long way to go (in just about any country I can think of) before we even come close to accepting Law's suggestions about multiple perspectives – public inquiries are designed to find the truth, the single reason for the disaster, even if it turns out there isn't one. But we don't live in a world where there are easy answers to difficult questions, and even technical problems can have multiple solutions depending on how they are approached and understood. There is a mismatch here between the political (and often societal need) for research to come up with answers and the sheer mess and muddle that the complex systems that we now live within generate.

It is the job of social research not only to conduct research that is methodologically robust, but which also meets the needs of those that commission it (my point in relation to the MoI example at the end of Chapter 6) and, even more broadly, the societies in which we live. If we are making an argument for public funding for work that does not demonstrate some kind of wider societal benefit, we might well find that funders are unwilling to help us. All research is the result of some kind of compromise – it is our job to be aware of the implications and tensions that result from the compromises that we have to make.

# Glossary

**abduction** A research strategy which attempts to contextualise research within a particular description of it, or from a particular theoretical perspective. It is a process requiring imagination, asking researchers to interpret their empirical findings within a particular framework. If we invite someone to 'take a Marxist perspective' on our data we are asking them to engage in abduction.

**convenience sampling** A sampling process sometimes more often used in qualitative research than quantitative research in which participants are chosen on the basis of the ability of the researcher to access the group.

**correlation and regression** Statistics which examine the extent to which two more sets of variables are related to one another.

**critical realism** A contemporary version of realism pioneered by writers such as Bhaskar and Archer that suggests that there is a world independent of our perceptions of it (realism), but also that social research has a key role in helping us to understand how ideas about the world can oppress certain societal groups, and should be used to help emancipate them.

**deduction** A research strategy based on testing theory using research observations, often associated with quantitative research methods.

**descriptive statistics** Statistics which provide the basic characteristics of data, including calculations of location (mean, mode, median) and dispersion (standard deviation, range).

**empiricism** The idea that knowledge is gathered through our sense experience of the world.

**epistemology** The theory of knowledge. It seeks to explore what makes knowledge, and what makes good knowledge. It asks how we know what we claim to know.

**hypothetico-deductive** The combination of hypothesis setting and deductive reasoning that forms the basis of experimental methods.

**induction** A research strategy based on building theory from observations, attempting to ground theory-building in research observations. Often associated with qualitative research strategies.

**interpretivism** The view of social research that suggests that we understand the social world through the constructions that people have made of it, and who reproduce those constructions through their activities. Interpretivists believe that the external world cannot be reached unmediated of these constructions – it can only be interpreted through them (hence interpretivism).

**methodology** The study of methods. It explores the usage of methods, comparing them to explore their similarities and differences and their underlying assumptions.

**mixed methods** Social research methods that mix both quantitative and qualitative methods. Methods can be run concurrently or one after the other, depending on the aims of the research design.

**ontology** The theory of being. The key ontological question in social research is the status of the world external to our conceptions of it. Does it exist independent of our conceptions, or does it depend upon those conceptions for us to be able to understand it at all?

**positivism** The view of research characterised by a combination of realism, treating the external world as existing independent of our conceptions of it, but which is accessible to us through our senses in a more or less unproblematic way. These observations lead to generalised laws which can be constructed using the scientific method, based on observing constant conjunctions and which can be subsequently verified by repeating the scientific test.

**qualitative methods** Social research methods which are typically non-numerative, and so are based on methods such as interviews and observation. Qualitative methods are typically text based, but newer methods make increasing use of visual techniques, sound and video as well.

**quantitative methods** Social research methods which are based on numbers in one form or another. Quantitative methods are typically deductive, and are extremely powerful in hypothesis testing because of their strong internal validity.

**random sampling** A sampling process which attempts to be representative of the wider population by everyone within the group having an equal chance of being chosen.

**retroduction** A research strategy, often associated with realist methodology, that attempts to reconstruct the conditions that must exist to explain the existence of observations. Making use of thought experiments and counterfactual argumentation, the framework which best fits the data can be found.

**stratified sampling** A sampling process similar to random sampling, but in which the population is split into groups that may be representative of it according to a theory being tested (e.g. class, gender, ethnicity) and participants chosen randomly within them.

# References

American Sociological Association (1999) *Code of Ethics and Policies and Procedures of the ASA Committee on Professional Ethics*. Washington: American Sociological Association.

Archer, M. (1995) *Realist Social Theory: The Morphogenetic Approach*. Cambridge: Cambridge University Press.

Ariely, D. (2008) *Predictably Irrational: The Hidden Forces That Shape Our Decisions*. London: HarperCollins.

Ayres, I. (2008) *Super Crunchers: How Anything Can Be Predicted*. London: John Murray.

Becker, H. (2008) *Writing for Social Scientists: How to Start and Finish Your Thesis, Book or Article*. Chicago: University of Chicago Press.

Benton, T. and Craib, I. (2001) *Philosophy of Social Science: The Philosophical Foundations of Social Thought*. London: Palgrave Macmillan.

Bhaskar, R. (1979) *The Possibility of Naturalism*. Brighton: Harvester Press.

Blaikie, N. (2003) *Analyzing Quantitative Data: From Description to Explanation*. London: Sage.

Bootle, R. (2009) *The Trouble with Markets: Saving Capitalism from Itself*. London: Nicolas Brealey.

Bryman, A. (2001) *Quantity and Quality in Social Research*. London: Routledge.

Burrell, G. (1997) *Pandemonium: Towards a Retro-Organization Theory*. London: Sage.

Byrne, D. (1997) *Complexity Theory and the Social Sciences*. London: Routledge.

Byrne, D. (2003) *Interpreting Quantitative Data*. London: Sage.

Carter, B. and New, C. (eds) (2004) *Making Realism Work: Realist Social Theory and Empirical Research*. London: Routledge.

Cassidy, J. (2009) *How Markets Fail: The Logic of Economic Calamities*. London: Penguin.

Clark, T. and Mangham, I. (2004) From dramaturgy to theatre as technology: the case of corporate theatre. *Journal of Management Studies*, 41(1): 37–59.

Clegg, S. (1989) *Frameworks of Power*. London: Sage.

Cohan, W. (2009) *House of Cards: How Wall Street's Gamblers Broke Capitalism*. London: Allen Lane.

Czarniawska, B. (1997) *Narrating the Organization: Dramas of Institutional Identity*. Chicago: University of Chicago Press.

Danermark, B., Ekstrom, M., Jacobsen, L. and Karlsson, J. (2001) *Explaining Society: An Introduction to Critical Realism in the Social Sciences*. London: Routledge.

ESRC (2005) *ESRC Research Ethics Framework*. Swindon: ESRC.

Evans, R. (2001) *In Defence of History*. London: Granta Books.

Fairclough, N. (1989) *Language and Power*. Harlow: Longman.

Fairclough, N. (1992) *Discourse and Social Change*. Cambridge: Polity Press.

Fairclough, N. (2000) *New Labour, New Language?* London: Routledge.

Fairclough, N. (2002) Language in new capitalism. *Discourse and Society*, 13(2): 163–166.

Flyvbjerg, B. (2001) *Making Social Science Matter: Why Social Inquiry Fails and How It Can Succeed Again*. Cambridge: Cambridge University Press.

Flyvbjerg, B. (2007) Five misunderstandings about case-study research. In C. Seale, G. Gobo, J. Gubrium and D. Silverman (eds), *Qualitative Research Practice*. London: Sage. pp. 390–404.

Freeman, S. (2005) *John Rawls*. London: Routledge.

Gamble, A. (2009) *The Spectre at the Feast: Capitalist Crisis and the Politics of Recession*. London: Palgrave Macmillan.

Gapper, J. and Denton, N. (1997) *All that Glitters: The Fall of Barings*. Harmondsworth: Penguin.

Glaser, B. (1978) *Theoretical Sensitivity: Advances in the Methodology of Grounded Theory*. Mill Valley: Sociology Press.

Glaser, B. (1992) *Emergence vs Forcing: Basics of Grounded Theory Analysis*. Mill Valley: Sociology Press.

Glaser, B. and Strauss, A. (1967) *The Discovery of Grounded Theory: Strategies for Qualitative Research*. New York: Hawthorne.

Graham, H. and McDermott, E. (2005) Qualitative research and the evidence base of policy: insights from studies of teenage mothers in the UK. *Journal of Social Policy*, 35(1): 21–37.

Greener, I. (2006) Nick Leeson and the collapse of Barings Bank: socio-technical networks and the 'Rogue Trader'. *Organization*, 13(3): 421–441.

Greener, I. (2008) *Healthcare in the UK: Understanding Continuity and Change*. Bristol: Policy Press.

Greener, I. (2009) Towards a history of choice in UK health policy. *Sociology of Health and Illness*, 31(3): 309–342.

Greenhalgh, T. and Peacock, R. (2005) Effectiveness and efficiency of search methods in systematic reviews of complex evidence: audit of primary sources. *British Medical Journal*, 331(7524): 1064–1065.

Guba, E. and Lincoln, Y. (1989) *Fourth Generation Evaluation*. Thousand Oaks: Sage.

Gujarati, D. (2009) *Basic Econometrics*. London: McGraw-Hill.

Hall, P. (1993) Policy paradigms, social learning, and the state. *Comparative Politics*, 25(3): 275–296.

Hammersley, M. (1991) *What's Wrong with Ethnography?* London: Routledge.

Hammersley, M. (1998) *Reading Ethnographic Research*. London: Longman.

Himmelfarb, G. (2004) *The New History and The Old*. Cambridge, MA: Harvard University Press.

Honigsbaum, F. (1989) *Health, Happiness and Security: The Creation of the National Health Service*. London: Routledge.

Jenkins, K. (1995) *On What is History? From Carr and Elton to Rorty and White*. London: Routledge.

Jessop, B. (2002) *The Future of the Capitalist State*. Cambridge: Polity Press.

Klein, R. (2006) *The New Politics of the NHS: From Creation to Reinvention* (fifth edition). Abingdon: Radcliffe Publishing.

Latour, B. (1988) *Science in Action: How to Follow Scientists and Engineers through Society*. Cambridge, MA: Harvard University Press.

Latour, B. (1991) Technology is society made durable. In J. Law (ed.), *A Sociology of Monsters, Essay on Power, Technology and Domination*. London: Routledge. pp. 103–131.

Latour, B. (2005) *Reassembling the Social*. Oxford: Oxford University Press.

Latour, B. and Woolgar, S. (1986) *Laboratory Life: The Construction of Scientific Facts*. Princeton: Princeton University Press.

Law, J. (ed.) (1986) *Power, Action and Belief: A New Sociology of Knowledge?* London: Routledge & Kegan Paul.

Law, J. (2004) *After Method: Mess in Social Science Research*. London: Routledge.

Lawson, T. (1995) *Economics and Reality*. London: Routledge.

Lee, N. and Hassard, J. (1999) Organization unbound: actor-network theory, research strategy and institutional flexibility. *Organization*, 6(3): 391–404.

Leeson, N. (1996) *Rogue Trader*. London: Warner Brothers.

Leonard, M. (2006) Teenagers telling sectarian stories. *Sociology*, 40(6): 1117–1133.

Levitt, S. and Gubner, S. (2007) *Freakonomics: A Rogue Economist Explores the Hidden Side of Everything.* London: Penguin.

Levitt, S. and Gubner, S. (2009) *Superfreakonomics: Global Cooling, Patriotic Prostitutes and Why Suicide Bombers Should Buy Life Insurance.* London: Allen Lane.

Mandelbrot, B. (2008) *The (Mis)Behaviour of Markets: A Fractal View of Risk, Ruin and Reward.* London: Profile Business.

Mason, P. (2009) *Meltdown: The End of the Age of Greed.* London: Verso.

McCloskey, D. (1998) *The Rhetoric of Economics.* Wisonsin: University of Wisconsin Press.

Milgram, S. and Bruner, J. (2005) *Obedience to Authority: An Experimental View.* London: Pinter & Martin.

Mol, A. (2002) *The Body Multiple: Ontology in Medical Practice.* London: Duke University Press.

Morgan, G. (1986) *Images of Organisation.* London: Sage.

Navarro, V. (1978) *Class Struggle, the State and Medicine.* New York: Prodist.

Pawson, R. (2006a) Digging for nuggets: how 'bad' research can yield 'good' evidence. *International Journal of Social Science Methodology,* 9(2): 127–142.

Pawson, R. (2006b) *Evidence-based Policy: A Realist Perspective.* London: Sage.

Pawson, R. and Tilley, N. (1997) *Realistic Evaluation.* London: Sage.

Pawson, R., Greenhaigh, T., Harvey, G. and Walshe, K. (2005) Realist review – a new method of systematic review for complex policy interventions. *Journal of Health Services Research and Policy,* 10(Supplement to Issue 3): 21–34.

Pinker, S. (2009) *The Sexual Paradox: Troubled Boys, Gifted Girls and the Real Difference between the Sexes.* London: Atlantic Books.

Rawls, J. (1995) *A Theory of Justice.* Cambridge, MA: Harvard University Press.

Reed, M. (1997) In praise of duality and dualism: rethinking agency and structure on organisational analysis. *Organization Studies,* 18(1): 21–42.

Rorty, R. (1999) *Philosophy and Social Hope.* London: Penguin.

Rorty, R. and Engel, P. (2007) *What's the Use of Truth?* New York: Columbia University Press.

Sayer, A. (2005) *The Moral Significance of Class.* Cambridge: Cambridge University Press.

Schwartz, B. (2004) *The Paradox of Choice: Why Less is More.* New York: HarperCollins.

Sebag-Montefiore, S. (1996) The bad boys of finance. *New Statesman and Society:* 22–23. 9th September.

Sennett, R. (2009) *The Craftsman.* London: Penguin.

Social Research Association (2003) *Ethical Guidelines.* London: Social Research Association.

Sorkin, A.R. (2009) *Too Big To Fail: Inside the Battle to Save Wall Street.* London: Allen Lane.

Spicker, P. (2007) Research without consent. *Social Research Update,* 51(Winter): 1–4.

Steinmo, S., Thelen, K. and Longstreth, F. (eds) (1992) *Structuring Politics: Historical Institutionalism in Comparative Analysis.* Cambridge: Cambridge University Press.

Strauss, A. and Corbin, J. (1998) *Basics of Qualitative Research: Techniques and Procedures for Developing Grounded Theory* (second edition). London: Sage.

Taleb, N. (2008) *The Black Swan: The Impact of the Highly Improbable.* London: Penguin.

Triana, P. (2009) *Lecturing Birds on Flying: Can Mathematical Theories Destroy the Financial Markets? How Financial Practice Differs from Theory.* London: John Wiley & Sons.

Weston, A. (2000) *A Rulebook for Arguments.* Indianapolis: Hackett Publishing.

White, P. (2009) *Developing Research Questions: A Guide for Social Scientists.* London: Palgrave Macmillan.

Wood, M. (2005) The fallacy of misplaced leadership. *Journal of Management Studies,* 42(6): 1101–1121.

Yin, R. (2008) *Case Study Research: Design and Methods.* London: Sage.

# Index

field work 27, 73, 97, 98, 137, 156, 159, 186
financial crisis 70, 140–141
Flyvbjerg, Bent 85, 98, 138, 153
focus groups 77–78, 155

generalisation 13, 54, 74, 80, 82, 84, 90,
    95, 98–99, 127, 129, 130, 137–138,
    139, 140, 141, 158, 159, 202
generative causation 15, 16, 18, 19, 40, 117,
    118, 119, 123, 152, 165, 166–167, 196
Glaser, Barney 96, 97, 98,
Google (including google scholar) 23–24,
    25, 35, 175
Graham, Hilary 35–37
Graphs 67
grounded theory xiii, 66, 88, 95–99, 100,
    101, 102, 109, 110,
Guba, Egon 105–106, 107

Hammersley, Martyn 73, 90–92
harm, avoidance of 52, 77, 144, 145, 147,
    148, 150, 197
hierarchy of evidence 24–26
historiography xiii, 2, 103–104, 109,
    127–128, 129, 139, 141
human geography 6, 126–127
hypotheses 3, 5, 7–8, 11–12, 13, 16, 18,
    21, 39, 40, 41, 61, 66, 71, 74, 83, 107,
    113–114, 137, 138, 167, 171, 186,
    201, 202
hypothetico-deductive approach 19, 39, 40,
    41, 61, 62, 74, 83, 113, 120, 123, 201

idealism 17, 19–20, 32–33, 40–41, 79–81,
    82, 99, 103, 104, 108, 115, 123, 139
impartiality 147–148
independence of social research 18, 107,
    108, 144, 145, 147–148, 149
induction (and inductive) social research
    3–4, 8, 12, 18, 21, 41, 61–62, 64, 72,
    74, 89, 95, 96, 137, 186, 201
inductive arguments 164, 167–169, 171, 172
interviews 2, 4, 5, 6, 7, 10, 39, 40, 43,
    75, 76–77, 86–88, 90, 93, 128, 149,
    150, 194

journals, academic 23, 25, 26, 27, 36, 50,
    83, 169, 170, 172, 182, 192, 197, 198

Latour, Bruno 17, 85, 94, 95, 96, 104,
    105, 106, 107, 108, 115, 116, 122, 132,
    166, 196
Law, John 17, 80, 94, 95, 96, 104, 105,
    106, 107, 108, 109, 111, 115, 116, 196,
    198–200

legitimacy 48, 75, 81, 89, 94, 104, 105,
    110, 193–194
Leonard, Michelle 155–156
Lesson, Nick 124
levels of analysis 120–124
Levitt, Stephen 139, 165
Lincoln, Yvonna 105–106, 107
Logic of appropriateness 1, 13, 18–19, 28,
    50, 86, 142, 150–151

Mandelbrot, Benoit 70
Marxism 14, 16, 129, 201
MAXQDA 101, 102
McDermott, Elizabeth 35–37
mean, median and mode 28, 57, 68–70
methodology 4–7, 19, 113–114,
    177–178, 202
Milgram, Stanley 134
mixed methods 2–3, 19, 40, 41, 71,
    194–196, 202
Mol, Annemarie 83, 110–111, 115,
    166, 200
monographs 25
Multi-vocality 104–105, 108, 178

naming and shaming 31, 183
    health policy 128–129
newspapers 26, 197
note-taking 17, 22, 26–27, 85–86, 88, 93,
    96, 106, 164, 180, 184
Nvivo 101

objectivity 17, 18, 32, 34, 44, 86, 87,
    103, 104, 107, 128, 139, 183, 195,
    196, 199
ontology 4, 6, 12, 19, 58, 90, 107,
    112–119, 121, 122, 139, 152, 157,
    158, 202
open and closed systems 13, 30, 131–133,
    139–140
organisation studies 39, 115, 126, 133–134,
    164, 178

Pawson, Ray 15, 31, 37, 178–180, 182–183
phenomenology 126–127, 129–130,
    138–139, 141
political science 14, 15, 108, 127–129, 139
population (in a sample) 8, 39, 41–42, 51,
    56, 62–66, 136, 137, 139, 162
positivism 12, 70, 74, 80, 81, 82, 83, 84,
    85, 86, 87, 88, 89, 99, 106, 107, 108,
    139, 151, 152, 196
postmodernism 12, 80–81, 82, 84, 128
primary research 1, 2, 4, 20, 88, 103, 109,
    128, 155

qualitative methods xiii, 2–3, 8–9, 18,
35–37, 73–92, 93–111, 137, 163, 166,
178, 194–196, 202
quantitative methods xiii, 2–5, 7–8, 15,
18, 19, 28, 35, 38, 40, 41, 51, 55–72,
74–75, 81–83, 85, 90, 106, 107, 109,
137, 166, 178, 182, 194–196, 202
questionnaires xiii, 38–54, 63, 65, 79, 86,
88, 109, 194, 195
questions, in questionnaires 42–49, 50
questions, in interviews 86–88
questions, research 2, 5, 6, 7–11, 27, 28,
50, 63, 75, 94, 137, 170–171, 186

Rawls, John 45
reading 23, 24, 26–27, 45, 90–92, 102, 128,
176, 192
realism 13, 14, 16, 17, 19, 20, 31–32, 33,
34, 35, 40, 41, 59, 60, 61, 79, 80, 81,
82, 84, 90, 91, 103, 104, 105, 107, 110,
113, 115, 116–119, 121–123, 125, 139,
152–153, 154, 158, 159, 160, 166, 178,
195, 196, 199, 201
realist review 31–33, 34, 35, 178–180
reflexivity 32, 50, 66, 70, 100, 106, 142,
148, 150, 152, 159, 162, 191, 193, 197
reliability 35–37, 103, 104, 105–106
research proposals xiii, 157–158, 172,
183–190
research synthesis 35–37, 105
response rates 38, 48, 51, 66
reviewing research 22–37, 174–182
Rorty, Richard 107

sampling 30, 36, 38, 39, 41, 42, 51, 62–66,
71, 74, 75, 80, 81, 135–137, 139, 178,
186, 187, 194, 201, 202
Sayer, Andrew 14
Schwartz, Barry 54
scoping research 35–36, 41, 137, 188, 193
secondary research 2, 4, 20, 109, 155, 159
Sennett, Richard 67

social policy 6, 29, 54, 128, 130, 133,
137, 179
Social Research Association 143–144
sociology 4, 14, 36, 67, 109, 115, 120, 129,
143–145, 178
sources 2, 22, 23, 24–26, 35, 103–104, 128,
146, 148, 172, 174, 175, 177, 180–181,
182, 192
standard deviation 69–70
SPSS 58, 67
statistical significance 8, 74, 114,
135–136, 165
Strauss, Anselm 96, 97, 98, 101
subjectivity 6, 17, 18, 20, 32, 33, 40, 44,
78, 81, 86, 87, 104, 108, 139, 153, 195
substantive significance 114, 135–136, 165
Super Crunchers 71–72
surveys xiii, 10, 30, 38–39, 66, 194,
195, 196
systematic reviews 29–31, 32, 33, 35–37,
177–178, 180, 182, 183

T-Lab 102
Taleb, Nassim Nicholas 70, 160
telephone interviews 88
Thatcher, Margaret 41
time 125–131, 177,
transcription 88–89, 102
Truth 4, 12, 13, 14, 17, 32, 59, 61, 80, 81,
87, 105–108, 113, 116, 119, 149, 195

validity 31, 36, 37, 43, 60–61, 71, 75,
76, 77, 78, 79, 80, 82, 83, 105–107,
139, 195
variables 7, 8, 11, 13, 18, 57–61, 67, 70, 71,
114, 131, 134, 158, 166, 194
voluntary participation 145–148

Wikipedia 23, 24, 35
Wittgenstein, Ludwig 58

Yin, Robert 137

DESIGNING SOCIAL RESEARCH